THE IMAGE OF AFRICA IN GHANA'S PRESS

The Image of Africa in Ghana's Press

The Influence of International News Agencies

Michael Yao Wodui Serwornoo

https://www.openbookpublishers.com

© 2021 Michael Yao Wodui Serwornoo

This work is licensed under a Creative Commons Attribution 4.0 International license (CC BY 4.0). This license allows you to share, copy, distribute and transmit the text; to adapt the text and to make commercial use of the text providing attribution is made to the authors (but not in any way that suggests that they endorse you or your use of the work). Attribution should include the following information:

Michael Yao Wodui Serwornoo, *The Image of Africa in Ghana's Press: The Influence of International News Agencies*. Cambridge, UK: Open Book Publishers, 2021, https://doi.org/10.11647/OBP.0227

In order to access detailed and updated information on the license, please visit, https://doi.org/10.11647/OBP.0227#copyright

Further details about CC BY licenses are available at https://creativecommons.org/licenses/by/4.0/

All external links were active at the time of publication unless otherwise stated and have been archived via the Internet Archive Wayback Machine at https://archive.org/web

Updated digital material and resources associated with this volume are available at https://doi.org/10.11647/OBP.0227#resources

Global Communications vol. 2 | ISSN 2634-7245 (Print) | 2634-7253 (Online)

ISBN Paperback: 9781800640412
ISBN Hardback: 9781800640429
ISBN Digital (PDF): 9781800640436
ISBN Digital ebook (epub): 9781800640443
ISBN Digital ebook (mobi): 9781800640450
ISBN XML: 9781800640467
DOI: 10.11647/OBP.0227

Cover design by Anna Gatti based on a photo by Duangphorn Wiriya on Unsplash at https://unsplash.com/photos/KiMpFTtuuAk

Table of Contents

Acknowledgements	ix
Introduction	1
1. Historical and Contextual Antecedents	11
2. Benefitting from the State of the Art	29
3. Theoretical and Conceptual Frameworks	63
4. Methodology	89
5. Portrayal of Africa: Results of Ethnographic Content Analysis	109
6. Postcolonial Trajectories of the Ghanaian Press: Discussing Actors, Conditions and the Power Dynamics	137
7. Discussing Africa's Media Image in Ghana: A Synergy of Actors, Conditions and Representations	165
Appendices	197
References	209
Index	233

In memory of

Alice Wodui Fekpe

1928–2019

Mum

In honour of

The School of International and Intercultural Communication

The collaborative graduate school founded by Prof. Dr. Susanne Fengler (TU Dortmund), Prof. Dr. Barbara Thomaß (Ruhr-University Bochum), Prof. Dr. Jens Loenhoff (University of Duisburg-Essen)

Acknowledgements

I am deeply grateful to my academic supervisors, Prof. Dr. Barbara Thomaß and Prof. Dr. Susanne Fengler who have been quite supportive of my journey into the academy. They have joined the ranks of other significant women in my life: my Mum Alice Wodui Fekpe, my sisters Margaret, Theodora and Regina, Dr. Hilde Hoffmann, Tina Bettels-Schwabbauer, Dr. Julia Lönnendonker, Elsie Acquaisie and Angelina Koomson-Barnes.

I am grateful to the School of International and Intercultural Communication (SIIC) and its hardworking team of professors. I am equally appreciative of Dr. Dirk Claas-Ulrich and members of my dissertation committee: Prof. Dr. Barbara Thomaß, Prof. Dr. Susanne Fengler, Prof. Dr. Annette Pankratz and Prof. Dr. Peter M. Spangenberg.

I am thankful to Michele Gonnelli, with whom I shared an office and several other private spaces. I am also grateful to the entire SIIC doctoral cohort including Caroline Lindekamp, Bettina Haasen, Till Wäscher, Florian Meißner, Darlene Nalih Musoro, Ann Mabel Sanyu, Marcus Kreutler and Abeer Saady. I am also indebted to workers of the Erich Brost Institute for International Journalism for all the friendly supports they have offered me during this research. I would like to mention in particular the warmth of Olaf Batholome, Monika Bartholome, Nadia Leih, Mariela Bastin, Fabian Karl, Raimer Simons, Gordon Wuellner and Carina Zappe.

I am grateful to the Ruhr University Bochum (RUB) Research School for providing funds for the study. I am thankful to my "secret doctoral committee," at the Gaylord College of Journalism and Mass Communication in the University of Oklahoma, USA, which included Prof. Dr. Gade, Prof. Dr. Craig, Dr. Shugofa and Rev. Fr. Emmanuel Nduka.

Living in Germany for the most part of this study, I can say for sure that I miss my time of worship at the New Apostolic Church in

Unna-Massen-Priest Christof Krebs and the late Frau Asta Kruger. I am especially thankful for my friend and doctor who took very good care of my health — Dr. Med. Christoph Päuser.

I have very vivid memories of the support from my academic mentor, Dr. Andrews Ofori Birikorang, who was such an inspiration to me every time I met with him. I am so grateful for the inspiration and phone calls from my family and friends in London. My sincerest gratitude goes to Mr. and Mrs. Eugene and Vivian Malcolm-Fynn, Mr. and Mrs. Joseph and Michaela Frimpong, Mr. and Mrs. Sakyi Djan and Mr. and Mrs. Sam Brew, Rosemary Akweley Charway and Francisca Aku Akubor.

Introduction

Media coverage of Africa has historically been analysed using different approaches and from the vantage point of different geographical locations. Academic literature of the late 1970s and 80s highlights the negativity and bias on the part of developed nations not only in the way they write about Africa but also regarding their control of international news flow due to the growing influence of a hegemonic private press (Nordenstreng, 2012; Sreberny-Mohammadi, 1997; Hawk, 1992; Sreberny, 1985; Stevenson and Shaw, 1984; Nordenstreng and Schiller, 1979; Galtung, 1971; Galtung and Ruge, 1965). This literature seems to suggest that a socially constructed discourse about Africa, which has come to be known as *Afro-pessimism*, has either improved in the wake of *Africa rising* discourse (Bunce, Franks and Paterson, 2017, Nothias, 2015; Ojo, 2014) or is in fact a non-existent myth (Scott, 2015). Indeed, recent publications argue that the claim of negative representation has no validity beyond certain few Western countries (Scott, 2017; Obijiofor and MacKinnon, 2016). New studies continue to adduce empirical evidence of Africa's negative portrayal in US elite press and of how this coverage spreads around the world (Gruley and Duvall, 2012). In this book, I trace these debates by examining the nature of the continent's coverage in the Ghanaian press with a focus on the dominant themes of representation, subject matter and tone of the coverage. I will also offer explanations for Africa's depiction in the press by journalists and editors, their newsroom exigencies and the world beyond these two contexts.

Background

Due to the historical implications of the use of communication technology by the Persian, Greek, Roman and British empires, communication across borders continues to occupy the minds of many researchers today (Thussu, 2000). However, an early attempt to explain the coverage of one country by another became prominent through the work of Johan Galtung, who introduced the Centre–Periphery model in which he attempted to explain the inequality within and between nations, and why that phenomenon was resistant to change. These inequalities and imbalances in international news flow, highlighted by Galtung, account for the persistent complaints of developing nations regarding their coverage in the Northern press (Galtung, 1971; Galtung and Ruge, 1965).

The attempts in scholarly literature to explain how nations cover each other were inadequate in establishing the necessary credibility of these imbalances. In fact, prior to the publication of UNESCO's MacBride Commission report (1980), the claims made by developing nations regarding their negative portrayal by Western media, which subsequently reinforced prejudices in the West, remained largely allegations. In addition to the UNESCO publication, several other studies, in particular those examining the portrayal of Africa in other countries, have been published (Bunce et al. 2017; Mody, 2010; Chang and Lee, 1992; El Zein and Cooper, 1992). The Western media has consistently refuted the claim that it represents Africa and other parts of the world through a negative lens. They argue that the term "Western press" is a generalisation referring to the press in the US and the UK. According to Jonathan Graubart (1989), the refutations by the Northern Hemisphere, led by the US, require a review. In the California Law Review, Graubart suggests that when the US evaluates proposals for change to the negative coverage of developing countries, it should move away from "the pious sanctity of its private press and rather attempt to pragmatically consider what steps it can take to further the economic and socio-cultural conditions in the Third world by reversing the consequences of centuries of negative coverage" (p. 631).

A detailed look at how African journalists portray countries on the continent could provide us with useful insights with which to assess the gravity of Western dominance over foreign news businesses, and help us to understand how this has promoted dependency and hegemony. Thus far, existing research efforts have described how the media in the dominant Northern Hemisphere (Western nations) continue to negatively represent Africa, with little improvement (Bunce, 2017; Nothias, 2015). Recent publications have analysed other developed nations beyond those already implicated and have found this entire claim to be a non-existent myth (Obijiofor and MacKinnon, 2016; Scott, 2015). These studies, however, do not deal with the way in which Africa is covered by the continent itself, while the few studies that do acknowledge this point, ignore (Obijiofor and Hanusch, 2003; Pate, 1992) the agency of sources that were employed in the coverage.

The Problem, Purpose and Significance

The relationship between the ideology of a country and its portrayal in the media has been investigated and expounded (Ofori-Birikorang, 2009; Van Djik, 2009; Snow and Benford, 2000). The media frames that appear in news have their roots in the several influences that shape their production and reproduction (Gruley and Duvall, 2012). However, most scholars have only analysed media content and have overlooked more deeply-rooted questions pertaining to their sources. To disregard the origins of news selection and their value is comparable to a thesis which argues that no relationship exists between media portrayal and its source. The argument that sources play a significant role in news construction is justified because the ideology of news rarely permits receiving journalists to make major changes to what their fellow journalists have communicated.

Journalists are committed to the questions of who, what, when, where, why and how. The important question that remains unanswered, however, is whether African journalists writing for their local newspapers are capable of any resistance towards the influences of the international press? We can only understand this issue when we begin to analyse their works. The investigation of African media output, focusing specifically on sources, provides a new angle to the debate of both quantitative and qualitative imbalance of news flow to Africa. In any case, Wrong (2017) highlighted the need for African media to show their resistance by assuming a more responsible role than their Western counterpart.

Motilola Akinfemisoye (2013), supported this observation by arguing that significant improvements in mobile telephony and Internet access on the continent present a glorious opportunity for circulation and access to counter-narratives and broader stories about Africa.

Instances where the values of a particular international news agency become the guiding principle of an African newspaper could be the result of several factors such as media ownership, training, access, professional affiliations and history (Hachten, 2004; Golding, 1977). Unfortunately, these explanatory components are often disregarded by researchers. My intention is to investigate the coverage of Africa within the continent itself, without the assurance, as Francis Nyamnjoh (2017) argues, that the African journalists will fare better or worse than their Northern media counterparts. Rather, I consider this book a commitment to plurality, in a way that gauges how the issues have evolved over the years and across borders. This book fills a scholarly vacuum by providing the first description of the continent's current portrayal in the Ghanaian press. This description focuses on dominant themes employed by the press, the sources utilised, subjects discussed and the reasoning behind the country's portrayal. This book also tackles decision-making regarding news selection, which extends beyond the events and the journalists in question to the social milieus of the newsroom and Ghanaian society in general.

The overarching purpose of this book is to describe how Ghanaian newspapers have portrayed the African continent in their foreign news pages and the subsequent issues that the portrayal raises. It will be important to examine the weight of influence each international news agency carries as a source in the Ghanaian press as well as the collective influence exerted by international media on Ghanaian media's coverage of the continent. The book evaluates the subsequent reasoning behind the kind of representation Africa receives from the Ghanaian press in terms of actors, conditions and practices. These specific objectives guide my enquiry, as the study aims:

1. To deconstruct the dominant themes, tone and subjects employed in the representation of Africa in the Ghanaian press and to discuss the deconstructed themes in relation to those employed by the media in the Northern Hemisphere

regarding the portrayal of Africa (Bunce et al., 2017; Hawk, 1992).

2. To determine the weight of influence of international news agencies (actors) as sources in the Ghanaian press (Obijiofor and Hanusch, 2003).

3. To evaluate the conditions and practices which shape the foreign news selection beyond news values, by uncovering both conscious and unconscious elements, from the perspective of the journalists, their work environment and the immediate world beyond the newsroom.

4. To investigate the nature of intermedia agenda-setting relationships between Ghanaian newspapers and transnational news agencies (Segev, 2016; Golan, 2008; Groshek and Clough Groshek, 2013; Roberts and Bantimaroudis, 1997).

Media representation and news selection about foreign *Others* have been debated extensively over the years. Indira Gandhi outlined the need for real change when she stressed the importance of self-reliance in these words:

> We want to hear African on events in Africa. You should similarly be able to get an Indian explanation of events in India. It is astonishing that we know so little about leading poets, novelists, historians and editors of various Asian, African and Latin American countries while we are familiar with minor authors and columnists of Europe and America (Gandhi, 1984, p. 16).

The approach in this book contributes to literature on media representation in three unique ways. Firstly, it contests media representation through the approach of postcolonial theory — which offers a more democratic re-reading of media text — questioning, reframing and rethinking representations about the West and Others (Shome and Hegde, 2002). It is essential to note that the use of postcolonial theory in analysing foreign news selection is not to emphasise the West and East divide, but to understand and explain how identity is represented in the politics of power. Secondly, international news flow is often considered as a product of gatekeeping factors (Chang and Lee, 1992) or event-oriented determinants (Eilders, 2006, 2006; Maier and Ruhrmann, 2007). Only a few studies have investigated intermedia agenda-setting as a possible factor (Groshek and Clough Groshek, 2013; Golan, 2008). Furthermore, most studies on news selection have been limited to content and frame analysis at the expense of a broad, explicit and multidisciplinary framework (Van Djik, 2009). In an attempt to capture the inherently ideological structures embedded in the news selection process, this study contributes to the literature on journalism research with a unique blend of ethnographic content analysis (ECA) and ethnographic interview. Although ECA is aimed at seeking a deeper insight into media text, it fails to provide the perspective of journalists and editors. This weakness is addressed by the application of detailed ethnographic interviews employing rigorous methodical techniques, which have enriched the findings in this book.

Guiding Questions

The study is driven by a compelling investigation into the portrayal of Africa in the Ghanaian press. Closely related to this issue are the further sub-questions that provide the context for a better understanding of this aspect of the study. The first research question (RQ1) — what is the overview of the coverage of Africa in the Ghanaian press — is divided into four sub-questions:

1. What subjects/topics/story types were mostly covered on the continent?
2. What were the dominant themes through which the African story was narrated?
3. What was the quality/tone of coverage (negative or positive or neutral)?
4. How comparable are RQ1 sub-questions a. b. and c. between the Ghanaian press and their Western counterparts?

The second research question (RQ2) asks: what is the weight of influence, both quantitative and qualitative, which individual international news agencies carry as sources in the Ghanaian press? The third question (RQ3) investigates the reasons behind the kind of representation Africa receives in the Ghanaian press in terms of conditions, practices and perspectives of the journalists. Finally, RQ4 asks how has the issue of intermedia agenda-setting preferences between the Ghanaian press and their foreign counterparts been reviewed, considering the phenomenon's evolution so far?

Outline of the Book

The details here reveal the arrangement of the various chapters of the book. Chapter 1 presents the historical and contextual backgrounds of the study. Beginning with a discussion of the UNESCO-commissioned MacBride and Sreberny-Mohammadi reports, the chapter opens up the debate of that era. The findings of Beverly Hawk's edited book on *Africa's Media Image* are outlined, in addition to the work of Mel Bunce et al. (2017). Ghana's evolving positionality as a strong Pan-African state is discussed, from the pre-independence through the post-independence era to the current Internet and digital age. Chapter 2 situates this study in the current literature as a way of benefiting from previous research. It discusses the meaning and usefulness of foreign news in general, while also discussing the conceptualisation of terms and expanding upon a discussion relating to the opportunities afforded by the digital and Internet era for a fuller understanding of the world. It continues to evaluate the various determinants of international news coverage. This chapter subsequently describes how Africa has been portrayed in the Western media alongside a discussion of the determinants of international news flow. This chapter zeroes in on the framework within which the African press operates and the influences of international news agencies, and Western education and training on this entire process. Chapter 3 examines the theoretical and conceptual frameworks of the study. The theories of newsworthiness, intermedia agenda-setting and postcolonial critique are discussed. The inter-relationships among the three theories are outlined, highlighting how they help in addressing the objectives of the study. The theoretical framework and hierarchical influence model of Pamela Shoemaker and Stephen Reese (2014) are recounted. Chapter 4 discusses the overarching methodology with a detailed outline of the various methods and procedures that inform the study. Ethnographic content analysis (ECA), a method that integrates qualitative and quantitative approaches to content analysis, is explained. This chapter also provides a rationale for the use of multiple methods (triangulation) for data collection as it pertains to this study. It encompasses the sampling methods and procedures employed, the units of analysis that were subject to examination, the period of study, as well as the steps and procedures carried out in the actual data collection in the field. The chapter ends with a discussion of validity, reliability and ethical issues, as well as coding instruments and protocol adopted for the study. Chapter 5 presents the findings of the ethnographic content analysis that emerged from the examination of articles on the foreign news pages in the newspapers studied. It discusses how the findings of the ECA complement purposes outlined for the research. The chapter ends with a comparison of Africa's image as portrayed in the Ghanaian press vis à vis the current literature. Chapter 6 focuses on the description of the findings relating to the ethnographic interview aspect of the data as a follow-up on chapter five. The ethnographic interview reveals the reasoning behind the foreign news selection process in Ghana from the perspective of the journalists and editors. The chapter outlines the qualitative weight of influence and the conditions shaping the foreign news selection. The workings of intermedia agenda-setting relationships are traced through the ethnographic interviews. All the findings are reduced to descriptions involving little or no discussions at that stage of the analysis. Chapter 7 discusses the findings outlined in Chapters 5 and 6 in line with the objectives of the entire study, in particular through an evaluation of each of the research questions posed in the Introduction. The chapter argues that the coverage of foreign news in the Ghanaian press reinforces existing postcolonial trajectories and relationships that contribute to the existing imbalance in international news flow around the world. The chapter further argues that the *soft-power* success of China's Xinhua News Agency not only represents South–South cooperation, but presents a new form of supremacy as a result of the relationship and engagement defined by imbalance of power relations and interactions between the Chinese and their Ghanaian counterpart. The chapter also focuses on the juxtaposition between the dependency of the Ghanaian press on international news agencies and its claim of an *African perspective*, thus suggesting that the entire scenario represents a resistance and subaltern ambivalence. However, to reach such a conclusion we must first consider to what extent resistance is truly effective. In reality, Ghanaian journalists have done less in practice to establish any potent resistance to their negative proxy coverage of the continent, which begs the question, does the efficacy of resistance exist only in its conception or can it be achieved in practice?

1. Historical and Contextual Antecedents

> Indeed, in the Marxist tradition, it is the object of faith that no aspect of society can be understood apart from its social and historical context (Shoemaker and Reese, 2014, p. 65).

In this chapter, the historical and contextual backgrounds of foreign news are discussed predominantly in terms of ideology, in particular focusing on the efforts of UNESCO. The New World Information and Communication Order (NWICO) debate is reviewed from the perspective of the MacBride and Sreberny-Mohammadi reports. Contemporary research efforts by Beverly Hawk (1992) and Mel Bunce et al. (2017) to further highlight the continuities and evolutions of the debate are discussed.

The historical and contextual position of the Ghanaian media is discussed in relation to its evolving nature. The pre-independence, or colonial, era of Ghanaian media is marked by a significant ambivalence towards press freedom. Led by the British, this colonial regime was credited with enabling an environment for growth of nationalist press in Ghana, while conversely imposing draconian laws which, in certain instances, limited press freedom. Post-independence, the Ghanaian press became more repressive than their colonial counterparts. The continuities of the post-independence era are traced to the current system of press which is in operation in this country today.

This chapter adopts a line of argument which follows the Western historical entanglements with Africa, especially Ghana, and their impact on the development of modern communication and journalism, leaving significant ideological footprints on the Ghanaian journalist's foreign news selection. The stark imitation of Western journalism education and

© Michael Yao Wodui Serwornoo, CC BY 4.0   https://doi.org/10.11647/OBP.0227.01

curricula by Ghana's media development process is further enhanced by media assistance programmes and training which continue to be dominated by development organisations and media professionals from the Global North (Schiffrin, 2010).

UNESCO and Ideological Trajectories of Global Communication Debate

The concept of New World Information and Communication Order (NWICO) occupied global media policy debates from the 1970s until the 1990s, amidst the strong ideological battle relating to decolonisation and the collapse of Soviet communism (Nordenstreng, 2011). These debates, initiated by 55 Non-Aligned Movement (NAM) members, received attention from professional and academic communities, and, by the 2000s, had been replaced by the concept of media globalisation. The NAM members argued that the existing order was neo-colonial and exhibited cultural imperialism, and, as such, provided developed countries with a greater control over media technologies, including the capacity to produce cultural products ranging from movies and music to news. The proponents of NWICO felt the need for a reversal of Western dominance and a balance in the current one-way flow of information from the Northern to the Southern Hemisphere. The developing countries claimed that they received less coverage from the press in the more affluent countries, which seemed to be more interested in disasters, famines and wars (Dakroury and Hoffmann, 2010).

The aim of the NWICO concept was to enable developing countries to exert a greater influence over their media, information, economic, cultural, and political systems in order to change the current global communication system. This change would prove imperative in undoing the current system in place, which, at the time, stood for an outgrowth of prior colonial patterns and control reflecting commercial and market imperatives (McPhail, 2006). This debate also covered the issue of human rights. Inextricably linked to the process of development and democratisation taking place, there was a call for explicit recognition of the right to communicate. The proponents argued that this right could only thrive in an environment which accommodated and facilitated the assertion of individual freedoms, thus leading to the liberal doctrine of a *free flow* of information (Hoffmann, 2010).

In 1971, Johan Galtung introduced the Centre–Periphery model as an attempt to explain the inequalities within and between nations and why such structures were resistant to change. His article, "A Structural Theory of Imperialism", divided the world into two parts with the dominant countries of the Northern Hemisphere as the "Centre" and the dependent countries of the Southern Hemisphere as the "Periphery". Galtung contends that the vertical interaction between the "Centre" and the "Periphery" is a major factor behind inequality among nations. He adds that "the feudal interaction structure is the factor that maintains and reinforces the inequality", serving as a protection for the continued existence of this inequality (Galtung, 1971, p. 89). In a review of Galtung's work, Hamid Mowlana (1985, p.21) came up with four hypotheses regarding the state of the world press system:

1. There is a preponderance of negative news events reported in the world press systems.

2. There is a much larger discrepancy in the news exchange ratios of "centre" and "periphery" nations than in the exchange ratios of "centre" nations.

3. "Centre" news occupies a larger proportion of the foreign news content in the media of "periphery" nations than the "periphery" news occupies in the "centre" nations.

4. There is relatively little or no flow of news among "periphery" nations, especially across colonial-based bloc borders.

Mowlana further reviewed previous studies that analysed the imperfections in the content of world news and identified five shortcomings (Mowlana, 1985, pp. 24–25):

1. International news is "Western-centric" since the sources of news, even in most of the developing countries, are Western news agencies and wire services.

2. Existing developing countries coverage focuses on negative or "bad" news — catastrophes, violence and corruption, rather than on "developmental" news or educational information, while the study conducted by Robert

Stevenson and Richard Cole (1984b) revealed that negative news is not only predominant in Western media, but in the developing countries media as well: a conclusion also drawn by Nwa'ndo Ume-Nwagbo in her study of African newspapers (Ume-Nwagbo, 1982).

3. International news tends to be shallow and oversimplified, in that it concentrates on political leanings of governments rather than on accurate and comprehensive coverage of conflicts affecting nations and people.

4. International news concentrates on the elite rather than on the masses.

5. Research shows that the emphasis of international news is on events rather than on factors leading to and causing the events.

The review of Mowlana (1985) came at a time when huge historical and ideological battles of influence were taking place. Kaarle Nordenstreng (2010) argues that the historical moments which gave rise to the MacBride report can be divided into five different stages, which partially overlap, spanning from 1970 to the new millennium. Nordenstreng defines these developments as the "global media debate" and argues that the elements of this debate predate the "pre-war League of Nations" (Nordenstreng, 1993a, p. 65). On the basis of such an account of history, one could argue that the New World Information and Communication Order (NWICO) was an old concept reorganised under a new umbrella. Nordenstreng (2010) clarifies that even though NWICO was located in mass media, its fundamental ethos was rooted in international law. H. Eek (1979) provides an insightful analysis which establishes that the *concept of order* was already included in the 1948 Universal Declaration of Human Rights. He subsequently argued that media and its freedoms were governed by an established framework of international law which promotes both freedoms and responsibilities.

Proponents and supporters of NWICO insisted that the activities of imperialism were not confined solely to the political and economic fields but also cover the cultural and social fields and, as a result, required a "concerted action in the fields of mass communication" (Nordenstreng, 2010, p. 2; Nordenstreng and Hannikainen, 1984). Advocates of NWICO offered analysis of press freedom in a way that problematised and deconstructed the concept's bias for neo-liberal ideals. In particular, Herbert Schiller (Schiller, 1984, 1976) highlighted the American *free flow doctrine* as an instrument of cultural domination.

The MacBride Commission was realised amidst the heated debate between imperialism and press freedom. The eventual report was sharply criticised by scholars for its compromising posture (Hamelink, 1981). Nordenstreng (2010) highlighted some differences in opinion on the Commission itself when he quoted remarks made by Gabriel García Márquez and Juan Somavía, both of whom disagreed with the US's new offer to develop communication infrastructure in the developing world as a way of dealing with the imbalances and inequalities highlighted. The insistence on the need to develop communication infrastructures in developing countries is correct and necessary, but it should not be overstated. It is not possible to solve contemporary communication problems through money and training alone. The idea of a Marshall Plan for the development of communications in underdeveloped countries is inappropriate and will tend to reproduce Western values and transnational interests within these societies. Actions in this field, if not carefully selected could reinforce minority power structures within third world countries or serve as a vehicle for cultural domination (Nordenstreng, p. 11). Cees Hamelink offered one of the strongest criticisms regarding the treatment of transnational news agencies in the report:

> The Report, although rightly pointing to the crucial role of transnational corporations in the field of international communications, did not sufficiently recognize that the new international information order is indeed likely to be the order of the transnational corporations. The "one world" the report ambitiously refers to in its title may very well be the global marketplace for transnational corporations (quoted in Nordenstreng, 2010, p. 11).

Aside from its criticisms, the MacBride report also posed several questions which were left unanswered, issues which, in today's climate, are arguably all the more prescient and require further attention. The report demanded the establishment of a New World Communication and Information Order (NWICO), a plurality of sources, the elimination of negatively-impacting monopolies, and the mentation of national media to prevent sole dependence on external sources. The eighty-two recommendations featured in this report have, in most cases, failed to be implemented (Hancock and Hamelink, 1999). However, the issues identified in the recommendations are still recurring with their emphasis on social impact instead of technology. According to Nordenstreng (2010), the issues should be pursued with an analytical approach, including much of what was proposed by the MacBride report without necessarily using the phrase *new world information and communication order*.

The MacBride Report: *Many Voices, One World*

The MacBride Commission gathered large data on "contents of information, accuracy and balance in facts and images presented, infrastructure for news supply, rights and responsibilities of journalists and organisations engaged in news gathering and distribution as well as technical and economic aspects of their operation" (MacBride, 1980, p. xix). Seán MacBride collated the entire report in keeping with the Commission's ethos. It was his estimation that, when goodwill governs the future, the resultant effect will be a new order to benefit all of mankind. The report indicates how, over the years, whenever there was a perceived challenge to the established order, different types of journalism (business press, sensational press, the opinion press, the crusading press) tended to mirror popular causes. In their report, MacBride and his team argue that there are "historical links that can be perceived today both in content of reporting and the way the newspapermen from those origins of journalism types conceive their socio-political responsibilities in the regions they are" (MacBride, 1980, p. 7). According to MacBride (1980), the modern concept of press freedom emerged as a reaction to the American and French Revolutions, which subsequently provided strong contextual background for its application. Having traced the historical context of written communication from its use by minorities to majorities, to its increasing commercial structure and outlook, the report establishes how the majority of these changes have resulted in "harmful disparities both between countries and within them, as well as towards diversity, pluralism and a great variety of communication patterns, both at various development levels and inside countries belonging to different socio-political systems" (p. 10). Based on these findings, the study then concludes that an evolution of the communication order represents the roots of the present-day communications system and therefore requires a thorough investigation. The report also mentions that information communication may facilitate the creation of wealth or, rather, a system responsible for the existing communication gaps which, as a consequence, may contribute to the widening of the breach between rich and poor nations.

The report argues that even though communication is a weapon of independence struggle and played a significant role in the quest of developing countries to improve their economic and political future, these benefits might be thwarted because of the continuous dominance and the power possessed by some nations over the technical and general resources within the sector. As a result, these endowed nations have imposed their ideas on developing nations.

The second half of the twentieth century witnessed over two billion people from almost eighty nations being liberated from manifest colonial domination. These liberations instigated feelings of agitation about the prevailing imbalanced world order. Many of the activists realised that the world's political, economic, scientific, technological, military, social, and cultural conditions had fostered dependence of a large number of nations on a handful of dominant ones. The MacBride report perceived cultural dependence, alongside political and economic dependence, to be a serious injustice which has historically been at the heart of dependency discussions. The study argues that "communication" has encouraged these discussions through "exchange between unequal partners, allowing the predominance of the more powerful, the richer and the better equipped" (p. 34). The report knowingly or inadvertently problematises discrepancies in power, as well as the influence these discrepancies have had on the structure and flows of communication.

This report frames my own line of research in its argument that inequality, specifically in the news, is a complex and varied phenomenon which manifests both quantitatively and qualitatively at various levels between developed and developing nations and among developing nations themselves. The MacBride report concludes that "doubtlessly, there is no single, universal criterion by which to measure these imbalances and disparities, since news values differ from one country to another and from culture to culture and even sometimes within a single country" (p. 36). The major argument against the agitation of imbalance by developing countries emanates from the *free flow* concept/ doctrine, which is an outgrowth of freedom of expression. This doctrine, which has been applied to collective human rights, has many flaws and, as such, has proved beneficial to developed nations and detrimental to vulnerable and less endowed nations. The report's recommendations were meant to discourage all unequal encounters while encouraging a communication order that benefits developing nations (Nordenstreng, 2010; Vicent et al., 1999; MacBride, 1980).

The MacBride report also suggests that the world's communication should be decolonised and democratised in order to propagate the concept of New World Information and Communication Order (NWICO) and commends the subsequent addition of the establishment of the International Programme for the Development of Communication (Kuo and Xiaoge, 2005).The relevance of the MacBride report to emerging developments in international communication cannot be over-emphasised. According to Robin Mansell and Kaarle Nordenstreng (2007), "many of the issues and dilemmas highlighted by the MacBride Report's authors exist today" (p. 15).

The Sreberny-Mohammadi Report:
Foreign News in the Media

In spite of the controversy of the MacBride report, UNESCO did not renege on its quest to inform the world about the representations of foreign countries. Indeed, the organisation (UNESCO) recommissioned the International Association for Mass Communication Research (IAMCR) to study the "image of foreign countries representing different social systems and development stages, as portrayed by mass circulated press in the countries concerned" (Sreberny, 1985, p. 3). The comparative study of twenty-nine countries examined diverse media systems at varied levels of development, political orientation and socio-economic organisation. The study offered refreshing, up-to-date information on the situation at that time, particularly with regards to international news flows in many parts of the world. Nwa'ndo Ume-Nwagbo (1982) described the report as the "most comprehensive set of studies on the new world information order undertaken in 1979–1980 by the International Association for Mass Communication Research (IAMCR)" (p. 41). The study traced its genealogy from the Brandt report through to MacBride and arrived at a single compelling result that has not yet been thoroughly unpacked. This then provided the IAMCR research team with a much-needed locus for another report. According to Annabelle Sreberny (1985), "one of the major areas of inequality and dependency in the existing information order, lies in the processing and dissemination of news" (p. 7). Even though this point, referenced by previous reports, was clearly pertinent, it was not acted upon. The authors of the Sreberny report denied that their study should be considered as an analytical justification to the New World Information and Communication Order debate. Rather, they stated that their principal intention was to "combat ignorance and prejudice on what was seen as a vitally important issue, to increase awareness, to make it more difficult for conventional rationalisations to be sustained and, to provide a sound base for informed policies and change" (p. 10).

Some of the findings of the Sreberny report are worth revisiting for their enduring instructive attributes. According to the report, "Africa as a region was repeatedly described as providing *dominant stories*, mostly in relation to Idi Amin and Uganda, and the elections in the then Rhodesia" (Sreberny, 1985, p. 52). However, the continent as a whole, in terms of overall quantitative coverage, only achieved a middle ranking. The report firmly implied that journalism's age-old news reporting selection dilemma was a problem of what to omit, not what to include. Sreberny established, in line with previous researchers, a quantitative imbalance and feudal interaction among developing nations:

> Perhaps more important than the question of whether the West is over-represented in international news is the problem of the several under-representation of certain other parts of the world. There is even a marked shortage of news about other developing regions in the media of any given developing nation, so that it is still true to say that "the peripheral nations do not write or read much about each other, especially not across bloc borders" (p. 52).

The study finds that the coverage of Africa and most developing nations is linked primarily to catastrophes and coup d'états. This is due to the fact that most media systems conceptualise news to be exceptional events, many of which occur in Africa, for example. The report also finds a great deal of homogeneity in the structure of international news across all twenty-nine media systems and therefore concluded that the free flow doctrine, in this instance, could not produce diversity. From this research, the study draws two overarching conclusions which retain a certain relevance today:

> The narrow determination of what constitutes international news, and the corresponding omission of certain kinds of events, actors and localities. The second has to do with the structure of bias and interpretation through which selected stories are actually presented. The relative weight and impact of each of these on those who receive the news, add the wider implications of this, remains to be assessed by other research (p. 53).

Africa's Media Image

Beverly Hawk's edited volume, *Africa's Media Image*, was influential in uniting scholars of journalism, communication and African studies together with journalists to share scholarly analysis and experiences. Traditionally, scholars tended to analyse the work of journalists without practical context and thus would mostly compare the journalistic output to idealistic scholarly standards. However, *Africa's Media Image* covers areas of research that are still highly relevant today, including the Cold War, aid, censorship, African-American press, African agency amongst others. Hawk (1992) argues that the "repertoires of knowledge, symbols, and a priori structuring of Africa are a Western creation" (p. 4). She observes that American readers, due to their lack of knowledge about the continent, usually require special contextual information with which to interpret the meaning of reported events coming as part of the African news. Hawk also demonstrates how media representation of the continent and contextual information regarding the reports coming from Africa were "limited by commercial and financial considerations of editors, the personal opinions of editors and correspondents, and press restrictions of host governments" (p. 4). This highlighted that, aside from Western metaphors and colonially-inclined perspectives, there were also practical challenges which contributed to the continent's media image.

The book reports that the re-contextualisation of African events for an American audience led to the borrowing of vocabulary from civil right movements and landmark US events. As a result, these events are deprived of their true context, which results in a distorted image of the continent. The increase in technological advancements on the continent coupled with a growing number African scholars and professionals around the world is to be commended but there is still a great deal to be done. Nonetheless, Hawk has recently argued in the foreword to Bunce et al. (2017) that changes in recent decades have magnified "African voices, technological advances in communication are transforming information about Africa and consequently the image of Africa around the world. With Africa as the motive force in African news, the continent has opportunity to claim agency over its image" (Bunce et al., 2017, p. xvii). Bunce et al. (2017) adopted a similar approach by bringing together scholars and journalists to assess the changes and continuities in the continent's media image. They have argued that increasing participatory and indigenous information flows have resulted in some form of continental agency on how African stories should be written. In the light of these, the *Africa rising* discourse and reflexive assessment by Western journalists, Bunce et al., argued forcefully that the continent's image in the Western press has improved, if only a little.

Ghana's Evolving Positionality

The literature described so far has primarily concentrated on the evolution of Afro- pessimism relating to the investigation of Africa's coverage. For instance, Hawk (1992) concentrates on the situation as it then stood in the 1990s, and earlier decades, from a US perspective. Bunce et al. (2017) extend their outlook beyond the US and trace the phenomenon globally from the 1990s through to the present day. What these two studies fail to acknowledge, however, is the evolution of Africa's negative image within the continent itself from a critical perspective. In response to this, my own study argues for depth over width, hence the selection of the case of Ghana for an ethnographic analysis. This research departs from Levi Obijiofor and F. Hanusch (2003), who attempted to study Ghana and Nigeria using quantitative content analysis and a survey.

An argument for considering Ghana's positionality in an investigation of *Afro-pessimism* can be made from several perspectives. Ghana, being one of the pioneers of Pan-Africanism, provided a fertile ground for liberation thinkers across the continent to fight for self-rule. According to Wilberforce Dzisah (2008), "Ghana is reputed to be the place where the early nationalist press in West Africa took a firm root, from where it extended to other colonies" (p. 76). The country attracted civil rights leader Martin Luther King Jr., among others, who strongly applauded the nation's independence. Soon after its independence, several initiatives were introduced by Kwame Nkrumah, the first President of Ghana, to promote the continent's story especially through the introduction of Foreign Service broadcasting and newspapers. The continuity of Ghana's leadership, in this respect, suffered a considerable blow when President Nkrumah's government was overthrown unconstitutionally in February 24, 1966 through a military coup d'état. The country endured several military coup d'états until 1992 when Flt Lt Jerry John Rawlings restored the nation to democratic rule. These scenarios have implications for the way the media operates today.

However, Minabere Ibelema and Tanja Bosch (2009) have argued that the dominance of the West African press is due to the fact that it is one hundred years older than its counterparts in East Africa and French-speaking African territories. They argued that it was "therefore no accident that Ghana — the country which led the way — became the first sub-Saharan African country granted independence, and continues to present a media that is remarkably unfettered and freest on the continent of Africa" (Ibelema and Bosch, 2009, p. 302).

Pre-Independence Era and Continental Posture

Charles Bannerman, considered to be the first African editor of a newspaper, established the *Accra Herald* alongside his brother Edmund Bannerman. Dzisah (2008) states that the Bannerman brothers "suffered persistent persecution at the hands of the British colonial authority for publishing stories which were at variance with the dictates of the imperial power" (p. 76). Prior to the efforts of the Bannerman brothers, the British colonial Governor, Sir Charles McCarthy, had established a newspaper in Sierra Leone before arriving in Ghana. It was titled *The*

Royal Gold Coast Gazette and Commercial Intelligencer and began circulation on 21 April 1822 (Barton, 2014).

William Hachten (1971) argues that the "development of mass communications in Africa, both past and present, in its nature and extent are products of European influences" since modern mass communication was not an "indigenous African creation" (p. xv). According to Hachten, this explains why differences in media systems are traceable to colonial experiences. More specifically, the role, played by newspapers in Anglophone Africa during the struggle for independence, was immeasurable and served as catalyst for modern nationalism especially during a period when Africans had no hand in the governance of their own countries (Karikari, 1992). The non-religious press in Ghana during this epoch displayed a radical and strong political commitment against colonial rule, a success story which is partly attributable to the British liberal model. An article from the maiden edition of *The Gold Coast Times*, published on 29 March 1874, summarises the struggle:

> In instances where the rights and interests of the people are disregarded, and attempts are made to tamper with them, and to put them down with a high hand, we shall be found at our post, prepared to perform our duty fearlessly and independently, regardless of the frowns of King or Kaiser (Jones-Quartey, 1975, p. 80).

The desire to publish a newspaper for Africans came from the African people themselves (Hachten, 1971). The initiatives did not usually endure but nonetheless provided an excellent repertoire of newspapers which followed the closure of the *Accra Herald*. These are *The Gold Coast Times, The Gold Coast Independent, Gold Coast Chronicle, Gold Coast People* and the *Gold Coast Express*. The colonial response to the vibrant Ghanaian press was a resort to sedition laws aimed at both the Ghanaian nationalist press and other nationalist figures from the West African sub-region living in Ghana (the Nigerian Nnamdi Azikiwe and the Sierra Leonean Wallace Johnson). These laws were dogmatically applied in the 1950s, when public tension for independence became widespread (Reports of the Commission of Enquiry into Disturbances in the Gold Coast, cited in Ekwelie and Edoga-Ugwuoju, 1985). The colonial authorities controlled the media development process in accordance with their economic and political interests, setting a bad precedent for newly independent states in Africa. F. B. Nyamnjoh (2005) explained that the governments of new states in Africa came to understand, from their colonial masters, that the power of media would propagate a particular political perspective and motivate the larger masses to action. For example, even following independence, the colonial powers still had interests in these new sovereign states and ensured that the press kept civil society in check according to Western expectations of a stable geo-region for investment. This was largely possible because most of the new sovereign states in Africa depended on Western technological and industrial resources for several aspects of their development process (Nyamnjoh, 2005).

Ghana's embeddedness in the African liberation struggle is not a new phenomenon. Frank Barton (2014) indicated that the first attempt to produce a newspaper for the whole of West Africa came from the Ghanaian leader J. B. Danquah in 1931. The *West African Times*, though founded by J. B. Danquah, was supplied by Reuters as a sign of Africa's rootedness within Western Europe. In fact, the nationalist press became so vocal that the British colonial regime decided to introduce the Mirror Group from the UK. The Group, according to Kwame Karikari (1992), almost crushed the entire nationalist press with its superior capital investments but it was eventually nationalised by Kwame Nkrumah soon after Ghana became independent. Several other newspapers emerged (Ainslie, 1966) in an attempt to reiterate the importance of self-rule. The *Asante Times* and Nkrumah's *Accra Evening News* were founded in 1947 for a similar purpose. According to Rosalind Ainslie (1966), "with the success of the *Accra Evening News*, Nkrumah again established the *Morning Telegraph* in Sekondi and the *Cape Coast Daily Mail*" (p. 58).

Post-Independence Era

Postcolonial press freedom in Africa was even more repressive than the colonial era. W. Joseph Campbell (1998) quoted the Nigerian publisher, Babatunde Jose, who claimed that postcolonial press in West Africa had relatively less freedom to publish than during colonial era. K. A. B. Jones-Quartey's (1974) account of the Ghanaian case was not different. While there were about forty newspapers circulating between 1931 and 1956, by the time Ghana became an independent state on March 6, 1957, only eleven newspapers were still in production. The irony was that even though the press had the potency to bring together the nation, this positive attribute was largely ignored. According to Dzisah (2008), this was partly due to the conduct of the opposition in splitting the country on tribal and regional lines. The benefits of post-independence press in Ghana were swiftly diminished by the political polarisation within which it operated. Nkrumah, who established a few of the nationalist newspapers and edited the *Evening News* as a private newspaper, was cited by Hachten (1971) expressing his disdain for the private press: "it is part of our revolutionary credo that with the competitive system of capitalism, the press cannot function in accordance with a strict regard for the sacredness of facts and that it therefore should no remain in private hands" (p. 168).

Post-independent press in Ghana had elements that were extremely unprofessional and destructive. The opposition newspapers openly supported secession of the country, an act that was deemed to have contributed to the drift towards civil and tribal war (Karikari, 1992; Hachten, 1971). While Karikari (1992) felt that the opposition newspapers, such as *The Ashanti Pioneer*, had lost their credibility due to their extreme tribal posture, Hachten (1971) disagreed, stating:

> Undoubtedly, the newspaper had loyal following and was a quavering but determined voice for freedom of expression in Ghana. The *Ashanti Pioneer* enjoyed an international reputation because it had always fought for its principles and its editors had gone to jail for them (p. 177).

In 1963, Nkrumah bought and nationalised *The Daily Graphic* newspaper with a daily circulation of 106,000 copies. *The Daily Graphic*, however, mainly retained its independence after it was nationalised, as a result of the newspaper's editors' resistance to a succession of oppressive governments, which in turn forced several editors into exile while others were forcefully and wrongfully removed from office (Asante, 1996).

The initial notion of Nkrumah to engage postcolonial press and journalism as an instrument of mobilisation for the development of a nation state was greatly undermined by press opposition (Awoonor, 1996). Successive military governments, having experienced what the press was capable of doing, maintained their locus of power spanning from the colonial powers era to Nkrumah's era of repressive press control. Initially, his proved relatively successful because both Independence and Republican Constitutions made no provision for press freedom except for Article 3 (i) of the 1960 Constitution which, according to Karikari (1998), stated:

> Subject to such restrictions as may be necessary for preserving public order, morality or health, no person should be deprived of freedom of religion or speech, of the rights to move and assembly without hindrance or the right to courts of law (pp. 164–65).

According to Karikari (1998), the newspaper licensing law appeared and re-appeared in several forms to limit press freedom especially in 1963 under Nkrumah. This was repealed by the multi-party parliament in 1970, was reinstated in 1973 only to be repealed once more in 1979. The Provisional National Defence Council (PNDC) government resorted to this law again in 1985.

However, from 1962 through to 1992, press freedom became very important in the Ghanaian constitution, allowing ordinary citizens to test the laws and their potential impact on a democratic Ghana. Before independence, Ghana had no electronic media other than Radio ZOY, set up by the colonial government that rebroadcast BBC programmes. In 1954, Radio ZOY was converted to Gold Coast Broadcasting Systems and to the Ghana Broadcasting Corporation (GBC) in 1956. Kwasi Ansu-Kyeremeh and Kwame Karikari (1998) suggest that post-independent Ghana "saw the mass media largely under government monopoly and control. From 1957 to 1981, one regime after another formulated its set of rules for the media (state newspapers, private newspapers and state electronic media) that proscribed private press activity and kept state-owned media under strict governmental controls" (p. 24). Newspapers, however, remained active throughout these struggles.

When Ghana eventually returned to constitutional rule in 1992, there were several provisions put in place which aimed at a free press, and the newspaper sector began to experience a considerable morale boost to effectively perform its watchdog roles. Following a long legal battle with the government during this period, the state monopoly over the broadcasting sector was deregulated to allow for private participation in broadcasting. Effective from 1996, the broadcasting sector was liberalised, facilitating the establishment of several private radio and TV stations in the country. Currently, there are five hundred and seventy-five (575) authorised FM radio stations and one hundred and forty-six (146) authorised television stations across Ghana (National Communication

Authority [NCA], 2nd Quarter/2020). The popular radio and TV stations and newspapers in Accra have active online presence. Some of the most popular online news websites include: Ghanaweb.com, Myjoyonline.com (Joy FM); Citifmonline.com (Citi FM); Peaceonline.com (Peace FM); Starrfmonline.com (Starr FM); Adomonline.com (Adom FM); Graphic.com.gh (*The Daily Graphic* newspaper); Dailyguideghana.com (*Daily Guide* newspaper); and Ghananewsagency.org (Ghana News Agency). It is important to indicate that the significant number of the articles which appear on online news portals (Ghanaweb.com) and radio stations are the same articles found on the front-pages of the popular newspapers (FES, 2014; Sikanku, 2011).

Newspapers remain the focus of this research because of their immense influence on media studies worldwide. David Altheide and Christopher Schneider (2013) note that a detailed analysis of print media data enables us to consider the social context in which stories are produced, and to examine the interaction between media representations and normative understandings/attitudes. Jennifer Hasty's findings (2005), which indicate that newspapers occupy the nexus of the Ghanaian media, are hardly surprising given that newspapers have remained crucial to the Ghanaian news discourse for a very long time. The centrality of newspapers in news discourse remains just as strong today, in spite of the massive proliferation of FM radio/TV stations. It is however imperative to include that newspapers in Ghana have become politically polarised in a manner that spells an end to their centrality at the country's press and political discourse. Investigative stories and bigger scandals critical of the current government are mostly published online by offshore news portal located in the Netherlands (Ghanaweb.com, modernghana.com).

FM radio/TV stations have extended the leverage of newspaper discourse with their newspaper reviews and morning show programmes whose discussions are heavily driven by newspaper content. The African Media Barometer Report (2014) confirmed this notion when it asserted that radio stations in Ghana often scavenge news from newspapers thereby enhancing accessibility to news found in newspapers. Few radio stations provide their own news and many of them simply "cannibalise" news from newspaper sources. Some newspapers run a small number of copies of their papers and circulate them to radio stations for use.

The potential to occupy a central national discourse is greatly increased when you appear in the newspaper (FES, 2014, p. 120).

The March 18, 2014 edition of *The Daily Graphic* newspaper in Ghana featured an editorial titled, "Newspaper Reviews Killing Print Media", which describes how the liberalised electronic media has drawn on newspaper content in their morning and late evening discussions. Some radio stations even read their news directly from the newspapers and these, according to the column, have resulted in declining newspaper sales.

Summary

This chapter provided the historical and contextual antecedents which render both the subject of foreign news imbalance and Ghana as effective choice of topics for this in-depth analysis. It encompasses the debate from the MacBride report, academic works led by Sreberny for International Association of Media and Communication Research (IAMCR), a collection of articles from Hawk and the recent work of Bunce et al. (2017). The MacBride report, which was written in response to imbalances that had been reported by developing countries arrived at very excellent conclusions. The Sreberny report sought to fill a gap of ignorance about representations of nations at the time and certain issues in international news that still required attention. The collaborative works of Hawk (1992) and Bunce et al. (2017) exemplified further academic investigation into the issue of representation and Western *Othering*.

Ghana has played a definitive role in African nationalism. This chapter recounts the country's history from pre-independence through to post-independence, to an overview of the current state of affairs of the Ghanaian media. This historical context largely accounts for the present situation of the Ghanaian press, which tends to be analysed without recourse to the history books. This chapter establishes why the Ghanaian case offers rich insight into the issues of ambivalence, continuity and understanding.

2. Benefitting from the State of the Art

This chapter summarises state-of-the-art research that has attempted to discuss the phenomenon of foreign news. The chapter begins with a description of foreign news and its usefulness to identity creation and recognition for both the reported nations and the dominant reporting nations. It offers useful definitions and conceptualisations and describes how Africa has been represented in the Western media — in particular, the use of negative images in this representation, which have become normalised over time. In turn, the chapter reviews the growing body of literature that argues that negative coverage of Africa in the Western press cannot be empirically supported (Nothias, 2017; Obijiofor and MacKinnon, 2016; Scott, 2015). It touches on how hegemony and representation of *Others* have become basic elements that the Western press uses to resist criticism and claim innocence. The effects of centuries of negative reporting on Africa and the continuing hegemony of foreign news production have contributed significantly to how Africans view themselves. This was illustrated with research that investigated the framework within which the African press was born and the influence of Northern news agencies on how the African press currently works.

The state of foreign news selection in Ghana is discussed with a focus on the history of journalism education in general, elements of colonial practice and the current liberalised media market. This chapter ends with a discussion on the way forward to improving foreign news coverage in and about Africa, along with the crucial opportunities and challenges new media technology offer in this regard.

Foreign News and its Usefulness

Even though foreign news is mostly evaluated negatively, as a false representation of reality, it nonetheless remains a dominant way for people around the world to inform themselves about each other, and to re-align events occurring across the globe to their local conditions. The usefulness of studying foreign news has mostly been grounded in research. Kwadwo Anokwa, Carolyn Lin and Michael Salwen (2003) refer to the increase in interaction among people and nations as a result of technology, and argue that in order to better describe this increase in interaction, researchers must examine the nature of communication and news among nations. This, in turn, will enhance international diplomacy and understanding of different nations. Melissa Johnson (1997) argues that "news about foreign countries matter because unrepresentative news can have a strong effect on media audiences" and "knowledge and conceptions about other nations, but positive exposure to mass media relates to positive images or accurate judgments about foreign countries" (p. 315).

Joseph Nye (2004) has hinted at the fact that *soft power* is also about *power over opinion*, especially in the current information era. Public diplomacy as an element of soft power relies on media communication to inform and influence the public (Guo and Vargo, 2017; Golan and Himelboim, 2016). T.-y. Ting (2010) holds the view that foreign news reporting has been influenced by a global consciousness — *foreign news going global* or *going transnational* — which re-established the genre's contemporary appeal.

Definitions and Conceptualisations

Pierre Bourdieu's (1998) description of the relationship between journalism and politics, while commenting on television, produced a definition that quite fits what we today call "foreign news". Bourdieu described TV as:

> a series of apparently absurd stories that all end up looking the same, endless parades of poverty-stricken countries, sequences of events that, having appeared with no explanation, will disappear with no solution — Zaire today, Bosnia yesterday, the Congo tomorrow (p. 7).

Supporting the illusory nature of foreign news, Bella Mody (2010) borrowed an allusion from Walter Lippmann to explain foreign news as our individual construction of a "picture in our heads" of distant places. These two descriptions reflect the understanding of Fergal Keane (2004) about his three decades career as a Foreign News Correspondent for the BBC World Service. He asserted that "since the end of colonialism, Western correspondents have stood in front of emaciated Africans or piles of African bodies and used the language of the Old Testament to mediate the horrors to their audiences" (p. 9). Foreign news on Africa should seemingly contain a sound bite from "white angels of mercy consisting of aid agencies, a brave white reporter and a backdrop of wretched African masses" (ibid.). Foreign correspondents and aid workers believed that, by doing so, the audience in Europe "related" better to the stories they were sending; "just as it's always been and always will be, they [the readers or audience] think, but for the goodness of our brave reporters and aid workers" (ibid.).

The representation of Africa as a failed and passive site in constant need of foreign assistance has occupied other researchers (Nothias, 2012; B'béri and Louw, 2011). The representation is not only unhealthy, but perpetuates some values and stereotypes through a kind of *register* that supports the continuation of oppression by the Global North (Said, 1978). Daniel Bach (2013) argues that the news narrative of Africa as the next business destination is also "an invitation to call back the ghosts of explorers, soldiers and sellers who each in their own way once discovered Africa" (p. 11). Because foreign news is a "major source of gaining knowledge, for most citizens of developed nations, about the foreign others" (Mody, 2010, p. 3), it occupies a crucial space in our knowledge formation. Ines Wolter (2006) continued this line of thinking and explained that the way the West perceives and reacts to people from different parts of the world depends largely on how these countries have been reported in the Western media. Victoria Schorr (2011) adds that negative reportage on Africa has implications for the flow of finance, trade and tourism to the continent and this informs intercultural relations too. Schorr's arguments were confirmed when audience research in developed nations suggested that media representations have an impact on how audiences in the Northern Hemisphere perceive Africa (Borowski, 2012). In Jo Fair's (1993) assessment of race in the construction of Africa's media image in the USA, she contends that the Western public's beliefs about the African continent, its people and countries, are largely informed by media-produced content, since no Western school system studies the continent in any significant form. Media coverage then remains a very useful element of education and a point of influence, relevant to understanding the representation of Africa among Western and non-Western societies, including African countries themselves. To Fair (1993), the problem is not just representation of Africa in the news media "per se, but the social implications and possible consequences for social representation and social reality are intimately entwined" (p. 1). She then argues that the historic exploitation of Africa was supported through the slave trade, colonial and postcolonial relations which continue to permeate Western representations of Africa with scope and complexity. Fair (1993) further suggests that representing some people as *Others*, and with negative images, serves to maintain and perpetuate social inequalities and "offer justification for the need to have colonised them" (p. 18).

Karikari (1992) suggests that the British colonial governments in Ghana, and other parts of Africa, used the Western press to propagate their agenda. This colonial tactic has not quite ended, according to D. M. Mengara (2001), since a predominantly racist view persists in the West about Africa, because the Africa we see today is European-made. Boulou Ebanda de B'Beri and P. Eric Louw (2011) contend that Africa has had no influence on or input into the negative and stereotypical representation it has received from Northern media organisations, and therefore does not have the ability to change the representation. With these arguments in mind, it is clear that media texts convey meaning and need to be handled in a manner that minimises negative portrayal. However, the investigation of international television news agencies by Chris Paterson (2011) drew our attention back to the concept of media imperialism, as he contended that the images we all share, and which substantially shape our political, economic and cultural lives, come almost entirely from two similar newsrooms in London. "This process of globalisation", he said, "is also a process of imperialism which has been hugely ignored in the globalisation discourse for the past three decades" (p. 18). Paterson provided further instances of how one could explore the extent to which contemporary imperialism has evolved to include

US and China, and how these countries have been made especially visible through the activities of global media (Paterson, 2017).

Mel Bunce et al. (2017) contends that the Northern press's news construction of Africa as a business destination — as a claim of improvement — still constitutes a postcolonial critique. But for the economic standstill and ageing population in the Northern Hemisphere, Africa would not have enjoyed this tag that it rightfully deserved. The *Africa rising* discourse has other contexts too. For example, as a new economic giant (China) appears aggressively to compete with the Northern economic influences on the African continent; for this reason, Africa needs to be better presented in the West as a place for investments opportunities. Apart from the fact that this isn't significantly different from the binary discourse of the Cold War, it is also contradictory to contemporary experiences of some journalists on the continent who are still faced with the *Old Testament* discourse, like Mohammed Amin recounted in an interview with Chris Paterson in 1995 (cited in Bunce et al., 2017, p. 2).

> There's a mentality. Nigeria — those elections a few years ago (1993) — and I was talking to my editor, wanting us to put in a crew in Nigeria. And the response was "Is there going to be trouble?" Well, my answer was, "There's a reasonably good chance there will be trouble, but this is an important country. Should we not be covering the elections? If there is trouble, of course, we cover the trouble as well". "Well", they said, "... if there are dead bodies on the streets of Lagos we've got to go in there". Now, you know, I am sick of that sort of an attitude! I wonder if the same editor would think like that if there are coming elections in Britain or France or America — that you've got to wait until there are dead bodies in the street... They think alike about Africa.

Again, Bunce (2015) claimed that local journalists' involvement in the field of foreign news production presents a diversity that results in healthy power dynamics, reflecting what African news should look like. But Salim Amin dissented from this claim when he argued, in the same collected edition, that Al Jazeera's launch was a perfect beginning with double capability and visibility on the continent compared to other international news media. However, the network was headquartered outside of the continent and "final decisions, on what the news must look like were taken by men and women with little knowledge of the continent" (Amin, 2017, pp. 96–97).

The growing need to cut cost in reporting on foreign countries has also resulted in a situation known in procurement terms as *sole-sourcing*. News *sole-sourcing* means buying agency material on specific items from one foreign news agency. This phenomenon significantly affects journalism's cannons of objectivity and impartiality, per the analysis of Paterson (2011), because it contributes to the "reinforcement of the hegemony of the two powerful news agencies in London and that is inherently partial" (p. 13).

Stuart Hall (1986, p. 86) similarly argued that the "media's illusive nature of presenting what it called an objective and impartial news, which usually either established a dominant ideological discursive field as a valid or partial explanation as comprehensive, remains contentious." When news agencies are running as businesses and even engage in mergers and acquisitions as well as increasing the shareholders' wealth, it becomes more difficult to accept that the views they express are free of interests and represent the public good. While the MacBride and Sreberny reports mentioned five dominant news agencies in the 1980s, Paterson (2011) confirmed the dominance of only two agencies, whom not even the mighty British Broadcasting Corporation (BBC), with all its foreign correspondents, can do without for a week.

The debate to validate the global media's power to influence foreign policy continues unabated. However, there is ample evidence presented by Piers Robinson (2002, p. 123) that media influences foreign policy. Robinson's argument supports the claim that "the CNN effect is a factor in influencing policy-makers' decisions to intervene during humanitarian crises." In a rather critical approach, Eytan Gilboa (2005) contended that even though the CNN effect had been exaggerated, it did not affect the fact that the global news networks play multiple roles in policy-making, diplomacy and international relations, and that rigorous theoretical and methodological frameworks are required to better establish the roles and their effects. It is quite clear then that the reporting of Africa in the global media needs to be accurate and comprehensive to be able to attract the necessary attention the continent deserves in order to develop. Indeed, Vincent Price and Edward Czilli (1996) substantiate the fact that among the several factors predicting news recall, the intensity of foreign news coverage is a good predictor of an audience's understanding of international affairs.

However, other scholars contest the direction of influence between the foreign media and Western foreign policy. Is it the Western media that drives US foreign policy or is the Western media driven by US foreign policy? Christian Fuchs (2010) supports the latter, arguing that the neo-imperialist project is significantly kept alive by the contemporary corporate transnational media, who act in line with US foreign policy. Hall (2013) makes the argument even more comprehensive when he stated that external participation in Africa has been dodgy with developed nations using international corporations in labour, resources, consumers markets and land to cover their real activities. However, Bunce et al. (2017) raised a thoughtful question: "Are these evolving interventions exploitative or cooperative, and does a discourse of neo-imperialism itself support a neo-colonial media image of Africa as a continent and one fifth of the world's population incapable of autonomy" (p. 7).

The editor of *New African* magazine, Baffour Ankomah, suggests that political ideology, Western government foreign policy, economic interest and *historical baggage* are the major reasons why Africa remains negatively reported in the Western media. In this statement, Ankomah (2011) implies that the Western press is driven by Western foreign policy. He further highlights the central role played by American political ideology in Western media reporting on Africa. To quote a cover story of the *New African* magazine, he notes that:

> if the western government foreign policy favours you, their media will favour you, their media will consider you, but if they are against you, then you cannot escape what Lord Beaverbrook referred to as a "flaming sword" which cuts through political armour (Ankomah, 2008, p. 12).

A classic example of Ankomah's analogy is the claim by Kirsten Bookmiller and Robert Bookmiller (1992) that the coverage of the Algerian War of Independence, from 1954 to 1962, labelled supporters of the resistance as communist-friendly and as a result of these sensational labels, many Americans were prevented from understanding the real issues of the Algerian war. This strategy supports America's foreign policy towards France. Public perception of Africa in countries where negative news is the order of the day remains negative, simply because, in most cases, the population exclusively relies on media information for understanding Africa.

As highlighted by Suzanne Franks (2006), an online BBC survey in 2004 reported a staggering 73% of its respondents in the UK were unaware of the Millennium Development Goals. The UK public's lack of awareness of these goals makes it more difficult for them to demand better coverage from their public broadcasters, and, because there is no demand for increased or improved coverage, the media coverage of such development goals diminishes. This occurs because most audiences in Western countries do not understand the frameworks put in place to overcome the challenges within the Millennium Development Goals, especially poverty, and the progress that has been made in that regard in the Global South. This results in a vicious cycle where Northern media practitioners argue that they are gauging the taste of their audiences, as if the audiences are capable of evaluating their "news tastes" under these circumstances.

The absence of regular correspondents and news attention on Africa is not the only factor affecting the quality of foreign reporting on Africa; longer television documentaries, providing adequate context and balanced education, are also in decline. The Third World and Environment Broadcasting Project has tracked television coverage of developing countries between 1989 and 2003; they reported that Africa received the least television coverage in terms of documentary and education programmes (Dover Barnett, 2004). Western news media's decision to focus on the Rwandan refugee crisis, as opposed to the Rwandan genocide, fits into a well-known, conventionalised understanding of Africa as a place where adverse events happen, and where Africans are in constant need of Western intervention and assistance (Girardet, 1996). The events reported on are homogenously negative in nature — a phenomenon referred to as "coups and earthquakes" syndrome by Mort Rosenblum (1979). A. L. Dahir (as cited in Akinfeleye et al., 2009) summarised the content of CNN and Reuters reporting on specific programmes and made allusion to what "the Nigerian journalist, Pascal Eze calls [...] 'PIDIC Perspective': poverty, instability, disease, illiteracy, and corruption" (p. 452). To Dahir, it does not matter who hosted the programme; the images are still negative even when people of African descent host programmes on Western networks. There is rarely space for an alternative view of Africans. H. W. French (2017) wrote to *The New York Times* complaining of an extraordinary approach by the network "to render black people of African ancestry voiceless and invisible". He described their work on Africa as a "scene of misery: people whose thoughts, experiences and actions were treated totally of no interest" (p. 38). Over the years, Western journalists and media owners have defended themselves by resorting to the argument that they are catering to a perceived taste of their immediate Western audience who require context for them to understand the news on Africa (Hawk, 1992).

Another act of defence is the Talloires Declaration, a conference held in France, to denounce UNESCO's promotion of New World Information and Communication Order (NWICO). The conference stated that "Press freedom is a basic human right" (p.16). Kaarle Nordenstreng (2010) offers two explanations to refute that declaration. First, the subject under international law from which "the right to freedom of opinion and expression" emanates is the *individual* (everyone) not the media (press). Second, the human right, which is invoked here, "comes with duties and responsibilities and could not be exercised in a manner that is dangerous to the interest of the international community" (p. 10) and preservation of peace and security. The popular "vast wasteland" speech by Newton Minow in 1961 to the American Federal Communication Commission (FCC) conference brings two elements to the fore that established the responsibility required of reporters in most Western democracies:

> First, what you gentlemen broadcast through the people's air affects the people's taste, their knowledge, their opinions, their understanding of themselves and of their world — and their future. Second, the people own the air. And they own it as much in prime evening time as they do at six o'clock Sunday morning. For every hour that the people give you ... you owe them something. And I intend to see that your debt is paid with service (p. 14).

Minow is asking for American journalists to be responsible about the quality of their service to the American people. Nordenstreng (2010) and H. Eek (1997) however, have asked for an extension of these principles to foreign countries or *foreign Others*. Nordenstreng (2010) argues that even though "NWICO was attacked as a curb on media freedom, in reality, the concept was designed to widen and deepen the freedom of information by increasing its balance and diversity on a global scale" (p. 3).

This section has explored some of the arguments regarding NWICO, the MacBride and Sreberny-Mohammadi reports. It also highlighted some of the defences Western journalists and institutions raise against the new world order request and how inconsistent their defence is in relation to international law. The next section describes the opportunities presented by the Internet and the digital era as a way of dealing with *foreign otherness*.

Opportunities in the Digital and Internet Era

The digital age brought with it a number of promises regarding how foreign coverage, both in the press in the Northern Hemisphere and the within the African continent, could improve. Many of these promises to tackle problems in foreign news reporting and journalism relied on ideas about the ease of the Internet. A prominent problem to arise was the issue of the 2008 Global Financial Crisis, resulting in the closure of foreign news bureaus. Levi Obijiofor and F. Hanusch (2011) describe the *lone person* reporter — an individual equipped with the necessary digital regalia to cover events around the world — as the innovation that will transform foreign news in many ways, both positively and negatively.

The sharp decline in foreign news around the world has been well established in media studies literature (Altmeppen, 2010; Wolter, 2006; and Franks, 2005). The most disturbing dimension of this phenomenon is that it counters scholars' predictions that the digital age would offer increased opportunities for wider global coverage. Indeed, Simon Cottle (2009) has expressed dissatisfaction with the capacity of journalists and media organisations to capture diverse issues of global concern. While the impact of technology is clearly visible in multiple ways, it has nonetheless defied the expectations of role allocation that occupied researchers at the beginning of the Internet era.

Rachel Flamenbaum (2017) describes how Ghanaians negotiated the social media terrain in a manner that puts the *Africa rising* discourse to positive use and engenders agency. She argues that a conscious effort took place to represent Ghana and Africa positively and with optimistic interpretations of experiences that have habitually been negated throughout history by Western countries. To Flamenbaum, the notion of *New Ghana* seems to reject the enduring narratives of negativity and economic failure that pervade postcolonial West Africa, both inwardly and outwardly. However, the fact that this social media activism has not become prominent on mainstream media demonstrates the limited extent to which this positive agency over narrating Africa has travelled beyond the continent.

Coverage of African News

The coverage of news in Africa has been investigated with varied perspectives and from different geopolitical positions. Harvey Feinberg and Joseph Solodow (2002) examine the long legacy of Africa's negative image through an exploration of the adage "always something new coming out of Africa", the origins of which can be traced to ancient Greece. They demonstrate that the phrase, which Aristotle made allusion to, was a proverb originating in Greece no later than the fourth century BC. As such, as Feinberg and Solodow argue, the phrase can be used as evidence for the long history of *Africa's Otherness*.

In line with the arguments of this book, the following sections will deal with the reporting of Africa in the press in the Northern Hemisphere, and the African press itself. This contrast will reveal the wide evolution of the systemic *Afro-pessimism* concept, especially in the African continent itself. This is not to argue that African journalists are not doing better than their Western counterparts in covering the continent, but rather that the present state of affairs is in part accounted for by centuries of domination, resulting in an endemic dependence syndrome. This argument is substantiated by the findings of this book.

It is also useful to highlight recent research finding that the coverage of Africa in Western countries was not as negative as previous researchers have argued; Obijiofor and Mairead MacKinnon (2016) argue that the concept of negative representation of Africa in the Western media could not be empirically supported in the case of Australia. They claim that the Australian press "devoted a modest amount of coverage to African news. All four regions of the continent received coverage" (p. 41). Meanwhile, Martin Scott (2009, 2015) argues that because studies asserting the prevalence of *Afro-pessimism* had barely covered North Africa, Francophone Africa, non-news genres, non-elite media and radio content, it is problematic for such studies to propose generalised conclusions regarding the nature of media coverage of Africa. He contends that the "assumption that representations are dominated by Afro-pessimism, for example, maybe accurate — but it is not currently substantiated by the existing evidence" (p. 191).

Reporting Africa in the Press in the Northern Hemisphere

Several aspects of the coverage of Africa in the dominant media of the Northern Hemisphere are presently examined. The most significant aspects are the nature and amount of coverage, and the possible reasons accounting for the nature and amount of coverage. Specifically, coverage is insignificant in terms of number, but significant in terms of negativity and stereotypical representation — a concept that has become known as *Afro-pessimism*. In this section, I review scholarly works conducted on the reasons for the nature and amount of coverage Africa receives in the Northern press.

The term *Afro-pessimism* suggests that Africa has little or no prospect of positive development (Schmidt and Garrett, 2011, p. 423; Evans, 2011, p. 400). *Afro-pessimism* can be very difficult to explain because it is an expansive concept. In this book, I adopt four parameters in order to evaluate it. The first parameter — in accordance with Bunce (2017), Anju Chaudhary (2001) and Susan Moeller (1999) — is subject matter: stories that focus exclusively on events that are negative in nature, such as famine, disease, wars, poverty and killings. The second parameter is the tone of the reportage, that is, when an event or policy is negatively evaluated on the whole, whilst ignoring positive aspects that are also crucial to the discussion. The third parameter is the omission or silence on some parts of a complex reality, either consciously or inadvertently, either because of a lack of native knowledge or because the media or reporting body in question adopts a simplistic posture in reporting complex issues (Nyamnjoh, 2017; Mody, 2010; Hawk, 1992). The fourth parameter is the negation of positive stories by framing them against an outdated or unrelated contextual background. For example, when Nigeria's new commitment to democratic changes of government is discussed as a positive, within the same reporting story, there is context material stating that "Nigeria is that West African country where 200 girls have been abducted by Boko Haram". Even though this is factual, one wonders what it is doing in a story recounting a positive event about Nigeria's democratic changes.

The Western media coverage of Africa, Africans and African issues has always been problematic, because these media reports are informed by Western ideas, ideology and political positions. Beverly Hawk (1992) explains this broadly:

> Africa is special because there is little common understanding between Africans and Americans to provide context for interpretation. Furthermore, unusual historical relations have shaped knowledge regarding Africa. These repertoires of knowledge, symbols and prior structuring of Africa are a Western creation. Where African news is concerned, then, American readers are in special need of contextualised information with which to interpret the meaning of reported events (p. 4).

Hawk (1992) added that the simplest way to communicate the African story in a comprehensible form, in limited space, is by reductionist colonial metaphors familiar to the reader, especially that of the tribe and collective "Africa". The resulting media image is a "crocodile-infested dark continent where jungle life has perpetually eluded civilisation" (p. 9). According to S. Franks (2005), the stories should fit into the usual frames of famine, disaster and bizarre traditional practices for it to make it in the Western media. Paddy Coulter, former head of communications at Oxfam and now with the Reuters Foundation, called for the need to sustain good reporting on Africa when he admonished journalists as follows:

> We need to break out of the cycle where editors complain that there are never any good ideas about Africa and producers claim that editors are never interested anyway. The challenge is to come up with imaginative and challenging ideas so that Africa continues to command serious coverage in years to come (Franks, 2005, p. 134)

Coulter's expression is an example of self-reflection and reflexivity; two crucial self- questioning elements that he and most other journalists lack during their training and practicing career. Mody (2010) highlights these concerns by asking, "whose version does the foreign news 'represent', anytime it is reported, what does it emphasise and what is it silent on?" (p. 13). According to Mody, journalists are limited by the conditions under which they work (deadlines, threats to their life, political hurdles and lack of language capacity) to answer those questions. Apart from the lack of reflexivity, "journalists forget either knowingly or unknowingly how stereotypes and myths which have under-girded colonialism remain unchallenged by both the Western media and the journalists themselves" (Mody, 2010, p. 3; Harth, 2012, p. 2).

David Slater (2004) argues that the West has not only failed to engage in self-reflection of its dark past, but it also has virtually no counter-representation from the developing countries. According to Amy Harth (2012), during the Cold War — where there was the representation of ideas and counter-representations based on individual bloc ideologies — African countries were engaged in liberation movements for the establishment of the right to self-determination. Harth further establishes that this preoccupation of the African people was even misreported as the ensuing conflicts were mostly constructed as proxy wars between the USA and the USSR within the Cold War paradigm. Harth (2012) contends that the overwhelming success of colonialism continues "to cause the Western media to perpetuate unquestioned ingrained stereotypes and myths that were created in order to justify colonial conquest and racially-based exploitation and these account for the continued under-representation and misrepresentation of Africa in the Western media" (p. 3). Francis Nyamnjoh (2017) calls for plurality in the perspectives on Africa, since such plurality recognises that the single Northern media perspective — with its exclusive prerogatives — is inherently misrepresentative of Africa because, like any other identity, the African identity is a work in progress.

The issues omitted or not reported are equally essential. One way to shape stories about Africa, to conform both to current policy objectives and to the conventional understanding of most US readers, is simply not to report them. "The single most common form of media misrepresentation" regarding the developing countries "is omission" (Mody, 2010; Parenti, 1993, p. 192). Hawk (1992, p. 6) continues by noting that "Africa is truly 'covered' by the Western press in the sense that important stories go unreported". There is also the neglect of the power of global corporations to investigate important issues like food, mass killings and crises (Shiva, 2009; Tunstall, 2008). Keane (2004) requested to see from his colleague journalists in the Western media, stories of resilient African newspapers, broadcast media and civic society working hard to improve the continent's fortunes. The story of Salim Amin, son of the famous cameraman Mohamed Amin of Nairobi, paints a pathetic picture of these omissions. He argues, "We cannot sell anything positive about Africa even though we do plenty of positive stories, on subjects other than war and disaster, but they are mainly for an African audience now, because we cannot move them internationally" (BBC History Seminar, 24 November 2004 cited in Franks, 2005, p. 133).

Oliver Boyd-Barrett (2004) argues that the over-reliance on official sources in foreign news reporting results in the neglect for causes, processes and consequences of events. Mody (2010, p. 16) supports this notion and further explains that "lack of ideas and explanations about root-causes obfuscates understanding that could lead to real change." Mody argues that the coercion from the West, which interrupted the indigenous development of Africa, Asia and the Caribbean, has its impacts on modern-day difficulties in the colonies. Discussing the troubles of the colonies, such as *poverty*, only from the perspective of civil war, corruption and incompetent institutions, is to say that colonisation, class relations, divide and rule, exploitations and structured injustices never existed, or if they did exist, they had no impact on the continent's path of development. Mody (2010) establishes that "hunger, disease, death and illiteracy are symptoms of a more basic structural cause that is historically situated and globally interconnected..." (pp. 16–17). Walter Lippmann (1922, p. 30) reasoned that there are images that limit journalists' access to facts, such as:

> artificial censorship, the limitations of social contact, the comparatively meagre time available in each day for paying attention to public affairs, the distortion arising because events have to be compressed into very short messages, the difficulty of making a small vocabulary express a complicated world....

Lippmann's assertions explained the shallow manner in which Western journalists tackle the reporting of complicated issues in Africa. However, all too often, the journalists appear to have a good idea already of the portion of these complications that relates to the contribution of colonialism and interconnectedness of the world today. Lippmann termed this as the *pictures inside* that so often mislead men in their dealings with the outside world. Even though Lippmann's main concern was with the *Self and Other*, these are the issues that have taken a macro shape in today's geopolitical debate.

The American journalism author, James Carey, substantiates Lippmann's assertions. He maintains that the idea of *explanation* is inconsistent with the profession of journalism's insistence on *facts*. No matter how useful explanation will be to a text, journalists are not interested because they do not have the space or time, and someone else must vet their work using simple objective and mechanistic rules. Boyd-Barrett (2004) defers from Carey's position, arguing that the propagandist and selective nature of US war reporting, could not be the result only of journalism's insistence on facts, but also ideology. Harth (2012) and Mody (2010) claim that the colonial hangover and geopolitical terrain of twenty-first century reporting are contributory elements to this debate. Joanne Sharp (1993, p. 491) gave a broader view to this discussion when she argued that the "mass media provide the context within which elite geopolitical texts are produced, disseminated and received." To her, this is crucial because the rippling effects of these press images, and public discourses on them, eventually get established as conversational wisdom. Garth Myers, Thomas Klak and Timothy Koehl (1996) investigate Western media coverage of Rwandan and Bosnian wars and demonstrate that, through such practices mentioned by Sharp, "many unequal power relationships are articulated, reinforced and perpetuated" (p. 22).

Frames with which Western media cover Africa have not improved because the actors have not changed. News agencies, according to Mody (2010) and Paterson (2011), have become hegemonic in nature, and are relied on by most Western news organisations to an extent unlike anything before. Bunce et al. (2017) observe a few improvements when comparing two time periods, which presents a hopeful look at the future; however, no consistent picture of change exists among the dominant Northern media organisations.

At this point, I will review some specific studies on the coverage of Africa in the Western media. The claim that Africa is hardly covered in the Western press has been established by many scholars (Galtung and Ruge 1965; MacBride, 1980; Sreberny et al., 1985; Hawk, 1992, Fair, 1993; Franks, 2005; Mody, 2010). However, one insightful approach to confirming these studies was the study conducted by Myers et al. (1996), using comparative research that analysed US newspapers' coverage of civil wars in Bosnia (Europe) and Rwanda (Africa). Rwanda recorded 560 articles and Bosnia 14,114 articles within the same period. Bosnia was covered twenty-five times more than Rwanda, irrespective of the magnitude of the conflict in Rwanda. The articles on Bosnia were twice more elaborate on strategies and tactics than the ones on Rwanda. There was significantly less/almost no usage, in many cases, of the terms "tribal" and "ethnic" in the description of the Bosnian war, while the Rwandan reports were filled more than forty times with these terms. Myers et al. (1996, p. 36) contends that the "US press depiction of Bosnia's war is that it is a logical and considered outcome of historical events while Rwanda's war is simply centuries-old tribal savagery." These negative frames, according to Myers et al. (1996), were constructed by the "US press almost entirely from non-Africa sources who depicted Africa as a timeless and placeless realm of 'tribal' conflict, the repository of deep-seated US fears of African 'Others'" (p. 21).

Moreover, there is also the issue of journalistic error. M. Robins (2003) analysed the coverage of the Sudanese Lost Boys by top US newspapers, and found that the stories were presented out of context and many of them contained discrepancies in the details of Sudan's civil war. Robin's study indicates that "rather than showing an increased sensitivity to international news, many newspapers just recycled incomplete images of Africa that fit into the American expectations and dominant foreign policy discourse in that country" (p. 45). Erroneous and negative press coverage of Africa is fundamental to the knowledge of the citizens in those Western countries where these publications are made. In a public attitudes survey, Deborah Lader (2007, p. 3) reports that "47 per cent of UK citizens use newspapers as a source of information about the lives of poor people in Africa." The results from Andrew Darnton's Public Perceptions of Poverty (PPP) study show that while tabloid readers were, on average, less likely to agree with the statement "we need trade justice, not free trade" (Darnton, 2005a, p. 12), broadsheet readers were, on average, more likely to be "very concerned" about poverty in poor countries (Darnton, 2005b, p. 6). Although the correlation between press coverage and audience understanding suggested by these studies does not prove causality, it does give a strong indication of the influence of Western media portrayal of Africa on the citizens of their respective countries.

In 2007, the President of Rwanda, Paul Kagame, admitted: "the constant negative reporting of Africa kills the growth of direct foreign investment. There have been suggestions that this is meant to keep Africa in the backyard of the global economy" (Ankomah, 2008, p. 146). In essence, some studies have linked Africa's negative media image to the perception of the continent held by some people and institutions in the Northern Hemisphere. H. M. El Zein and Anne Cooper (1992) examined *The New York Times'* coverage of Africa for roughly two decades. They found that Africa constituted 15% to 20% of all international news coverage and over half of the continent's countries were never mentioned at all. For those mentioned, 53.8% to 87.7% of the coverage related to crises. Africa received extremely little front-page coverage except in a few cases concerning brutal warfare. Due to the concepts of "pack and parachute journalism" (Fair, 1993, p. 9) and the growing hegemony in global newsgathering, this particular example is unlikely to differ from the situations elsewhere in most Western nations. The Voluntary Service Overseas's *Live Aid Legacy* studies, cited in Scott (2009), investigated the nature of the negative portrayal of Africa and found that perceptions of Africa were markedly different from perceptions of other areas of the developing world. The study identifies that negative frames found in Africa consist of poverty and famine, and these conditions are understood to be the result of circumstantial and "natural" factors.

A. S. de Beer (2010) launched a new conversation, arguing that, due to globalisation, news media content could no longer be pinned to a territory or to previous binary concepts as national/international, core/periphery. Beer argues for a disruption of these binary categorisations, both because these binaries do not exist in reality, and because the assumption that Africa is predominantly reported as a hopeless continent is itself changing, especially as a result of the significant progress that has been reported in the work of Minabere Ibelema and Tanja Bosch (2009). In line with this thinking, Scott (2015) suggested that Africa's "negative" representation in the US and UK press has little empirical evidence supporting it. To him, the claim that the coverage is characterised by essentialisation, racialisation, selectivity, ethnocentric ranking and predictions lacks a typology until fairly recently (see the typology of *Afro-pessimism* in Nothias, 2015). He further refers to the body of literature making such claims as reliant on "widespread vagueness surrounding the ontologies of Africa and the ways in which representations of Africa are understood to contribute to the construction of Africa" (p. 206). Toussaint Nothias (2017) provided further empirical support for Scott's work through textual analysis of British and French newspapers –complemented by interviews. He found that the claims about the coverage of Africa being systematically *tribal* and *dark*, relying predominantly on *Western voices* and homogenous in portrayal, are not empirically supported.

Reporting Africa in the African Press

This section provides a review of previous studies that have focused on how the African press reported the continent, as a whole, and some events in particular. The coverage African countries receive from each other reflects in some instances their foreign policy. John Lent (1976, p. 181) argues that foreign news reporting in developing countries depended on their ties with the superpowers, colonial background, relationship with neighbouring countries, economic infrastructure, governmental stability and professional training of journalists. Due to those factors, countries in Western Europe and North America have become a "semi-permanent" option for these developing countries. Nigerian coverage of foreign news has been linked to the country's foreign policy and socio-cultural ties (Nwuneli and Udoh, 1982; da Costa, 1980). O. E. Nwuneli and O. Dare (1977) found that the recognition of the People's Movement for the Liberation of Angola (MPLA) government by Nigerian federal government led to an increase in the volume of news about Angola in the Nigerian press around that time. In addition to this foreign policy move by the Nigerian government, the Nigerian press also depended heavily on foreign news agencies for their coverage, confirming Lent's (1976) assertion regarding proxy coverage through colonial- and superpowers.

Emmanuel Alozie (2007) studied the pattern dominating the coverage and analyses of the 1994 Rwandan crisis in two leading African newspapers: the Kenyan *Daily Nation*, and the Nigerian *The Guardian*. He found that both papers attempted to explore the background and implication of the crisis more than their Western counterparts. This success was attributed to their "greater understanding of the underlying matters that affect the continent" (p. 226). The proximity of Kenya to Rwanda and their national interest in the crisis resulted in prolonged coverage and a deeper background, compared to Nigerian coverage of the crisis.

The Framework of the African Press

In this section, the conceptual explication of how the African press reports itself is introduced. This is followed by a discussion of the influence of transnational global news media on the African press, the goals of Pan-African News Agency (PANA) press, the relationship between new media technologies and foreign news, and previous research on how selected African media reported some countries on the continent.

The colonial domination of the African continent for centuries significantly shaped the way people on the continent and elsewhere formed their identity. To Frantz Fanon (2008, originally published 1952), this resulted in a situation where the colonised lost the possibility for autonomous cultural identity, and where legitimacy can only be gained through the taking on of Western ideals. Stuart Hall (1997) equally demonstrated that negative representation of a group of people affects the group's self-identity, which becomes shaped by how they are seen by others.

In the light of these assertions, coupled with Galtung and Mari Ruge's seminal findings (1965) — that a feudal interaction structure keeps dominated nations in the periphery, with little or no communication within or between these nations — no analysis of the African press should ignore the powerful impact of the past, and the way in which it re-enacts itself even today. This lack of news flow among African countries, coupled with an increasing conglomeration within the international news agency sector, makes the African news organisations even more vulnerable, than their European counterparts, to depending on agency materials for much of their work. Nyamnjoh (2017) explains that the call for African perspectives is not a claim that African journalists will escape stereotypes and misrepresentations when reporting the continent; it is rather a call to recognise that other views exist.

One of the uses of investigating foreign news flow among African countries, as in this study, is to show how Africa has been affected by both the psychological mechanism described by Fanon and the hegemonic conglomeration of the foreign news agency sector (Paterson, 2011). These perspectives on coverage have thus far been absent from the discussion, as previous studies (Akinfeleye et al., 2009; Pate, 1992 and Sobowale, 1987) concluding that African media were doing no better than their Western counterparts failed to investigate the predominant sources employed by the African press in these reports, and the roots of journalism education on the continent. Equally crucial is the economic capacity of the African press and the worldwide growing hegemony within the foreign news sector.

One crucial element in informing ourselves about one another is *education*. Since most African countries do not study the continent well enough within their school systems or through exchange programmes, a palpable knowledge gap exists across the continent itself that plays into the idea of relying on the former colonial master's news about the continent. Kuselwa Gongo (2007), in analysing South Africa's *Sunday City Press* newspaper, in the light of the paper's repositioning as distinctly African, concludes that *City Press* could not uphold the ideals of the African Renaissance and African nationalism in its reporting of Africa since much of what it reported only related to Africans in South Africa: "the huge knowledge gap about the continent among the South African reporters and editors was a major defect" (p. 147). In a speech to the Editor's Forum of NEPAD (New Partnership for Africa's Development), former South African President, Thabo Mbeki, asked African journalists to report on Africa especially effectively, because they were first Africans to become journalists, and it is paramount to put an end to the dangerous *state of unknowing* about the continent (Mbeki, 2003).

Western Education and Media Assistance

Diffusion of modernisation and innovation and its spread around the world can be traced to different forms of dependence by most developing countries on their developed counterparts. The relatedness of journalism training to the lingering Cold War diplomatic strategy of influence and spread of democratic governance has been established in media studies literature (Miller, 2009; Becker and Tudor, 2005). Ellen Hume (2004) argues that the developed nations came to appreciate, based on the experience from Eastern Europe, that "providing assistance to local, independent media is a vital way to promote freedom and democracy" (p. 110). Some scholars have traced this continued support for the media in developing countries to historical antecedents. Thomas McPhail (2006) argued that the world communication system we live in today is "an outgrowth of prior colonial patterns reflecting commercial and market imperatives" (p. 13). In fact, media culture is "transnational" in that it operates on a global scale, and is being produced by transnational media-conglomerates who have a good understanding of the linkage between the "logic of media and the logic of transnational capital" and the "satisfaction transnational elites" stand to get (Rønning, 1997, pp. 13–15).

James Scotton and Sharon Murphy (1987) argue that the adoption of the American model on the African continent was partly due to the choice of sponsors of journalism training on the continent at the time. Winston Mano (2005) holds the view that transnational media organisations undermine various democratic processes in Africa, but often these disruptions are covered by their exercise of a positive influence on media development across the continent (Barker, 2008). These arguments represent reinforcements of previous positions held by scholars on Africa's historical entanglements. Walter Rodney (1981) posits that the aim of British colonial education, which is still prominent in African universities, was to turn the African into a "fair-minded English-man" (p. 248). Ali Mazrui (1978) asserts that whether the education be British or French, the "African might, therefore, be regarded as the reflections of the total cultural orientations of the countries which ruled them" (p. 12). The fact that the African artists can be noticed from their colonial background is evidence of "the phenomenon of cultural dependency in all its ramifications" (p. 13).

Scotton and Murphy (1987), referring to Mazrui and others' line of argument of Mazrui, contend that "African students even at the university level were taught to be critical of all values they have learned previously in the African setting" (p. 13), which results in the disowning of previous African values and taking on new Western ideals as a sign of being educated. They argue that journalism education programmes in Africa are largely patterned directly on those in Europe and the United States to an extent that these programmes could be moved to the US, for example, "without changing texts, curriculum, or instructors" (p. 12). They also argue that the resistance to the adoption of a complete American model in the newly independent African states, staged by Britain and France, through the offer of various journalism training programmes in Europe were rather damaging, because it resulted in a competition over influence, rather than prioritising the development of the African press.

The lack of change reported by Scotton and Murphy can be traced in the argument of Terje Skjerdal (2012) that the African journalists today "regard themselves as members of a wider professional community beyond the continent while simultaneously maintaining a local identity" (p. 649). This provides a hint of the new space, which is partly Western and partly African. However, this conceptual hybrid space is characterised by a lopsided relationship. J. K. Domatob (1988) argues that the lopsidedness of this power relation is evident in the heavy dependence of sub-Saharan African media on neo-colonial status quo with regards to "training, policies, technology, news values, language, and advertising" (p. 151). Domatob further argues that an attempt to decolonise the Western model of communication and the "ideology of dependence remains difficult" (p. 171). The application of Western media practices in the African context unequivocally represents a reinforcement of neo-colonialism (Banda, 2008a) and undermines and misrepresents local culture (Sesanti, 2009).

Nancy Holm (2016) maintains that the entire *Bologna Process* to standardise journalism education across Europe has contributed to the formation of best practices, which she argues, always conflicts cultural values. In her case study of Denmark, Holm posits that the acceptance of Anglo-American on-camera presentation styles violates deeply-held Danish cultural values. She further asserts that cultural values matter and journalism educators need to pay attention to them even in the era of globalisation. According to Guy Berger (2014), "the ethos is one of journalism schools worldwide that relate to media experiences and educational recipes, which are assumed to be applicable worldwide" (p. 33). Berger concludes with this underpinning argument that journalism education around the world is not same and, as such, African institutions teaching journalism have begun defining their own specificity, with regards to excellence, in this heterogeneous communication field. This leads us to our next section, which discusses how technology is affecting dependence on Western agencies and shaping foreign news reporting worldwide. By answering some of the rhetorical questions posed by Obijiofor (2009, pp. 51–52), we will be better placed to understand the context we are dealing with:

> ... how have technological changes such as Internet impacted the image of Africa in the western media and to what extent have African news organisations been able to source their news without relying on multinational news agencies?

New Media Technologies, the Internet and Economic Rationality

William Hachten (2004, p. 87) sets the tone for this sub-section:

> If Africa is to develop economically and politically in the coming years, Western news media must do a better job of reporting events there. But even more important, African nations must acquire free and independent news media of their own — news systems that utilize the new information technologies communication satellites, global television, high-speed computer exchanges — that most of the world now uses.

Hachten's advice is ever more important because the "internet and the application of information technologies have caused far-reaching changes within work processes and routines in most industries around the world especially digitalisation of value chains and content have demanded a strategic change in perspectives within the media industry" (Zerdick, Picot, Schrape et al., 2001 cited in Schoeder and Stovall, 2011, p. 23). The Internet and its applications have had an influence on organisations, contents and journalists. The Erich Brost Institute's research into German foreign correspondents in the USA reveals increased use of emails and VoIP phoning, frequent visits to employer's websites, regular monitoring of online fora and access to their field of news by their editors in Germany. These present real changes in the way foreign correspondents have worked over the years (Hahn, Lönnendonker, and Schröder, 2008). Hachten and Scotton (2012) assert that technology is one of the crucial elements that has caused substantial changes to the gathering of foreign news. "In the nineteenth century, the news was collected by reporters who later used telephones, and then the telegraph to transmit them. For news from abroad, the press relied on journalist's letters carried by ships and then later by telephones, comsats and now Internet" (pp. 170–71).

They add that foreign newsgathering today requires the journalists to work with and rely on several other non-media professionals. According to Mark Deuze (2008), journalists are either sceptical or supportive of new changes occurring in the newsroom because such "changes in the institutional and organisational arrangements of their work in the past had resulted mostly to downsizing, lay-offs, less staff, budget and resources cut" (p. 8). However, "early adopters in the newsroom are excited if the changes help them in the way they do their work" (p. 9).

Catherine McKercher (2002) argues that technological convergence and corporate concentration must be understood usually as an opportunity for media owners to acquire new sources for profit, extending their grip on production and distribution of news. Even though some scholars hold the view that technological changes have influenced the practice of journalism for the better, others disagree and Deuze (2008, p. 4) sees the end of journalism in sight, especially as becomes increasingly entwined with other forms of communication such, as public relations and advertising:

> The boundaries between journalism and other forms of public communication — ranging from public relations or advertorials to weblogs and podcasts — are vanishing, the internet makes all other types of news media rather obsolete (especially for young adults and teenagers), commercialization and cross-media mergers have gradually eroded the distinct professional identities of newsrooms and their publications (whether in print or broadcast), and by insisting on a traditional orientation towards the nation, journalists are losing touch with a society that is global as well as local...

In addition to the many ways these changes affect journalists, journalistic news itself faces some problems concerning credibility and accountability. However, Joanne Yau and Suliman Al-Hawamdeh (2001) argue that credibility issues usually affect less established media houses, while transnational news organisations — such as the BBC, CNN and *The New York Times* — have migrated their traditional media credibility to the digital front. These influential traditional news media organisations (CNN, CNBC, Bloomberg and the BBC) continue to be more influential because they "have made it their business to make sense of the world for readers and viewers via various strategies to manage attention and present information" (p. 9).

A study on Nigeria and Singapore reports as low as 28% of journalists stating that new technologies have promoted ethical journalism. Also crucial to this study is the way these technological changes play into the preceding arguments of the coverage of Africa by African journalists. According to Obijiofor and Green (2001), these avenues of sources available to the African journalists include the official websites of renowned newspapers both in developed and developing countries, television, radio and the web. The problems presented by these technological opportunities are equally enormous for journalists in developing countries. Obijiofor and Hanusch (2003) report that, due to lack of training and re-training of journalists in Africa, the know-how to effectively apply these technologies are greatly hindered. Coupled with this is the sheer lack of access to computers and the Internet. Investigating the impact of new technologies on newspaper journalism practice in Nigeria and Ghana, Obijiofor (2003) reports that the technologies have improved rather than harmed the quality of newspapers and this was a view held by almost 90% of the respondents; "One major aspect of that improvement is that new technologies help journalists to save time in their work. Other improvements in quality of newspapers include the accelerated speed of production, enhancement of newspaper aesthetics through colour photography and ease of crosschecking spelling errors with the aid of the spell check software" (p. 54). Another aspect of Africa's image that received attention in this study is the influential role of Western media. Relating this to technology provided a basis on which to discuss whether or not new technologies have improved Africa's image in the Western media. Frances Harding (2003, p. 69) argues that the visual images of Africa in the Western media are the way they are because of two factors: "First, the development of technology and subsequent access to it; and second, the ideology and ethos that inform the use of the technology." Drawing on the media in several countries on the continent of Africa and in the UK, Harding traces the different ways in which the media produces and presents visual images of Africa. She further argues that there are similarities and differences between the distinct technologies; each produces its own images of Africa, and these differ greatly. One could argue that African countries have the ability to challenge the war-ridden images, with which they are frequently represented, using technology.

The decreasing cost of satellite receiving dishes, broadband, and equipment required for broadcasting have, according to Samuel Fiest (2001), led to major changes in broadcasting and print media. On broadcasting, he believes "digitalisation has already begun to dramatically shrink the size of broadcasting equipment. Modern transmission requires only a few suitcases of gear" (p. 710). On print media, Fiest argues,

> a photographer or journalist for that matter can file their stories from anywhere around the globe either through wireless telephone or satellite phone and those images can be published in a newspaper or magazine, or it can be published immediately on a Website (ibid.).

Closely related to this technological revolution is the cost involved in maintaining a foreign bureau and how the technology renders most journalists redundant by offering better approaches to achieving the same goals. Hachten and Scotton (2012, p. 176) reported between "$150,000 and $250,000 per annum as the cost of maintaining a foreign news bureau." They argued that it was not surprising that the higher this cost rises, the more predominant the reliance of both African and international news organisations on wire services will become. Susanne Fengler and Stephan Russ-Mohl (2008) reasoned in a similar way when they described "journalists and media owners as rational actors seeking to maximize materialistic and non-materialistic rewards (e.g. attention, reputation, fringe benefits) and these explain why, how and under what kind of restrictions journalists trade information for attention with their sources, calculating risks and benefits" (p. 667). By these arguments, it is clear that the decision of what to publish and how to publish it is no longer a major journalistic decision, but rather one that is strongly driven by economics. Obijiofor and Hanusch (2012), and Fengler and Russ-Mohl (2008) have all mentioned "pack journalism" and "parachute journalism" as concepts that have become permanently part of the journalism profession in response to cost-cutting. In "pack journalism", due to limited resources to cover events and the pressure to meet deadlines, journalists resort to cross-checking facts and omissions from other journalists and, eventually, there is only one account of an event. Franks (2005) and Wolter (2006) believe that flying a journalist to a country to cover an event as it occurs, and leaving immediately or a day after, has greatly destroyed the quality of foreign news reporting. The movement of the journalist so quickly to the next hotspot means all improvements in the last issues covered are not reported. In the era of cost-cutting, it has also become much clearer that the harsh economic conditions under which the media constructs its messages have impacted either the messages themselves or the processes. Researching readership taste provides a great tool for participation from the readership and an opportunity by the journalists to improve their targeted delivery of messages. According to Achal Mehra (1988, p. 2) readership surveys or market research are normatively designed to enable a newspaper to:

> identify the profile, needs and desires of its readers...Market research companies routinely compile newspaper readership profiles, including distribution of readers by age, sex, income levels, occupation, education, race, household size, and consumption patterns. Using advanced statistical techniques, like factor analysis and demographic tables, it is now possible to locate and define clusters of customers. It is also possible to develop the psychographic profiles of readers. The information is critical to advertisers making decisions on placing ads for particular products in a newspaper. But the information is also a gold mine for editors as well to identify the interests of their readers.

In turn, Rüdiger Schulz (2008) draws a distinction between readership research as media advertising research — where the ultimate purpose is for advertising — and editorial readership research — which is closely linked with academic reception studies aimed at gaining fundamental insights into readership/audiences. He underscores the far-reaching economic significance of media advertising research as a basis for its dominance. The major reason why such surveys are conducted is improvement in newspaper sales.

Influence of Transnational Western Media on the African Press

Arguing that there are influences on the African media regarding the way they report themselves is not an exaggeration looking at the enormous donor-driven activities on the continent. However, in the midst of these challenges, Charlayne Hunter-Gault (2008) calls for a change in both the way the continent is covered currently and a movement away from the distortions of the past with a resolve to write "Africa's new news" (p.

107). Fundamental to this goal is journalism education and newsroom socialisation across the continent. However, these two core-training processes are rooted in Western concepts and supported by Western donors. Eventually, this makes any attempt at paradigm shift almost impossible. Scotton and Murphy (1987) argued that religious and social customs and African languages except Swahili were banned or suppressed by Western actions or pressures. The independent African states left behind by colonialism could no longer communicate in the same languages and this resulted in the "African languages themselves largely becoming irrelevant in the areas of government, education and mass media" (p. 12). Ghana and Tanzania nationalised foreign-owned newspapers immediately after they became independent states, due to their perception of foreign ownership being incompatible with independent states and the fear of influence on the African media. However, they still maintained Western language and technologies.

The historical influence of the BBC World Service mentioned by Peter Golding (1979) remains enormous, and is still relevant going forward. According to Scotton and Murphy (1987), there has been remarkable inactivity to change journalism education programmes in Africa which have been largely modelled directly on those in Europe and the United States. The efforts of the African Council on Communication Education (ACCE), the only continental organisation of journalism educators, has attempted to make African journalism training relevant to Africa's social and cultural situation with a view that this results in African values playing the dominant role in African mass media. Within the UNESCO International Standard Classification of Education, most Africans qualify to be called educated since any group of socialisation in schools, homes, family and communities that brings about learning is acceptable as a form of education (Thompson, 1981). But according to Mazrui (1978), even university students under colonial rule at one point became the instrument to promote and control change.

Journalism education was one of the areas that the European academics could not easily infiltrate from the start because journalism, according to Karikari (1992), was a liberation tool mostly in Ghana where other intellectuals within the sub-region converged to push for self-rule. Nnamdi Azikiwe, the Eastern Nigeria political leader and editor of the *West African Pilot,* and Kwame Nkrumah, former President of Ghana, had used the press already as a tool for liberation movements before independence and were favourable to an American vocational style of journalism education. Nkrumah established American-style journalism education at the Ghana Institute of Journalism in 1958, but Azikiwe wanted Nigeria's first programme closely linked with a university. The structure, staff and much of the curriculum, including the journalism programme, were imported from the American universities almost completely without any changes (Okafur 1971 as cited in Scotton and Murphy, 1987, p. 14). The American model of journalism training at the university level became highly popular and even as early as 1935 journalism training had begun at the American University in Cairo. Later, the Universities of Cairo and Dakar started their own journalism training programmes that were modelled upon the American system. "It was inevitable that mass communications and journalism would have a Western structure in all its facets across Africa" (Scotton and Murphy, 1987, p. 15).

It was unfortunate that African approaches to reaching large audiences, such as through the chief's *Speakers* (the *Gongon beater*) in Ghana (the Gongon beater is the man who broadcasts the Chief's messages to the local community using a metallic instrument, a stick and his bare voice), was not quite integrated into this new curriculum. According to Golding (1977), the adoption of the American journalism training model itself amounted to an ideological transfer. Golding describes several transfers from Western nations to newly independent states, especially professionalisation.

Professionalism, to Golding, is a form of "integration into a dominant global culture of media practices and objectives as developed in the media of the advanced societies through three mechanisms: institutional transfer, training and education, and the diffusion of occupational ideologies" (p. 294).

Golding (1977) contends that "more specific ideologies appear as models of good practice and implicit statements of acceptable and unacceptable standards which are mostly contained in programme materials imported from overseas media" (p. 299). As the colonies continue to broadcast these programmes for years, both the audiences and the staff in the developing countries became bound to emulate them in style, philosophy and format. This is what Golding (1977) refers to as "professionalization becoming imitation" (p. 299). Two debatable professional ideologies inherent in all the transfers over the years include impartiality and objectivity of broadcasting in its provision of news. Therefore, the so-called public broadcasters on state payroll under Ministries of Information or Communication were made to work under a system where the broadcasting institution was expected to completely separate itself from the state.

According to Scotton and Murphy (1987), the professional values of objectivity and freedom from government restraints appealed to journalists in various social settings. This is perhaps because it provides autonomy at a minimum risk, but journalists in most African countries barely recognise that they are enjoying such autonomy because of the general public and not because of themselves. Another interesting ideological position put forward by Daniel Patrick Moynihan requires journalism to be antagonistic by all standards. He argues that:

> It is the mark of a democracy that its press is filled with bad news. When one comes to a country where the press is filled with good news, one can be pretty sure that jails are filled with good men (cited in Hachten and Scotton, 2016, p. 208).

While these assumptions turned into best practices that the African press had to imitate as a sign of professionalism, this was merely one of the numerous approaches available. Francis Kasoma (1996) describes it as a "tragedy facing African journalism that the continent's journalists have closely imitated the professional norms of the North" (p. 95). Anya Schiffrin (2010) adds that the challenges facing the media in sub-Saharan Africa are enormous and therefore likely to render journalism training by the plethora of foreign organisations less effective. However, because donor-driven training does not pay attention to the enormity of the challenging context within which the journalists in Africa work, they tend to ignore elements that can make the trainings effective. Again, Schiffrin's argument about whether or not the programmes of assistance have any objectives is quite revealing.

The influx of these competing actors, programmes and ideological socialisation on journalism training, coupled with the lack of a harmonious African model of journalism training, led Skjerdal (2012) to argue for a continuing debate regarding the independence of Africa's media. The growing influence of Chinese engagement on the African continent seems to include the media as well. H. D. Wu (2016) confirms that China's attempt to promote deep bilateral diplomatic and economic relations has resulted in the provision of their own content and points of view since 2009. Analysing the case of South Africa, Wu describes the limits and potential of China's engagement in public diplomacy. Herman Wasserman (2016) argues that increased influence of China on the African media space is not only limited to the spread of Chinese state press (Xinhua News Agency, *China Daily*, China Central Television and China Radio International) but includes flows and contra-flows of private media capital in South Africa. According to Wasserman, China's initiative to spread *soft power* through its media in South Africa is highly constrained for several reasons from the perspective of the journalists. He contends that:

> Soft power initiatives could potentially be amplified by journalists if they were to use Chinese media as their sources because this would allow local stories to be framed by Chinese perspectives. However, this would not happen if journalists did not consume Chinese media or if the Chinese perspective on news events were rejected (Wasserman, 2016, p. 18).

The argument both Wasserman and Wu seem to be engaged in are anchored on the assumption that the consumption of Chinese media by South Africa journalists would amount to soft power success for China. This study offers empirical evidence that contributes to the debate about China's soft-power influence in Ghana.

Daya Thussu, Hugo de Burgh and Andin Shi (2018), with their comprehensive exploration of the Chinese media in general, cite an estimated $7 billion set aside to be injected into external communication and expansion of Chinese broadcasting networks around the world. These investments are aimed at "promoting China's views and vision to the wider world and countering negative portrayals of the country in the US-dominated international media" (Thussu et al., 2018, p. 2). However, the intense commercialisation and injection of private capital into the Chinese media coupled with an ambitious quest to compete globally has pushed the Chinese government to transform their subsidised public media from being a "financial drain into a profit-making global industry" (Hachten and Scotton, 2016, p. 114). Xin Xin (2017) added that Xinhua's financialisation, via Xinhuanet, is a state-administrated initiative that supported Xinhua's own business ambitions. Having been successful in raising very large private capital, a state player like Xinhuanet's financialisation does not alter the control of the state on Chinese news media output at the moment. This may, however, change in the future because private shareholders who have invested huge sums of money could soon be expecting returns which might drive the entire Chinese media sector toward a Western capital model.

The inauguration of the Pan-African News Agency (PANA) in the 1980s marked the beginning of the continent's commitments to sharing a common approach to discuss problems and signs of progress. It also, according to J. J. Haule (1984), marked "ideological differences between them and their Western counterparts" (p. 113). This approach, in principle, is not different from the European Union television channels, whose broadcasts are aimed at telling Europe's stories of hope, despite the several financial crises, and Brexit, that have hit them in recent times. PANA is equally a response to the badly-needed balance in world information flow, and to correct the qualitative and quantitative shortcomings of news circulation within the continent (UNESCO, 1981). However, according to Haule (1984), PANA Press has not achieved the needed influence that was initially predicted of its activities. As a result, the African press still reports Africa from the perspectives of Western news agencies. The very economic tag that news has taken seems to be the major issue PANA could not overcome. The resource-rich countries have devoted resources to covering Africa that far outweighs PANA's budget.

Summary

This chapter reviewed previous literature touching on the core issues of how both the Western and African press report the continent. The chapter established the usefulness of foreign news and its historical antecedents and debates on *Afro-pessimism*. The determinants of foreign news coverage were broadly discussed and linked to why Africa remained largely uncovered. The performance of the African press in covering the continent was also reviewed and related to how the continent was covered by the Western press. The influences of transnational news agencies, technology, colonial history, education and the emerging effects of Chinese soft power or public diplomacy were described as elements difficult for the African journalists to resist because they have unconsciously internalised these elements of socialisation.

3. Theoretical and Conceptual Frameworks

This chapter is divided into three main parts: the introduction, the theoretical review and the frameworks of the study. It discusses the linkage of the three theoretical approaches beginning with an overview of the theories and how they have been deployed in previous research, with emphasis on strengths, weaknesses, limits and recommendations that will eventually form the basis for this study's theoretical and conceptual design.

The superimposition of the postcolonial theory on the theories of newsworthiness and intermedia agenda-setting is categorical in nature. This does not mean that the postcolonial theory is more useful than the two other theories; it only signifies the overarching critical impulse of it. The positioning of these theories in the model only represents the way the study conceives of their analytical application. What is new about this approach is that the weaknesses of the theory of newsworthiness, for example, to explicate meso- and macro-level influences on news selection decisions are minimised because other theories within the integrated framework can be used.

Firstly, it is argued that any model predicting news selection decision must incorporate intermedia influences, because they are real both in intra-nation and inter-nation agenda-settings (Du, 2013; Golan, 2006; Vliegenthart and Walgrave, 2008; McCombs, 2005). Lei Guo and Chris Vargo (2017) have further solidified the place of intermedia agenda-setting in international news flow debate through a theoretical mapping (using big data) of how news media in different countries influence each other in covering international news.

Secondly, arguments in this regard tend to claim that news factors and intermedia agenda-setting have not been developed to explain macro-level ideological influences that disrupt the innocence of Eurocentric knowledge around journalism and that question what is broadly described as globalisation, which also is imperial in nature (Paterson, 2017).

Thirdly, the question of why some countries are more newsworthy than others, and the similarities and differences in the scope of international news presented in different languages and cultures, has been theoretically tackled using the current global communication order, Internet and online media. Elad Segev (2016) argues that international news affects our perception of the world; in his new book, he explores international news flow on the Internet by addressing those key questions in a manner that combines both theories of newsworthiness and international news flow.

The review of Vincent Anfara and Norma Mertz (2006) demonstrates that the theoretical framework does not have a clear and consistent definition among qualitative researchers. However, the study adopted the idea that the "theoretical frameworks are any empirical or quasi-empirical theory of social and/or psychological processes, at a variety of levels (e.g., grand, mid-range, and explanatory) that can be applied to the understanding of phenomena" (p. 27). A conceptual framework, on the other hand, is not very different from a theoretical framework. According to Matthew Miles, Michael Huberman and Johnny Saldaña (2014), "a conceptual framework explains, either graphically or in narrative form, main things to be studied — the key factors, variables, construct — and the presumed interrelationships among them" (p. 20). It could be argued that conceptual frameworks are founded on theory/theories and as such represent the specific direction by which the research will be undertaken by identifying "who, what will, and will not be studied" (Miles et al., 2014, p. 21). The conceptual framework in this present study is deduced from the theoretical framework with more focus on the specifics of the study's arguments.

Theoretical Overview

In this section, the theory of newsworthiness, intermedia agenda-setting and the postcolonial theory are comprehensively reviewed as theoretical concepts. In turn, it is outlined how their application to this study offers new ways to understand them. The complimentary appreciation of these theories is to demonstrate that theoretical innovation is not to say that previous theories do not exist but to strengthen their weaknesses in their new applications especially to areas where they have not been significantly combined.

Guo and Vargo (2017) argued that the practice of measuring a country's salience in foreign news coverage as a measure of its newsworthiness does not provide a good understanding of how news flows around the world because it lacks the ability to predict a country's capacity to set the agenda for other countries. To capture both phenomena — being newsworthy and setting the news agenda for other countries — emerging studies must investigate the role of different countries in the international news flow from "different theoretical standpoints, including the intermedia agenda-setting theory" (Guo and Vargo, 2017, p. 518). To deal with these dynamics, intermedia agenda-setting theory is applied critically, in this study, to unveil how such journalistic co-orientations and reuse practices occur. Beyond this analysis is also a sublime but evident ideological element related particularly to the coverage of Africa: postcolonial relationships, which require a critique because of the very imbalanced nature within which it contributes to the coverage of Africa in Ghana.

Theory of Newsworthiness

Newsworthiness is one of the most utilised theories to explain how and why journalists select news. While some scholars rely heavily on psychology and perceptions of journalists in terms of both what makes news and what their audience's interests are, others concentrate on the organisational and professional routines rooted within the journalistic practice. But, at its basic level, the theory uses the concept of news factors to trace news selection back to the specific qualities of events, which are suspected as the determinant of the news value of an event and hence the decision of journalists regarding whether or not that event is newsworthy. According to J. F. Staab (1990, p. 424), most scholars trace the "rudimentary form of this concept to Walter Lippmann" while in a few exceptional cases, the authors refused to mention Lippmann's work.

The myth surrounding news is defined by Pamela Shoemaker (2006, p. 105) as a "primitive construct whose existence is not questioned"; it is also "passed down to the new generation of journalists through a process of socialisation" (Harrison, 2006, p. 118). Jerry Palmer (2000) describes the workings of news values as "a system of criteria which are used to make decisions about the inclusion and exclusion of materials and transcends individual judgements, although they are, of course, to be found embodied in every news judgement made by a particular journalist" (p. 45). Arguing for the useful place of the theory of newsworthiness even until today, Jürgen Wilke, Christine Heimprecht and Akiba Cohen (2012, p. 304) state that:

> Scholars who have studied international news have typically looked to global factors to explain the variability in coverage and much of these research assume that international news coverage reflects the power structure among nations. However, the crafting of media messages, including those focused on international events, is also subject to local influences. Such influences include organisational factors, the local community's power and corporate characteristics (p. 304).

Staab's (1990) explication of the theory challenges the assumption that "several news factors determine the news value of an event and therefore the selection decision of journalists" (p. 424). Christiane Eilders (2006); Shoemaker (2006); Staab (1990) and Rüdiger Schulz (1976) have all argued, in the sense of these frameworks, that the concept of new factors cannot be said to explain the actual process of news selection and "its validity is rather restricted to the questions of how far news factors determine size, placement and layout of news stories" (Staab, 1990, p. 246). The use of causal explication for news selection becomes even more contested within this area of research. Most studies on news factors have employed the causal models, which argue that news is selected or published because of its particular qualities (news factors) and an existing objectivity consensus about these qualities. Shoemaker (2006), however, cautioned that this causal model is weak because "news is a social construct, a thing, a commodity, whereas newsworthiness is a cognitive construct and a mental judgment. Newsworthiness is not a good predictor of which events get into the newspaper and how they are covered. Newsworthiness is only one of a vast array of factors that influence what becomes the news and how prominently events are covered" (p. 105).

As Stuart Hall (1997) argues, representation does not entail a straightforward presentation of the world and the relationships in it. For Hall, *representation* is a very different notion from that of *reflection*. By selecting news, in the first place, the media represents the world rather than reflects it. These social processes are difficult to causally predict because they are iterative and unconscious, except that some of those causal predictions make several underlying assumptions that basically defeat its potency to produce an accurate account of the prediction.

The definition of events within the concept of news factors has faced both ontological and epistemological difficulties related to the subject-object relationship. Staab (1990, p. 439) clarified these difficulties when he argued against the exclusive power allotted to events which makes it look like events in themselves are capable of determining news selection:

> Events do not exist per se but are the result of subjective perceptions and definitions. However, scholars have assumed, at least implicitly, a congruency of events and corresponding news stories. However, this does not fit the structure of news coverage especially in the political area because most events do not exist in isolation, they are interrelated and annexed to larger sequences. Employing different definitions of an event and placing it in a different context, news stories in different media dealing with the same event are likely to cover different aspects of the event and therefore put emphasis on different news factors (ibid.).

The object-based approach to news selection argues that events have some specific characteristics that are attractive to journalists; the more of these characteristics an event seems to possess, the more likely it is that journalists will select it. The argument that the nature of an event itself is the biggest predictor of newsworthiness to journalists ignores the subject-object relationship (Staab, 1990). A subject-based approach to the debate argues, on the other hand, that factors beyond the nature of events are responsible for news selection decisions, and they are quite independent of the events in general (Gans, 2004; Herman and Chomsky, 2008; Van Djik, 2009). For this study, I examine how subject-object based relationships blend together to determine news selection.

Andreas Schwarz (2006), in search of validation of these ideas, tested the theory of newsworthiness by Johan Galtung and Mari Ruge (1965) in Mexico, a non-Western country. Even though he confirmed all the hypotheses he had tested, as a replication of the Galtung and Ruge study, he cautioned that the "relationship between news factors and editorial emphasis that have been found do not necessarily prove that news factors are relevant criteria for the initial selection of news for publication" (p. 59). Deirdre O'Neill and Tony Harcup (2009) maintain that news values can help us understand how some occurrences are marked as "events", a label which eventually gets them selected as "news". This theory can also help us explore how some aspects of the selected event get emphasised, while other aspects are downplayed or excluded. To O'Neill and Harcup, in addition to these insights, "news values sometimes blur the distinction between news selection and news treatment" (p. 171). This lead us to the meso-level of the theoretical discussion, where the attention of the analysis shifts from journalistic behaviour to how organisational needs and culture influence the selection process.

Intermedia Agenda-Setting

Apart from the events themselves informing us about their selection or external factors influencing their selection, there is also an inter-organisational borrowing which is also the result of a lifelong socialisation process within the journalistic industry. Much of the research considering this phenomenon has described it as an aspect of agenda-setting theory. In fact, Maxwell McCombs (2005) labels intermedia agenda-setting as the fourth phase of agenda-setting theory, which explores the origins of the media agenda. He further argues that this phase and all other preceding phases of the agenda-setting theory need to "continue together as active sites of inquiry" (p. 118). According to McCombs (2005), agenda-setting theory progressed a little further than the original focus when researchers began asking: "If the press sets the public agenda, who sets the media agenda?" He further explains that the patterns of news coverage that shape the media agenda result from "the norms and traditions of journalism, the daily interactions among news organisations themselves, and the continuous interactions of news organisations with numerous sources and their agendas" (p.

548). He adds that journalists routinely seek to validate their sense of news by observing the work of their colleagues from elite media and this practice has ushered us into what he calls the "intermedia agenda-setting era", which comprises "the influences of the news media on each other" (p. 549). To assess the intermedia agenda-setting, Guy Golan (2006) and Joe Foote and Michael Steele (1986) compare the similarities in stories' leads by different media organisations. They argue that "two of the three networks had the same lead 91% of the time, and all three had the same lead 43% of the time" (p. 19).

Rens Vliegenthart and Stefaan Walgrave (2008) offer a comprehensive explanation to intra-nation intermedia agenda-setting by arguing that the process of intermedia agenda-setting is moderated by five factors, namely, lag length, medium type, language/institutional barriers and election or non- election context. Ying Roselyn Du (2013) explores the mass media's agenda-setting function in a context of increased globalisation to see if the theory of agenda-setting works within the global setting. She finds that "inter-nation intermedia influences" provide a new approach to move the journalistic co-orientation phenomenon to cross-national intermedia comparisons (p. 19). She holds a sceptical position towards the idea that national journalists will reduce negative coverage of the developing nations by international wire services because "Western news organizations have, in some occasions, found some of the reports by national media inaccurate" (p. 142). Yie Xie and Anne Cooper-Chen (2009) argue, in support of Daniel Riffe (1984), that in the case of international news, "borrowing or shortcuts can save enormous amounts of time and money" but that comes with a risk of inaccuracies in national accounts (p. 92). The global nature of news selection leads us to the next theoretical approach in this study, which is the application of postcolonial theory.

Postcolonial Theory

According to Shrikant Sawant (2012, p. 120) "postcolonial theory investigates what happens when two cultures clash and one of them with accompanying ideology empowers and deems itself superior to the other." To A. Prasad (2003), postcolonial theory is a critique that "investigates the complex and deeply fraught dynamics of modern

Western colonialism and anti-colonialism resistance and the on-going significance of the colonial encounter for people's lives both in the West and in the non-West" (p. 5). These definitions comport with the ideas of Bill Ashcroft, Gareth Griffiths and Helen Tiffin (1995), who argue that the way to reconsider Eurocentric and Western representations of non-Western worlds is to unsettle and disrupt the canonical text and theories and their implicit binary operations of "us" and "them".

Like all paradigms of knowledge, postcolonial theory has its fair share of criticisms and contestations within and outside the milieu. Firstly, the very name *postcolonial* attracted the attention of some scholars, who considered that as a premature celebration of the end of colonialism, a phenomenon the world is centrally imbricated in (Sawant, 2012). Secondly, the diverse, open-door approach of postcolonial studies to many fields of inquiry presents a serious challenge to an accurate conceptualisation of the field (Shome and Hegde, 2002). Thirdly, postcolonialism, also referred to as postcolonial studies, due to its vastness, runs the risk of unwittingly assuming that all colonial experiences were alike and, by so doing, falls prey to the binary scheme of colonial and postcolonial.

The growth of further binary conceptualisations within the colonised, for instance, depending on race and gender, are crucial for analysis as well. A binary mode would not improve this area of knowledge, however, the unlimited vastness in its conceptualisation is equally constraining. Examples of discursive practices already in use include slavery, dispossession, settlement, migration, resistance, representation, difference, race, gender, class, otherness, place, diaspora, subaltern, sexuality, hybridity, mimicry, ethnicity and many others, all of which have been discussed as part of the wider area (Goldberg and Quayson, 2002; Ashcroft et al. 2001). With these contestations come the clarification for communication scholars put forward by Raka Shome and Radha Hegde (2002), who discuss the integration of postcolonial studies and communication studies. They see postcolonial studies as an interdisciplinary field that theorises the problematics of colonisation and decolonisation. They, however, caution that a mere chronicling of the facts of colonialism would not qualify as a postcolonial study. This is because postcolonial theory within the critical theory tradition is interventionist and a political approach by nature. They argue, "Postcolonial theory does not only theorise colonial conditions but also why those conditions are what they are, and how they can be undone and redone" (p. 250). To Shome and Hegde, a postcolonial study must offer "an emancipatory political stance or interventionist theoretical perspective" in examining issues as a mark of the theory's critical impulse (p. 250). Shome and Hegde sum up the uniqueness of the milieu of postcolonial theory within the critical scholarship tradition in these words (p. 252):

> ... Postcolonial theory provides a historical and international depth to the understanding of cultural power. It studies issues of race, class, gender, sexuality, and nationality, that are of concern to contemporary critical scholarship by situating these phenomena within geopolitical arrangements, and relations of nations and their inter/national histories.

In the study presented in this book, it is demonstrated whether or not the journalists are aware of the complexities behind the use of sources and how they have either ignored or resisted this phenomenon. Two concepts within the terminologies of postcolonial studies have been crucial for my analysis: internalised oppression and hybridity.

Fanonian Internalised Oppression

Frantz Fanon (2008) argues that in an attempt of the coloured peeople to escape the association of blackness with evil, they don a white mask, or think of themselves as a universal subject equally participating in a society that advocates an equality supposedly abstracted from personal appearance. This is done through internalising, or "epidermalising", cultural values into consciousness, which results in a fundamental disconnection between the black man's consciousness and his body. Under these conditions, the black man is necessarily alienated from himself. Paul Gilroy argues that the concept of epidermalisation emanates from a complex combination of philosopher-psychologist's phenomenological ambitions, that privilege a certain way of seeing and understanding of sight. Gilroy (2000) argues that the concept suggests a perceptual regime in which the racialised body is bounded and protected by its enclosing skin. He then critiques it by stating that the "idea of epidermalisation points towards one intermediate stage in a critical theory of body scales in the making of race. Today skin is no longer privileged as the threshold of either identity or particularity" (p. 47). Dilan Mahendran (2007) refutes Gilroy's notion, stating that he has confused the lived experience of race for its representation. Mahendran argues (p. 193),

> It is the representation of blackness and its commoditisation in popular culture that Gilroy sees as shifting in the history of 'raciology' and not the lived experience of showing up black which has been durable in the long history of racism in the West..

Epidermalisation represented for Fanon a pathological metaphor to describe colonial conditions which would cover both perceptual and physical anti-black racism and the primacy of sight that the black-skinned man can never escape. In *Black Skin, White Mask*, Fanon says "I am overdetermined from without. I am the slave not of the idea that others have of me but of my own appearance" (p. 87). By this, he provides a notion of internalised oppression known generally as epidermalisation of inferiority (Fanon, 2008) and this has caused some people of colour to accept their subjected position as being the *natural order of things*. Fanon did not stop articulating this point. In *Wretched of the Earth*, he makes a refreshing appeal:

> Come, then, comrades, the European game is finally ended; we must find something different. We today can do everything, so long as we do not imitate Europe, so long as we are not obsessed by the desire to catch up with Europe (Fanon, 2001, p. 251).

Fanon saw imitation as a major hurdle for the newly independent states not because he wanted a complete divorce, but because he feared that imitation could play into the disruption of the psychic realm that had already taken place during the colonial encounter.

Bhabha's Hybridity and Third Space Intervention

It is clear from the works of Homi K. Bhabha (1994) and Ashis Nandy (1988), how the psychic realm of the colonised operates. The sublime nature of globalisation of speech to the advantage of the Western world, and the cravings of the colonised to legitimise their quality through imitation of the coloniser, is further exacerbated by the lingering influences of Western education, training and ownership of knowledge. Bhabha (1994) argues that changes in the psychic realm that were inflicted on the colonised during the colonial experience are very active even in postcolonial times. According to Bhabha (1994), in this era, the ruling is predominantly through capital flows rather than through force of military. Bhabha, however, acknowledged (p. 38):

> The historical connectedness between the subject and object of critique [...] shows that there can be no simplistic, essentialist opposition between ideological misrecognition and revolutionary truth. The progressive reading is crucially determined by the adversarial or agonistic situation itself; it is effective because it uses the subversive, messy mask of camouflage and does not come like a pure avenging angel speaking the truth of radical historicity and pure oppositionality.

The concept of the psychic realm in the work of Fanon represents a concept of *submissive imitation*, which assumes that the colonised is a passive alienated subject living on the edges of two worlds and constantly seeking legitimisation. But the necessary legitimisation by the coloniser in the postcolonial space — even in the era of globalisation — is still categorised and operated with a binary framework, such as "developed and developing"; "East and West"; "poor nations and rich nations". Fanon describes this concept fully using the term mimicry.

Bhabha, a staunch reader of Fanon, however, digresses from this essentialist conceptualisation of the colonised, arguing instead that the imitation practised by the colonised is not homogenous, but rather metonymic resemblance, repetition and difference. To encapsulate this idea, he coined the description of "almost the same but not quite" (p. 86). Bhabha (1994) then introduced the term *third space* as a place of hybrid identity that emerges from the fact that the colonised had to live on the edges of two worlds after being psychologically persuaded to imitate their ruler in language, attitude and worldviews. The changes in the way the psychic realm of the colonised works are more permanent than the structural elements that colonisation enforces (Bhabha, 1994 and Fanon, 2008).

Apart from these, Bhabha sees the performative practices of the postcolonial relationship as a subversive imitation, rather than submissive, which is characterised by fragmentations, contradictions, cracks and inconsistencies rather than binary oppositions. To him, the significant racial and cultural differences that exist between the world of the coloniser and the colonised is beyond binary categorisation and opposition. There are, in Bhabha's observation, "disabling contradictions within the colonial relationship" that expose the vulnerability of coloniser's discourse and allows the emergence of "subversive performative practices" (Ashcroft et al. 2007, p. 37). Bhabha (1994) tackled what shall constitute a hybrid performance as well.

However, his definition of hybridity is highly nuanced. He states that "hybridity is a camouflage" (p. 193), and that hybridity is the way "newness enters the world" (p. 227). He adds that, in his conceptualisation, the space of the postcolonial relationship is an ambivalent one "where cultural signs and meaning-making have no primordial unity or fixity" (pp. 28–37). Though these descriptions are difficult to empirically set out, for Bhabha, small differences, slight alterations and displacements — whether conscious or unconscious — are crucial for the agenda of subversion. He further offers a conceptualisation of how this hybrid resistance is performed to allow one to recognise it:

> Resistance is not necessarily an oppositional act of political intention, nor is it the simple negation or exclusion of the "content" of another culture, as a difference once perceived. It is the effect of an ambivalence produced within the rules of recognition of dominating discourses as they articulate the signs of cultural difference and reimplicate them within the deferential relations of colonial power-hierarchy, normalization, marginalization and so forth (Bhabha, 1985, p. 82).

Zehra Sayed (2016) offers an empirical description, focusing specifically on India, by arguing that the hybridity conditions described by Bhabha have led to a simultaneously "*in-ward* and *out-ward* looking dialectic, a symptom of the postcolonial identity" which is exhibited by the Indian media industry, and especially by actors within foreign-owned news agencies (p. 20). Marwan Kraidy (2002) brings Bhabha's debate more closely into the realm of communication when he explains that even though the concept of hybridity has been applied variously to describe mixed genres and identity, it is still rare to see the conceptualisation of it at the heart of communication theory. He argues that because hybridity is a widely used concept, "the recent importation of it to areas such as intercultural and international communication, risks using the concept as a merely descriptive device, that is, describing the local reception of global media texts as a site of cultural mixture" (p. 317). Kraidy also argues that the use of hybridity as a descriptive device presents ontological and political quandaries. Ontologically, Kraidy (2002) sees hybridity not "as a clear product of global and local interactions but as a communicative practice constitutive of, and constituted by, sociopolitical and economic arrangements" (p. 317).

While the pursuit of this present study is no different, my research is unique in the sense that it provides an approach which can be used productively to discuss new debates over how the resistance of the colonised should be described. When will an act suffice as resistance and how do we judge this? Bhabha (1995) answers with a framework to gauge the resistance element in the imitation of the colonised by arguing that the whole postcolonial relationship involves a "process of translating and transvaluing cultural difference" (p. 252), thereby establishing that — whether in the world of the colonised or the coloniser — no monolithic or essential cultural features exist. This disruption on both sides, no matter how small, constitutes a resistance of sorts.

Essentialism versus Agency

The definition of essentialism offered by Diana Fuss (1989) introduces the concept from the perspective of its critiques (p. xii):

> Essentialism is typically defined in opposition to difference; the doctrine of essence is viewed as precisely that which seeks to deny or to annul the very radicality of difference. The opposition is a helpful one in that it reminds us that a complex system of cultural, social, psychical, and historical differences, and not a set of pre-existent human essences, position and constitute the subject. However, the binary articulation of essentialism and difference can also be restrictive, even obfuscating, in that it allows us to ignore or deny the differences within essentialism.

Bhabha highlights the contradictions inherent in colonial discourse in order to underscore the coloniser's ambivalence with respect to his position toward the colonised *Other*. The simple presence of the colonised *Other* within the textual structure is enough evidence of the ambivalence of the colonial text, an ambivalence that destabilises its claim for absolute authority or unquestionable authenticity. This is a basic response to Fanon's perspective, in which the colonised is robbed of all agency and, consequently, he/she pursues an imitation of the master. In addition to the fact that the role of the colonised in his/her imitation of the coloniser is completely ignored in the dominant literature, in postcolonial studies, the locus of agency is located in the postcolonial relationship which involves the colonised.

Hierarchical Influences Model

Studies analysing media content must make explicit the *symbolic environment* within which the content is situated, in order to delimit the two blurring areas of research — what shapes the content and what impact it has (Reese and Lee, 2012). The Hierarchical Influences Model of Shoemaker and Reese becomes significantly useful for organising the theoretical concepts in this study. This hierarchical model has philosophical underpinnings that ought to be clarified early enough to situate its use in this study. The *media as a mirror* hypothesis, which argues that media reflects social reality with little distortion, is attractive to journalists because of its power to render content neutral. Shoemaker and Reese (2014) make a categorical statement about media content when they assert that media content is "fundamentally a social construction, and as such can never find its analogue in some external benchmark, a mirror or reality" (p. 4). What is crucial for studies on media content is the negotiation of this philosophical premise in an organised manner.

Due to the multi-faceted nature of influences shaping media content, it is crucial to organise this study's theoretical framework with a broadly acceptable hierarchy. Just like Shoemaker and Reese (2014), this study argues that exercising a hierarchical organisation offers "more clarifications, definitions, assumptions and empirical indicators and relationships for the theoretical groundings of any research work" (p. 5). As such, locating the theoretical framework proposed in Figure 3.2 within the Hierarchical Influences Model requires contextual adjustments and re-modelling that is useful for this research.

The Shoemaker and Reese Hierarchical Influences Model is made up of five layers of influence. The theoretical perspectives that provide the basis for factors shaping media content have been laid bare by Todd Gitlin (2003) and Herbert Gans (1979) as follows:

1. *Content is influenced by media workers' socialisation and attitudes.* This is a communicator-centered approach, emphasising the psychological factors impinging on an individual's work: professional, personal and political.

2. *Content is influenced by media organisations and routines.* This approach argues that content emerges directly from the nature of how media work is organised. The organisational routines within which an individual operates from a structure, constraining action while also enabling it.

3. *Content is influenced by other social institutions and forces.* This approach finds that the major impact on content is external to organisations and the communicator: i.e., economic, political and cultural forces. Audience pressures can be found in the "market" explanation of "giving the public what it wants."

4. *Content is a function of ideological positions and maintains the status quo.* The so-called hegemony approach identifies the major influence on media content as the pressures to support the status quo, to support the interests of those in power in society (Shoemaker and Reese, 2014, p. 7).

The latest model of Shoemaker and Reese (2014, p. 9) has five levels of analysis: individual, routine, organisation, social institutions and social system as shown in Figure 3.1.

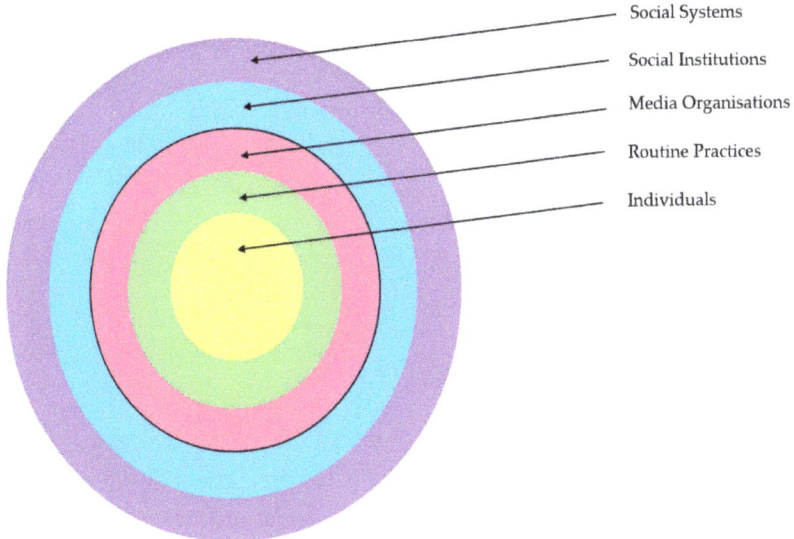

Fig. 3.1 The Hierarchy of Influences Model (Shoemaker and Reese, 2014, p. 9). Figure created by author (2020).

Individual Level

The individual level seeks to describe the creators of media content and how individual character traits provide a context within which they appreciate their professional roles. This level recognises the agency of individual journalists or media workers as actors under a larger professional constraint which eventually determines their actions. According to Shoemaker and Reese (2014), the power of media creators includes personal traits and idiosyncrasies that have been exhibited mainly through professional and occupational channels. The issue of digital communication and its appeal to individualism as an influential determinant of identity is clearer now than before. Located within the ideas of Manuel Castells (1996), the emerging networked relationship limits the workings of institutional analysis and rather draws attention to the relationship between the *self* and the *net*.

As a conceptual guide, the Hierarchical Influences Model considers the individual level as a constituent of personal demographic characteristics, background factors, roles and experiences of the communicator within his/her domain of profession. Shoemaker and Reese propose an interrelation of these factors by arguing that "the communicator's personal background and experiences are logically prior to their specific attitudes, values, belief" and they also precede "professional roles and ethical norms" (p. 209). One such element, according to them, is education. Education, particularly journalism education, has influencing roles that both as a general background factor and as a preparation of communicators for their career (p. 214). The interaction of the elements in this level alone require significant attention by itself so as to determine its composite influence on the entire hierarchical model.

Routine Level

"It is clear that routine and organisational levels overlap conceptually" (Shoemaker and Reese, 2014, p. 167). Shoemaker and Reese argues that "content emerges directly from the nature of how media work is organised" (p. 7). These routines and organisational arrangements that are recurring in nature over time, tend to form seemingly visible structures to which content must adhere. This defining structure could either be constraining or enabling or both at the same time. According to Shoemaker and Reese (2014), the routine level represents the immediate constraining or enabling structure of the individual, and the authors distinguish these from organisational level influences, which they argue are just larger patterns of the routine level influences that are more remote to the individual journalist. According to Shoemaker and Reese (2014), "ultimately routines are most important because they affect the social reality portrayed in media content" (p. 168). Shoemaker and Reese contend that routines are the practical response of journalists to difficulties, considering that they and their organisations continue to have very limited resources.

Organisational Level

Influences at the organisational level are similar to those at the routine level, but are more distinct from those at the individual level. Shoemaker and Reese (2014), where this level is concerned, highlight variables such as "ownership, policies, organisational roles, membership, inter-organisational interactions, bureaucratic structures, economic viability and stability" (p. 130). Distinguishing the organisational level of analysis from the routine level is not necessarily indicative of them being independent domains, however, there are "sufficiently unique attributes of each level" (p. 134) that could qualify them to be studied separately. The phenomena where modern organisational management has had members ultimately answering to owners and top management is significantly highlighted. This is where content and staff sharing within convergence platforms have become interlinked. The question that remains unanswered is how the structure of organisations reflect their allocation of resources, especially as a response to their environment. The practice that has so far been observed has signalled the danger of diminishing media autonomy, especially since the media must cohabit with those who finance it, or those who wield beneficial influence. As such, the power relations as they exists at this level relate closely to the influences these interconnections have exerted on content.

Social Institution Level

The distinguishing feature of this level from the three other levels is the fact that its factors lie outside both individuals and formal organisations themselves. According to Shoemaker and Reese (2014), this level illustrates that the media exist and operate within the inextricably connected power centres of society, which may either coercively or collectively shape content in many ways. The pertinent questions referred to at this level relate to ideology, inter-organisational field and outcomes of institutional forces.

There are proposals for considering media as a homogeneous political actor with counter influences on and from other actors and democracy in general. The field theory perspective speaks of how economic and cultural capital as a form of power has shaped specialised services into fields with peculiar internal homogeneity resulting from contingent historical path dependency.

Under this level, Shoemaker and Reese (2014) analyse sources as actors that shape power dynamics within the news selection decision. They argue that intermedia agenda-setting at some levels is a social institutional phenomenon. Shoemaker and Reese first discuss the blurring lines between the routine levels and social institution level when it comes to sources. They establish strongly that "sources of content wield important influence" (p. 108) on media content. When sources are routinised, they can be treated at the routine level. They justify the treatment of sources at social institutions level by emphasising the systemic influence they wield. Journalists are largely influenced by their sources in creating messages and this is quite clearly outlined by Gans (1979, p. 80) when he defines sources as "actors whom journalists observe or interview, including interviewees who appear on air or who are quoted in magazine articles and those who only supply background information or story suggestions." When these sources become institutionalised then they take on systemic attributes and their influences fall squarely within the institutional level of analysis.

Social System Level

The social system level according to Shoemaker and Reese (2014) represents the base upon which the other levels rest because of its focus on the social structure and its cohesive tendencies. Grounded in Marxist thinking, the analysis at this stage relates strongly to the notion that society is inextricably linked to its social and historical context, a comprehensive appreciation of which is required to be able to establish in whose interest individuals, routines and social institutions eventually work. These are embedded within the question of value, interest and power. Media content portrays how social actors impose their will over other actors in society. However, the symbols created by these power relationships are not neutral forces because news is essentially about the powerful, either about their ideas or their interpretation of events.

The debate about globalisation occupies this level of analysis. While some scholars argue that globalisation is just an idea of increased emphasis on the general awareness of other places (Nohrstedt and Ottosen, 2000), others have taken a more critical look at the phenomenon of diffusion and reception of Western ideas from political, economic and cultural systems, broadly under the bracket of cultural imperialism (Paterson, 2017, 2011). For Michael Elasmer and Kathryn Bennett (2003), the major preoccupation about this area of research, so far, is the use of conspiracy theory as the prelude to discovering how "contemporary international intentions and behaviours of states have amounted to various forms of imperialism" (p. 2).

The complexities in the description of globalisation were clearly marked out by how different scholars perceived the increasing international social relations.

Anthony Giddens (2003) describes the phenomenon using the term "local transformation", with which he explains the process of interaction between foreign media products and ideas from the world's urban centres with other parts of the world. He argues that these relationships might be causally related, through a complex mechanism of global ties in the world markets. Diana Crane (2002) argues that these diffusions and receptions could be better delimited as "cultural globalisation", which is the "transmission of various forms of media across national borders without necessarily impacting any homogeneous attributes because the parts" in the first place do not finely fit into the national context (p. 1). A more gradual approach to this conceptualisation of globalisation argues that the concept is happening but within and among "regional power centres" (Hawkins, 1997, p. 178). Therefore, globalisation represents a relationship between regions rather than nations. Crane (2002) further contends that these *cultural regions* are not necessarily dependent on geographical, linguistic and cultural proximity. Daniel Hallin and Paolo Mancini (2004) offer a rather basic rendition of globalisation by describing it as a term which helps scholars to avoid stating the obvious, which is the "expanding and imposing of single social imagery" (p. 27). Due to these complexities, Shoemaker and Reese (2014) discussed this level of analysis using four sub-systems: ideology, culture, economics and politics.

Towards a Theoretical Synergy

In this section, the theoretical and conceptual frameworks of the study are presented with diagrams detailing which theoretical lens provides which insights for a particular aspect of the study and how these individual insights could be linked together to provide the necessary answers for the research questions.

According to Miles et al. (2014), the framework could be "simple or elaborate, commonsensical or theory-driven, descriptive or causal" (p. 20). The study presented in this book adopts a simple theory-driven and descriptive framework. That is, the position of a theory within the framework shows which level of approach will be adopted in its analysis: descriptive, predictive or explanatory. The models employed incorporate both theoretical and conceptual ideas. They specify very important ideas, identify which relationships are likely to be meaningful, and pinpoint what data is required to deal with such meanings.

Conceptual Outlooks of Actors and Questions

Like Eilders (2006), Schwarz (2006), Johnson (1997), and Staab (1990), this study proposes that news selection research should be comprehensively approached at the micro-, meso- and macro-levels of analysis. The theory of newsworthiness is applied in this study to the behaviour of journalists in selecting the news. These are represented as micro-level investigations, which correspond with individual level analysis in the Shoemaker and Reese (2014) model. It is, however, crucial to note that the assumptions in this study differ in some ways in comparison with the entire argument of Shoemaker and Reese because the theory of newsworthiness was conceptualised significantly at the routine level in the Shoemaker and Reese model. However, Shoemaker and Reese argue that the day's news is influenced by many factors and therefore "influences from all levels of analysis determine the day's news; they are not as visible a target" (p. 172). The basic rationalisation in this study is that news factors and values are individual behaviour and attributes that most journalists gained through education, either in school or on the job. Even though most news organisation have compelling styles to which all newly employed journalists must adapt, the bottom line is that each journalist learns differently, and applies and interprets these values and styles differently. Due to this agency of cultural reception, I argue that news values and newsworthiness are significant at the individual level analysis, first and foremost. It does not imply that others could not use it at the routine and institutional levels since any individual behaviours routinised or institutionalised become routine and institutional level analysis respectively. The analysis here could be descriptive (percentages, means and correlations) or predictive (Golan, 2008; Wu, 2000).

In this study's framework, the theory investigates organisational arrangements of these influences as the basis for news selection in Ghanaian media organisations. Even though in foreign news selection one can even at this point propose socio-cultural elements, this study considers these influences at the meso-level. The meso-level in this study corresponds to two levels of analysis in the Shoemaker and Reese Hierarchical Influences Model: routine and organisational levels. Elizabeth Skewes (2007), relying on the accounts of Richard Benedetto of *USA Today*, states that journalists especially on campaign press planes (p. 97):

> don't think in terms of what the public wants to know, how can I help them know. They think of it in terms of [...] what does my colleague want to know? What can I show my colleagues that I know that they don't know?

Intermedia agenda-setting has therefore become a real theoretical consideration for every news selection decision, and this is even further determined by a complex economic and ideological reasoning. Postcolonial theory is employed as a macro-level analytical tool in this study. It seeks to affirm that foreign news selection in Ghana has something to do with economic and political relationships; political ideology and social structure as well as several elements in the micro- and meso-levels which are consciously and inadvertently influenced by these vast and complex historical relationships. Thus, this ideological function is considered an overarching element in the theoretical framework which actually explains the superstructure of power and its dynamics when it comes to foreign news.

Frameworks of the Study

The study presented in this book considers the politics of communication as central to the understanding of our modern globalised society and calls for a more socially responsible problematisation of international communication. Figure 3.2 presents the theoretical framework, which blends the three different theories and levels of analysis.

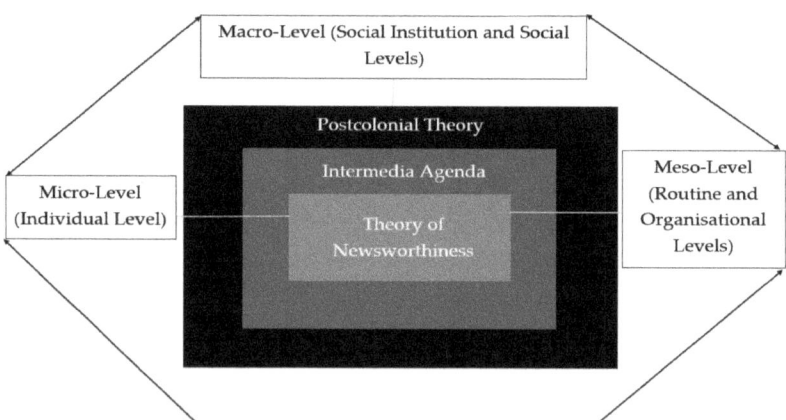

Fig. 3.2 The study's theoretical framework. Figure created by author (2020).

The three theories represented in the framework are the theory of newsworthiness as a micro-level analysis, which corresponds to individual level analysis in the Shoemaker and Reese hierarchical model. The theory is used to investigate the journalist's behaviours and understanding of what makes news. The intermedia agenda-setting theory is used to explain all organisational arrangements that affected the news selection process at the meso-level, which is conceptualised to involve both routine and organisational level analysis in Shoemaker and Reese's hierarchical model. The major questions of business and relationships have caused media organisations to depend on each other and these are interrogated at this level. Finally, the postcolonial theory provides an explication of how the other two levels are influenced by ideological elements at the super-structure level. The superimposition of the postcolonial theory is due to its nature as a critique and its use in this study as an explanatory level theory. The social institution and social system levels of analysis in Shoemaker and Reese model were collapsed together and embedded in the critical impulse of the postcolonial theory.

Figure 3.3 represents the conceptual framework of this study and it provides a cogent approach to tackle the data collection and analysis by showing subjects of interest, processes and the interrelationships between them. The framework proposes that three levels of factors do influence foreign news selection: journalist's behaviour, organisational arrangements and ideological functions. Even though there is an assumption that the process begins from the micro-level to organisational level upwards, this continuum can be equally iterative and reflexive. This means the process can begin from an ideological or organisational level or one can move up and down along the continuum to seek illumination. In this framework, there is no clear way of measuring the potency of each stage of the process against the others since the path is fluid and construed in human choices. But the fundamental understanding is that no matter where the process begins in the continuum or whichever stage wields more power along the fluid path, the resultant effect is that foreign news selection decisions are determined by all these interdependent and interrelated mechanisms, which eventually affect Africa's media image in the Ghanaian press.

The conceptual framework in Figure 3.3 is open to the assumption that the constituents of influence — individual journalists, organisational and ideological functions — can each independently contribute to the way Africa is covered in the Ghanaian press. As a result, the direction of influence from these three rectangular boxes is indicated in thick black, showing maximum influence. However, based on sociological dimensions of the framework, it is suggested that the influence of these three levels could either be measured jointly at the *foreign news selection* filter domain of the figure (where the influence of each level is dependent on the special circumstances of a particular day) or measured individually.

The individual measurement of these influences, in Figure 3.3, reflects subject-oriented and object-oriented debates, in which some scholars argue that news selection is a practice that ought to be investigated at the level of the journalists and their personal traits because there are sound criteria for objective news selections that journalists know well (micro-level). Others argue that news organisations significantly shape the journalists when they arrive at their premises and, as such, researchers must rather be concerned with how this socialisation takes place. The last argument hinges on the ideological elements that societal influences carry and that are exerted on the news institutions in general. In this study, all these ideas are incorporated in Figure 3.3, but with a new possibility where the news selection decision could be comprehensively described as the result of these three elements (influences), which meet at the *foreign news selection filter* stage.

3. Theoretical and Conceptual Frameworks

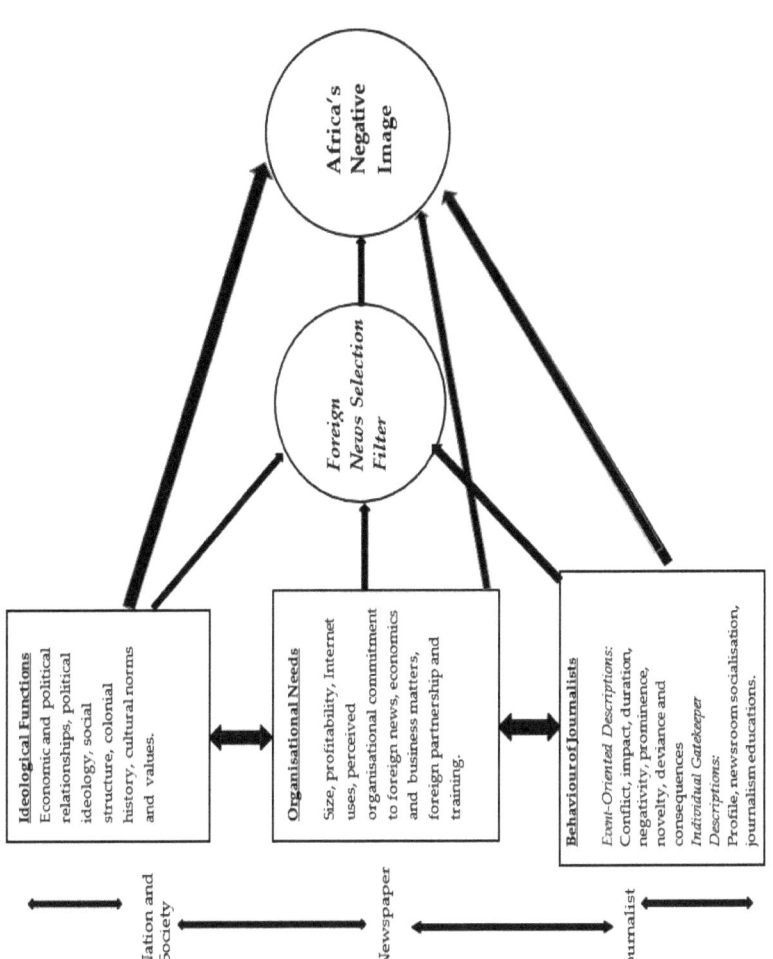

Fig. 3.3 Conceptual framework. Figure created by author (2020).

4. Methodology

In this chapter, I present the methods and procedures employed to answer my research questions (outlined below). The chapter is divided into six sections. The first section deals with the research design and rationale for the use of different methods (triangulation) for data collection. The second section discusses the sampling, while the third tackles the rationale for the choice of the newspapers and provides a detailed description of the selected newspapers. The fourth section describes the unit of analysis and period of study. The fifth section describes data collection and analysis. The sixth section demonstrates validity, reliability and ethical issues, coding instruments and the conceptual design for the ethnographic interview.

It is imperative to recall the research questions that were asked in the Introduction and to proceed with how to answer them through data collection and analysis. The four research questions that were set for the study presented in this book are:

RQ1: How was Africa depicted in the Ghanaian press?

1. What subjects/topics/story types were mostly covered on the continent?
2. What were the dominant themes through which the African story was narrated?
3. What was the quality/tone of coverage (negative or positive or neutral)?
4. How comparable are RQ1 sub-questions a. b. and c. between the Ghanaian press and their Western counterparts (Bunce, Franks and Paterson, 2017)?

RQ2: What is the weight of influence, both quantitative and qualitative, which individual international news agencies carry as sources in the Ghanaian press?

RQ3: What, from the perspective of the journalists, accounts for the kind of representation Africa gets from the Ghanaian press in terms of condition, actors and practices?

RQ4: How did specific intermedia agenda-setting relationships evolve?

The two-step data collection strategy started with an ethnographic content analysis (ECA), while the second step involved an ethnographic interview. The first step of empirical data collection started after receiving official written permission in line with the ethical requirement of the study to collect newspapers in the University of Cape Coast Library. The quantitative aspect of the content analysis revealed the weight of influence an individual international news agency carried as a source. This involved counting the number of foreign stories sourced from each of the international news agencies over the period of two years. The news stories that appeared on the foreign news pages of each of the four newspapers were counted. As part of step one, I collected ninety-six editions of the four major newspapers for the ethnographic content analysis that sought to reveal the dominant themes of depiction African countries received in the Ghanaian press.

The second step of data collection was conducted in twelve intermittent weeks from April–July, 2016. I spent two weeks each with the four selected newspapers interviewing the journalists and editors and observing the entire foreign news selection and production processes.

Research Design

Research design is a strategy of inquiry that gives procedural direction for the design of a study, whether within qualitative, quantitative or mixed-method approaches (Creswell, 2014). The purpose of the design can be explorative, descriptive, explanatory and a combination of the three, plus other purposes. Sequential and typological designs are less suitable for qualitative research because any component of design in the qualitative paradigm requires reconsideration and modification throughout the research process in response to new developments, which are inevitable (Maxwell, 2012). For Colin Robson (2011), the qualitative research design is an inductive process that hardly follows a sequence or strict pre-determined plan; it is flexible and not fixed. Therefore, making this design explicit from the outset of the study is like subjecting its strengths, limitations and implications to self-debate in order to construct and reconstruct it through the entire research process. In my two-step research approach, all three purposes of the research design were followed. While the ethnographic content analysis of the first step was exploratory and descriptive, the ethnographic interview provided explanatory illuminations to the initial findings.

Ethnography

According to John Creswell (2004), ethnography is a design of inquiry in which the researcher studies the shared patterns of behaviours, language and actions of intact groups in a more natural setting over a period of time mainly using observations and interviews for data collection. E. G. Guba and Y. S. Lincoln (2005) provided a broader clarification of ethnography as a design located across critical theory, constructivism and participatory paradigms. The ethnography design in this research applies two methods: ethnographic content analysis and ethnographic interview. Ethnographic content analysis (ECA) is a hybrid method that draws from both quantitative and qualitative approaches to capture narratives and numeric descriptions of a text in order to deconstruct meaning from it (Altheide, 1987; Altheide and Schneider, 2013).

Ethnographic interview, on the other hand, represents the application of different interview genres punctuated by observations (Bernard, 2002; Spradley, 1979). The use of these methods of inquiry provides a stronger case for the validity of the study as a whole. Content analysis is also ethnographic, that is, reflexive and circular in approach, right from data collection through analysis to interpretation. Ethnographic content analysis is "systematic and analytic, but not rigid" (p. 68). As with conventional content analysis, information is organised by categories and subcategories, but with an ethnographic approach, other categories are "allowed and expected to emerge throughout the study." This thinking has been previously corroborated by Klaus Krippendorff (1980), who argued that content analysis examines recorded communication texts, especially when the meaning of the message is embedded in the text itself.

The express use of methods grounded in ethnography (ECA and ethnographic interview) is a basic compelling rationalisation for the use of ethnography as a design to investigate news selection culture among Ghanaian newspapers. The very theoretical and conceptual arguments of this study are based on the notion that news production is the result of several forces exerting influences from varied levels. Geert Jacobs, Henk Pander Maat and Tom van Hout (2008) identified these influences and processes within the concept of news management, which they argued revolves around a "triumvirate of news access (source-media interaction), news selection (editorial decision making) and news production (entextualisation)" (p. 2). Paola Catenaccio et al. (2011) propose that emerging research in media must consider the concept of news management from a threefold perspective of the text, professional practice and interaction. They establish that "ethnographic, field-based, and interaction-orientated news production research is needed with researchers sitting in on the story meeting, looking over the journalists' shoulders at the computer screen, out on assignment, and listening to the water cooler or coffee break chat" (pp. 1845–46). These were the guiding elements of data collection.

Operational Definitions

Afro-Pessimism

Africa's negative media image, and the general perceptions people have about the continent, have been discussed broadly under the concept of Afro-pessimism, which Toussaint Nothias (2012) defines loosely as the inability of Africa to overcome pressing challenges related to poverty, health, development or governance. Relying on previous literature, Nothias argues that the uniqueness of the Afro-pessimism discourse, when applied to news media, leads to the delineation of five analytical components: "essentialisation, racialisation, selectivity, ethnocentric ranking and prediction" (Nothias, 2012, p. 1). In the study in this book, the definition of a negative media image of Africa is deconstructed through normative and critical perspectives. Normative perspectives rely largely on previous research while critical perspectives offer latent meaning, based on what is present — or what was expected to be present — in the news articles. The issue of homogenisation of the continent, for example, is a normative idea that has existed for a long time now. Again, in this study, there was a search for the reasoning and conditions behind the reoccurrence of these images, especially their spread on to the African continent itself. As a conceptual guide, Afro-pessimism represents all news stories focusing *fully on negative or natural disaster* on the continent (Bunce et al., 2017, Miller, 1999), wholly negative evaluation of policies and events (excluding natural events), omission or silence on some parts of complex reality (Nyamnjoh, 2017; Mody, 2010), and positive stories negated with unrelated contextual and historical background (Hawk, 1992).

International/Transnational News Agencies

When one considers international news agencies, traditional international newswire services — such as Reuters, Associated Press (AP) and Agence France-Presse (AFP), among others — come to the fore. However, in this study, all foreign news organisations cited as sources of international news articles in the Ghanaian press are categorised as international news agencies, and these include foreign wire services, transnational global media and other foreign news organisations.

Sampling Procedures

The major aim of sampling in research is to obtain a representative sample that satisfies the scientific approach to studying media content. According to Daniel Riffe, Stephen Lacy, and Frederick Fico (2014), the need for content analysis studies to sample units of content and time can create confusion as to which population inferences are applicable. They recommend that the researcher should make clear whether inferences concern content, time or both; this is because the appropriate dimension of inference (content or time) is based on which was selected with a probability sample. Matthew Miles, Michael Huberman and Johnny Saldaña (2014, p. 31) hold the view that sampling strategies in qualitative research should be theoretically, conceptually and purposively driven, rather than a search motivated by "randomness" and "representativeness." David Altheide and Christopher Schneider (2013) support this assertion with their observation that in some cases, a simple random sample or stratified sample could systematically distort an understanding of news coverage of an event. Both sides to this argument are insightful for my research because while the newspaper organisations were purposively selected, the content selection was randomly done using a constructed week approach that takes account of each day of the week.

The four selected Ghanaian newspapers (*The Daily Graphic*, *Ghanaian Times*, *Daily Guide* and *The Ghanaian Chronicle*) represent two ownership structures (state and private) with the highest circulation figures (FES, 2014). These newspapers are well recognised, reliable and have regular foreign news pages. However, specific editions to be included in the study were determined by the particular analysis of the stage of the research. While stage one adopted a census of all editions (content analysis), stage two (ethnographic content analysis) employed the constructed week approach in order to unearth the dominant themes Africa was depicted with. Using the two-constructed week approach involved selecting twelve editions of each of the four newspapers to represent a year and this is repeated for the second year; thus twenty-four editions of each newspaper were examined over the two-year period. This gave me a total of ninety-six editions in total. With an average of four stories per newspaper, I analysed approximately 250 articles that related to the coverage of Africa over the period under review. There were three different screening exercises to eliminate duplication of articles. After the screening exercise, 180 articles were considered distinct and unique for analysis.

The ethnographic interview is the core element of the second phase of the data collection and analysis. At this stage, I sampled journalists and editors who worked directly on the foreign news pages of the selected newspapers. In all, there were eight such interviews punctuated with newsroom observations. The design and interpretation of the ethnographic interview data benefited from the findings of the initial content analysis. The approach of using different sampling procedures for different stages of the research process is called multi-stage sampling, a practice where one or more sampling decisions and techniques are chosen at the different stages of the same research (Riffe et al., 2014).

Selection of Newspapers

While there are many newspapers in Ghana, the Friedrich-Ebert-Stiftung (FES) report (2013) identifies, in terms of consistency of printing and circulation, the top ten newspapers. Within the limits imposed on this study by time and resources, I selected the top four of these newspapers: *The Daily Graphic*, the *Ghanaian Times*, *The Ghanaian Chronicle* and the *Daily Guide*. The *Ghanaian Times* and *The Daily Graphic* are state-owned newspapers with the largest circulation. *The Ghanaian Chronicle* and *Daily Guide* are the largest circulating private-owned newspapers.

With a "daily circulation of 100,000" copies, *The Daily Graphic* remains the highest circulated newspaper, followed by the *Ghanaian Times* with "80,000 copies". *The Ghanaian Chronicle* and *Daily Guide*, the two private-owned newspapers, followed in the ranking with a daily circulation of "45,000 and 22,000" copies respectively (Friedrich-Ebert-Stiftung, 2013, p. 29). These four newspapers constitute about 92% of daily newspaper circulation in Ghana.

Table 4.1 Parameters of Newspaper Selection

Newspaper	Daily Circulation (DC)	Ownership Type	Position in National Circulation	Cumulative % of DC
The Daily Graphic	100,000	Public	1st	34
Ghanaian Times	80,000	Public	2nd	67
The Ghanaian Chronicle	45,000	Private	3rd	84
Daily Guide	22,000	Private	4th	92

Source: FES, 2013.

The total Daily Circulation (DC) of 286,500 represents 100%, out of which the individual newspaper circulation percentages and positions were calculated.

Apart from the circulation angle, newspapers can also be selected on the basis that they possess an international newsgathering ability and extensive foreign affairs coverage (Wells and King, 1994, p. 654). According to Andy Ofori-Birikorang (2009), newspaper selection decisions could also consider the longstanding popularity of a newspaper in the publishing history of a country. Clement Asante (1996) and Kojo Yankah (1994) have both pointed to the continued relevance of these four selected newspapers overtime for research and longitudinal analyses.

Units of Analysis

The entire foreign news article constituted the unit of analysis for the content analyses. A foreign news article is defined to include any news story that relates to any country other than Ghana. For the purposes of this study, all those articles that appeared on foreign news pages were analysed. This study did not analyse foreign sports news because it did not have the characteristics that met the objective of this study.

To determine the weight of influence individual transnational news agencies carried as sources, the unit of analysis was the byline of all articles published within the study period. Where the bylines had no indication of a visible source, the "lead" of the story was "google-searched" to discover the media organisation that packaged the story. And when the source of the article is still not traceable, it is counted as "unsourced". Generally, the units of analyses included the headlines, lead, paragraphs and bylines.

Data Collection

The first step of data collection was content analysis during the stage of exploratory research. The second step involved the ethnographic interview. The first step was designed to provide information for the conduct of the ethnographic interview. Katrin Voltmer and Hendrik Kraetzschmar (2015) argue that showing interviewees their own work in a reconstructive interview provides "a bridge for the interviewee to reflect on the process that led to that piece, including outside pressures, editorial routines and own beliefs at the time of writing" (p. 32). These elements work together to produce rich data which otherwise would not have been possible.

I conducted a purely quantitative count of sources to show the weight of influence carried by each transnational news agency as a source in the Ghanaian press. This was followed by Altheide's ethnographic content analysis technique to capture both narratives and numeric description of the foreign news articles. To achieve this, I allowed categories/codes to emerge from the data. Due to this, pre-existing codes used for initial ideas were eventually modified and new codes added to demonstrate the specific characteristics of the data. This meant I had to rely on the careful reading and re-reading of the data text in order to capture the text and its meaning, as well as the contextual meaning. I engaged with the text by doing multiple readings of every news story sampled to gain a general understanding of the contents. Descriptive notes were taken at every stage and further explored using the MAXQDA search string tool, which allows you to search for a combination of words together.

A second close reading of the text was conducted to identify the "discursive strategies" that lay within the text (Bertrand and Hughes, 2005). During this stage, I identified recurrent coverage issues or topics, and noted the various themes that emerged. I later categorised these notes on a thematic basis by assigning names and labels (codes) to them. These categories were then quantified into frequency distribution tables which supported the analysis (code frequency table). These led to a deeper interpretation of each of the selected news stories to determine latent meanings and significance embodied in the text. Through this process, I took the analysis of the news stories beyond its overt meaning. The analysis was in-depth, more culturally situated and profoundly contextual.

The content analysis relates only to a text under review. Although some inferences are applicable in content analysis, the design can neither test causal relationships between variables nor guarantee that the sender or the receiver shares the same attributed meaning. To minimise this weakness, per D. K. Lal Das (2008), I collected significant data through ethnographic interviews with the four selected newspapers to supplement the findings of the initial content analysis.

Ethnographic Content Analysis (ECA)

The use of Altheide's ethnographic content analysis approach meant that the processes of the analysis were reflexive and interactive with the researcher (not protocol), occupying the central position of the investigation, although protocols were later developed as a guide (Altheide, 1987; Altheide and Schneider, 2013). Trained coders with little or no supervision coded the manifest issues of the source(s). The second part of the first phase of the content analysis related to how Africa was depicted in the selected newspapers. After a close reading of at least a half of the stories was achieved, I developed content categories and frames, some of which were predetermined from a theoretical perspective and from existing literature, while other codes were allowed to emerge from the data. Categories and themes coded were not mutually exclusive because the categories largely overlap each other. The design of the coding categories was conducted in a manner that provided for both narrative and numeric descriptions to be captured. The preliminary approach in this study was to seek certain words and examine their association and proximity in various parts of the news article, including headlines. The news articles had several *thematic spaces* (operationally defined as foreign news article parts, which included the headline, sentence, lead, and paragraph).

I first conducted a Boolean search for words such as "crime", "killings", "development", and "human rights". This was followed with searches for "war", "famine" and "poverty", and these represented theoretical sampling, from a postcolonial perspective, of how the ideological structures contained in media texts define the foreign *Other*. The search for ten words before or after these words ("war", "famine" and "poverty") was conducted in line with Altheide's (2000) design for tracking discourse.

To determine the direction of the story as to whether they were positive, negative or neutral, I adopted the definition used by Anju Chaudhary (2001, pp. 33–34) in his analysis of negative news in Western and developing countries newspapers. According to Chaudhary, negative reportage includes negative stories about diseases, accidents and natural disasters. It includes unforeseen events that have caused personal injuries or destruction to life and property, as well as responsiveness to disaster relief. These categories, in Chaudhary's research, appeared in articles on "oil spills, famines, floods, earthquakes, droughts, fires, pestilence and diseases" (p. 33). These issues were subjectively and contextually defined and determined by Chaudhary because the discourse before, during and after an earthquake can be positive too, depending on how it is depicted. Positive news, according to Chaudhary is defined as "information about cure of diseases, relief efforts for families experiencing earthquakes, droughts, fires, pestilence and diseases. Others include a drop in fire accidents and improved air safety records" (pp. 33–34). Neutral foreign news was defined as stories that "involved both positive and negative in an equal measure or neither positive nor negative" (p. 34). Beyond Chaudhary (2001), three other conceptualisations of negative stories or Afro-pessimism were adopted for the content analysis. These included the tone of the analysis, omissions or silence on improvements and the negation of positive stories with negative contextual background information. The definitions informed the construction of a protocol to obtain data on topic, categories, emphasis and grammatical use of these words (war, famine and poverty) as nouns, verbs, adjectives and adverbs. The protocol included narrative descriptions as well as numerical or alphabet codes. It had space for notes and comments where necessary (see Appendix I).

Conceptual Design of the Ethnographic Interview

Usually, ethnography is associated with the immersion of the researcher in the field setting for an extended period of time, but it has also been argued that ethnographers work in settings in which complete immersion is unnecessary (Whitehead, 2005). I employed the ethnographic approach to ensure that I did not miss any of the cultures at play in the newsrooms, which I see as mini-societies. It assisted me in obtaining emic validity, which is the avoidance of a situation where responses to interview outside of natural contexts (newsroom and editorial meetings) may represent ideal culture instead of real or explicit culture. This could occur as a result of other factors, such as social desirability or tacit reality. Due to this, James Spradley (1979, p. 9) advises that if the "reality is tacit, the researcher through ethnographic fieldwork supported by repetitive, iterative and situational observations and interviews could unlock the meaning involved".

I adopted such an iterative view of continual observation, questioning, making inferences and repeating this process until most questions were answered with the greatest emic validity. I started the ethnographic encounters with an informal interview that had no conscious structure. For the first two days, I imposed no controlling structure and I simply recorded some conversations I remembered after the day's work. From the fourth day onwards, I then started to influence the direction of the conversations based on the research objectives. This continued with sit down semi-structured interviews and, later, with structured interviews. The process was repeated among the four selected newspapers. To synthesise the various experiences expressed by the journalists in the individual interviews and observations, I developed some structured interviews with all the journalists working for the foreign pages of the four newspapers. The conceptual outlook of this process as presented in Figure 4.1, which is a pictorial view of the process adapted from T. L. Whitehead (2005), H. R. Bernard (2002) and Spradley (1979).

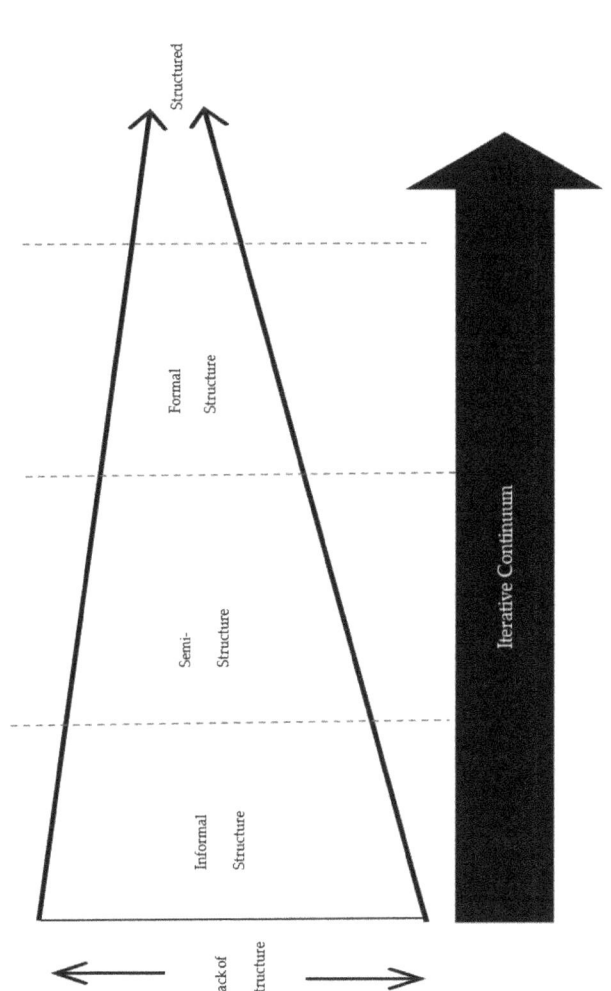

Fig. 4.1 Conceptual view of the ethnographic design. Figure created by author (2020), adapted from Whitehead (2005), Bernard (2002) and Spradley (1979).

The focus of both the interview and observation gains its shape and structure as the researcher moves through the progressive interview genres — from lack of structure, to a fully structured interview, by the end of the fieldwork. It is important to note that the iterative continuum along which the study flows is fluid, flexible and reflexive. This movement along the continuum is fundamental for such a reflexive model in order to generate ideas, re-question the process and make changes for the betterment of the insights of the study.

Data Analysis

According to Bernard (2006) "analysis is the search for patterns in data and ideas to help explain why the patterns are there in the first place" (p. 452). He adds that no matter the research paradigm, whether quantitative or qualitative, analyses ultimately are all qualitative" (pp. 452–56). This is because following all their analyses — factor, cluster, regression etc. — the researcher will still have to link the findings to other findings in literature through the interpretation of the figures. My analyses allowed for a deep assessment of the interview transcripts. I listened to each interview before conducting the next one, especially on the same interviewee. I read the interview transcript and the thick description of my fieldnotes twice. This resulted in a unique appreciation of the conversation, in a highly intimate manner. My pre-data preparation approach meant I could avoid coding individual words, or line-by-line coding. Instead, I concentrated on coding meaningful bits of the data, which collectively preserved each story's contextual richness (Ayres, Kavanaugh, and Knafl, 2003).

The use of postcolonial critique, predominantly, in understanding the data, meant using some preconceived codes (deductively) in the register of this tradition, but it equally meant I needed to give attention to inductive codes in order to capture new insights of my data which could account for the nuances of resistance discussed by Homi K. Bhabha (1994). It was clear to me that exclusive deductive coding produces a premature exclusion and closure to innovative analytical approaches and insights inherent in my data; I therefore avoided it.

Qualitative Analysis Guide of Leuven (QUAGOL)

The ethnographic interview significantly represented an explanatory-level analysis in this study. I used the Qualitative Analysis Guide of Leuven (QUAGOL) as a guiding document (Dierckx de Casterlé, Gastmans, Bryon, and Denier, 2012). QUAGOL divides the analysis process into two major parts: (1) thorough preparation of the data and coding process and (2) actual coding process using qualitative data analysis software. These two parts form what is referred to as first cycle coding (initial coding), and second cycle coding, which refers to pattern formation and linking codes (Miles et al., 2014). But the overarching task of my approach was the discovery of cultural themes. A theme, in the first place, is a postulate declared or implied, one that usually controls behaviour or stimulates activity, and which is "*tacitly* approved or openly prompted in a society" (Opler, 1945, p. 198). Spradley (1979) offers a definition for "cultural theme as any cognitive principle, tacit or explicit, recurrent in a number of domains and serving as a relationship among subsystems of cultural meaning" (p. 186).

To begin the analysis process, I conducted a mock analysis. Firstly, I undertook a thorough re-reading of the individual interviews, because each respondent was interviewed several times (average ten times). At this stage, I corrected mistakes on the transcripts, underlined phrases and made notes of thought-provoking statements and ideas. Secondly, I developed a narrative interview report of one-page on each interviewee vis-à-vis the research topic. By doing this, I render vivid interviewee's stories about foreign news selection in his/her daily work. I also condensed the stories to an abstract form through paraphrase and summary. Thirdly, I converted the narrative interview report into a conceptual interview scheme. I achieved this through the clustering of data into concepts. At this stage, I replaced concrete experiences with concepts. I avoided all-embracing concepts by describing each concept with the necessary indication of its content. Bernadette Dierckx de Casterlé et al. (2012) maintain that this stage supports the trustworthiness of the process of analysis. Fourthly, I conducted a test of the appropriateness of my conceptual interview scheme by looking iteratively again into the interview data to see if I had ignored a concept or over-emphasised another concept. This resulted in the reformulation and completion of the conceptual interview schemes. I resorted to further testing of the appropriateness of the conceptual interview scheme with the strategy of constant comparison across different newspapers and different roles of the journalists. I then drew up a list of concepts to start coding with. Finally, I began the coding process itself after describing this process in detail to the research team at the doctoral school presentations. Using the MAXQDA software, I rendered these preliminary concepts into codes. I provided no hierarchical organisation of the codes and no linkages. All that mattered at this stage was coding meaningful concepts and providing enough comments regarding the reasoning behind each code. The second cycle coding for the development of patterns, data interpretation and reporting followed with three primary strategies: keywords-in-context, constant comparison, and thematic analysis.

Keywords-in-Context

Keywords-in-context is a qualitative data analysis strategy that can increase the understanding of the researcher (Fielding and Lee, 1998). This is where I looked for specific words in the register of concepts and how they are utilised by the interviewee in the descriptions, especially as part of words before and after the concept's appearance. This string of words analysis allowed for context, initial concept description and an account of how concepts evolved in the body of the conversation (Altheide, 1994).

Constant Comparison

Constant comparison is a more popular qualitative analysis technique developed by Barney Glaser and Anselm Strauss (1967, 2006). According to Matthew Miles et al. (2014), even though it was developed for grounded theory, constant comparison can be used to categorise actors, states, events and actions into an abstractly defined class of concepts that could either be predefined or emerge from coding and memos. To Miles et al., subsuming particulars into the general class of concepts is a "conceptual and theoretical activity in which you shuttle back and forth between first-level data and more general categories that evolve and develop through iterations until the category is saturated" (p. 286).

They argue that the success of this process of abstraction is dependent significantly on how the researcher clearly links the study's conceptual framework and research question, as I have done in Figure 3.3. Through this figure, one can clearly identify which category of data sets should provide answers for which research questions. The constant comparison across the newspapers (*The Daily Graphic*, the *Ghanaian Times*, the *Daily Guide* and *The Ghanaian Chronicle*) and roles (reporter, page editor and editor) used both "enumerative induction" (instances going in the same direction) and "eliminative inductions" — testing the appropriateness of hypothesis against alternatives as a way of seeking rationalisation of the conclusions (Miles at al., 2014, p. 292).

Theme Analysis

Theme analysis is, according to Spradley (1979), a cultural analysis with a less developed technique for conducting it. So from Spradley's definition, themes can be tacit or explicit, they could have a relationship with each other in the broader cultural system and they could appear and re-appear in several domains. The first strategy proposed by Spradley (1979) for analysing themes is immersion. This is a complete surrender of one's mental life to a new culture. This does not necessarily mean spending years on the field. In its simplified form, Spradley argues that multiple interview sessions could be intercepted with pauses that are entirely dedicated to the appreciation of a piece of data collected before proceeding to the next interview and observation. The study presented in this book adopted this approach, as explained in the two-step research design. Making a cultural inventory is another way of improving immersion, but it also represents the second procedure itself. To avoid losing the easy familiarity with the data, the interviews were transcribed throughout the night before the next interview session. Cultural contradictions, social conflicts, informal techniques of social control, acquiring and maintaining status and solving problems (Spradley, 1979) are some of the suggestive frameworks for identifying themes, representing the third approach. From transcription and correction of transcription to coding, these indicators remained a target for the analysis. These strategies and approaches fall within the general approach of this study described as iteration and reflexivity. During the main analysis, there were still several phone calls and emails sent to interviewees regarding gaps that needed to be clarified.

Validity and Reliability

Issues regarding the validity of qualitative research have been scrutinised in recent times, because quantitative researchers are required to see their equivalence of validity being demonstrated in the qualitative paradigm as well (Creswell and Miller, 2000). Natasha Mauthner and Andrea Doucet (2003) have argued that reflexivity, which is one way to demonstrate quality, can be operationalised from "personal, interpersonal, institutional, pragmatic, emotional, theoretical, epistemological and ontological influences on our research and data analysis" (p. 413). They debunked the neutrality of data analysis methods and techniques and rather called for researchers to put reflexivity into practice by moving it from its current abstract position to a pragmatic and hands-on research activity. Michael LeCompte (2000) calls on qualitative researchers to provide a detailed articulation of their reflexive strategies in practice.

Content Analysis

It is crucial also to point out that validity cannot be assumed, and the way research reports are presented must welcome the opportunity for critical reflection by readers. According to David Altheide and John Johnson (1994, p. 496), showing "how we claim to know what we know is as useful as the very claim to what we know". The quantitative content analysis method relies on the face validity of its categories and bylines, which are coded verbatim from the articles.

The Daily Graphic newspaper was unique, due to layout and outlook changes. Although there were some attributions to international news agencies, full stories usually were not sourced within the bylines. The researcher devised a solution for this by typing out the "lead" of the story in a "google search". This approach revealed which international news agency actually packaged that story. After this was clarified, the test of reliability recommended with arithmetic formulae did not really offer solutions because the pool of newspaper articles was manually gathered through stages. The quantitative elements being coded were manifest, meaning that they only needed to be counted and recorded in the worksheet by three different groups of coders (two in each group). We were, in all, six coders and we changed groupings each day. In determining the manifest elements of the weight of the transnational news agency as a source, a few coding discrepancies occurred. These were mostly arithmetic errors that were eventually resolved through the exchange of code sheets for summation after the close of the working day during the coding process. That is, coders cross-checked the code sheets of other coders. We resolved very crucial counting errors through this strategy, which was revealed during the pilot test.

Krippendorff (2004, p. 13) argues that even multiple interpretations of textual matters need to be reliable in the sense of being replicable by other researchers, or described as the same or similar by independent analysts. With both quantitative and qualitative operations, I adopted the necessary steps to deal with reliability, validity and ethical issues in this study.

Field research in Ghana meant returning home for me, and my connection with the place proved useful because I felt at home and received favours from people in the media industry that I have known through my practice as a broadcast journalist and a journalism teacher. My familiarity with Ghana helped with access issues. I have not worked for the mainstream print media before, so the experience was new in some respects. I knew how to approach my interviewees effectively, having lunch with them and speaking broadly about non-research subjects. Even though I spent only three weeks at each newsroom, some of the interviewees started to address me as one of their own, and spoke candidly and comprehensively to me in sincere conversations. I succeeded in eliminating the initial fear of social desirability reported about Ghanaian journalists in research interviews (Hasty, 2005). While analysing, I reflected on my involvements in order to minimise any biases that might influence my interpretation. One advantage that my close involvement brings is the emic view that I possess of the research field and the data, which is unique.

Another validity check adopted in this study is prolonged engagement (Lincoln and Guba, 1985, pp. 301–04; Creswell, 2014, p. 250; Yin, 2011, p. 79). I spent a prolonged time on the field, and through this approach I developed an in-depth understanding of the phenomenon under study and succeeded in conveying details about the site and the people — details which lend credibility to the narrative accounts written for each interviewee.

The use of thick description throughout Chapter 4 in describing scenes, actors and situation is a form of validity check in qualitative research. Triangulation of data sources through extensive content analysis, newsroom observations and interviews gave me several opportunities to ask and validate the crucial questions of how the foreign news selection in Ghana is shaped in terms of actors, conditions and practices.

Another important internal validity check in this study was member checking. In line with this, I shared an initial case analysis with participants to seek further illumination where necessary. This does not represent approval from the interviewees or their validation. Where no new ideas emerged, the suggestions of the interviewees were abandoned. Testing the data collection and analysis protocols provided assurances that the protocols met the specific purposes of the investigation and the protocols were effective enough to elicit the necessary information required to answer the questions of the research.

Ethical Issues

Study participants are very valuable to every study. Miles et al. (2014) posited that the researchers and their research participants need some explicit agreement on what their expectations look like very early on in a research process. During the exploratory research, I received an invitation from the editors of the four newspapers to conduct my research. They jointly signed an agreement letter after I presented an introductory letter from my graduate school outlining my interests in this research project. To be sure that the study experienced the flexibility required in qualitative research, I remained open to regularly checking ethical agreements and negotiating them where necessary, especially on issues of anonymising some of the participants when they requested it.

5. Portrayal of Africa
Results of Ethnographic Content Analysis

This chapter presents the results of the ethnographic content analysis (ECA), which relates to the four selected newspapers. The weight of influence, dominant themes of portrayal and the subject and tone of the coverage of Africa in Ghanaian newspapers were determined. The quantitative weight of influence individual transnational news agencies carried as a source were analysed, one newspaper after the other, before moving the analysis to the aggregate level where the influence of international news agencies as a whole were discussed. The results of the ECA and ethnographic interview (EI) are reported in this chapter and the next; while the synergies are discussed in the final chapter. The motivation to combine results of both the ECA and EI is to strengthen and offset each approach's weaknesses. After all, the EI was developed with results and insights from the initial ECA to comprehensively uncover the reasoning behind the coverage of Africa from the journalists' perspective and newsroom setup. This allows the findings and conclusions of the study to fit together as a whole.

Quantitative Influence of International News Agencies

The weight of influence (quantitative) international news agencies carry as a source in the selected Ghanaian press individually and collectively were analysed using content analysis. *The Daily Graphic* newspaper dedicated the highest number of pages to foreign news — usually between two to three pages on a daily basis, except when the newspaper was oversubscribed with advertising, and except on Sundays, when no edition is produced. For a period of two years the paper published

4,287 foreign news articles in total. Table 5.1 provides details of the international news agencies these articles were sourced to:

Table 5.1 Sources of foreign news in *The Daily Graphic*

Sources	Articles	Percentage (%)
BBC World Service	2,517	58.70
AP	636	14.85
AFP	339	7.91
Xinhua	231	5.39
Reuters	221	5.16
Others	127	2.96
Own Reporters	107	2.49
Unsourced	106	2.47
CNN	3	0.07
Total	**4,287**	**100**

Source: field data (2015).

The British Broadcasting Corporation (BBC World Service) remains the most cited source over the two-year period. *The Daily Graphic* newspaper which had the highest number of news articles relied on the BBC with over 58% of its foreign news sourced to the British broadcaster. This newspaper's manner of selection of foreign news, which was positively skewed towards the BBC, also demonstrated a low level of diversity.

The inadequate diversity is visible in the number of articles sourced to the category of Others, which involved many other international news agencies apart from the ones that made it onto the code sheet. The elite ideology of this newspaper is magnified once more by its reliance on just a few well-known international news agencies, such as the BBC, Associated Press (AP), Reuters, Agence France-Press (AFP) and, more recently, Xinhua News Agency. Apart from the BBC and AP, which were more influential than the Xinhua News Agency, the likes of Reuters, Cable News Network (CNN) and Al Jazeera did not compete well with the Chinese news agency. The Chinese Xinhua News Agency joined the race for the quantitative influence just a little over decade ago, and produced a performance below AP and AFP but slightly above Reuters, CNN and Al Jazeera. CNN performed very poorly in this newspaper as a source. The category of *own reporter/correspondent* includes stories sourced to *The Daily Graphic* reporters or correspondents, both home and abroad, which were indicated in the byline as such. This category was dominated by stories mostly written by Ebo Godwin in Togo about that country's democratic struggles. The second influential set of stories related to the coverage of press conferences on the North China Sea crisis between China and Japan.

Another important category noticed in most previous foreign news studies was Unsourced. This included stories that had no author indications, no source quoted and no attributions cited. Considering the professional pedigree within which *The Daily Graphic* operates, 106 unsourced news stories, especially when compared with the other smaller circulating newspapers, is surprisingly high. It is useful, although, to state that this phenomenon started from mid-2013 onwards. Beginning in this period, the newspaper had a major change in design and outlook that turned *bylines* into names of cities where events took place. The page editor also decided that stories written by her would not bear her name.

The *Ghanaian Times* newspaper dedicated two pages on a daily basis to foreign news coverage, and recorded a total of 3,761 articles over the course of the period.

Table 5.2 provides details on how these articles were sourced:

Table 5.2 Sources of foreign news in the *Ghanaian Times*

Sources	Articles	Percentage (%)
BBC World	2,535	67.40
Xinhua	486	12.92
Reuters	324	8.61
Others	118	3.14
AP	71	1.89
Own Reporter	66	1.76
AFP	63	1.68
CNN	58	1.54
Unsourced	40	1.06
Total	**3,761**	**100**

Source: field data (2015).

The BBC remains the most cited source over the period also in the *Ghanaian Times*, providing the sources for 67.4% of all foreign news. The *Ghanaian Times* newspaper had increased diversity in the way it sourced foreign news, considering how individual constituents performed in Table 5.2. The diversity could be described as better, in comparative terms, than what exists in *The Daily Graphic*. The Others category came in fourth position in the ranking with over 3%, which indicates a slight improvement when compared with *The Daily Graphic*, although the performance of the BBC alone skyrocketed, with over 67%. The *Ghanaian Times* uses Xinhua News Agency as a source twice as much as *The Daily Graphic* does, even though both newspapers have a similar agreement with the Chinese news agency. Linked to its historical formation, the *Ghanaian Times* regularly recognises its reliance on the Northern media organisation as a failure inconsistent with its mandate as a Pan-African newspaper. They are always seeking avenues through which to diversify their sources of foreign news. But until the present day, characterising the *Ghanaian Times* as a Pan-African newspaper is inaccurate, considering their current reliance on foreign news agencies. The Chinese Xinhua News Agency is the second most influential source, with a performance above AP, Reuters and AFP. The category of Own Reporter includes stories sourced to reporters and correspondents at the *Ghanaian Times*, both home and abroad. This category of source was, as in *The Daily Graphic*, dominated by press conference coverage of the North China Sea crisis between China and Japan. The newspaper appeared to be the platform where the media battle between China and Japan (regarding the North China sea) was fought in Ghana. The *Ghanaian Times* also recorded the lowest number of Unsourced news stories. Even the few cases counted as unsourced news were marked as such due to issues clearly relating to unavailability of space on the bottom print margin, and these cases were usually indicative of a normal printing error.

Reuters became the third most cited foreign news source, performing better than AP, AFP and CNN. The *Ghanaian Times* newspaper held Reuters in a similar level of respect comparable to the BBC World Service. That is why it was even surprising to see Xinhua beyond Reuters. CNN, for the second time, performed poorly as a source of foreign news, which makes it clear that the two public newspapers in

Ghana do not rely on the work of the American broadcaster. The CNN effect, which is explained as the American international broadcaster's dominance on foreign policy discourse in the States and in the media in other countries, cannot be upheld here. The category of Own Reporter in the *Ghanaian Times* also constitutes less than 2% of the newspaper's total news articles over two years. This shows high level of dependency on others international media organisations.

The Ghanaian Chronicle dedicated one page, and occasionally two pages, per newspaper for the type of foreign news that fell within the scope of this study. The paper recorded 2,317 articles for the two-year period, making their coverage the fourth highest among the selected newspapers. Table 5.3 provides details on which transnational news agency sources constituted the coverage.

Table 5.3 Sources of foreign news in *The Ghanaian Chronicle*

Sources	Articles	Percentage (%)
BBC World	1,314	56.71
Others	636	27.50
CNN	250	10.79
Unsourced	41	1.77
AFP	33	1.41
Own Reporter	26	1.12
AP	10	0.40
Reuters	7	0.30
Xinhua	0	0
Total	2,317	100

Source: field data (2015).

The *Chronicle* is rather unique in their reliance on foreign news organisations as source. Although, like the other newspapers, the Own Reporter category is as strikingly low as less than 2%, they demonstrated a higher level of diversity in their sourcing of foreign news. The source category of Others represents all other foreign news organisations other than the ones listed on the code sheet. In essence, they most frequently used other major news organisations than any other newspaper in the sample for this study. However about 50% of this figure (636) came from

Al Jazeera alone. Just like the *Ghanaian Times*, the Chronicle newspaper cited the source of most of their stories except in cases where there was not enough space at the bottom of the newspaper for citing sources. However, there was no single story sourced to Xinhua News Agency and yet the *other* category was the second highest. This shows that their diversity was widespread. CNN recorded 10.79% as the source of the coverage at a third position. This meant that apart from the BBC, CNN was the next single most cited foreign news agency in this newspaper. This is sharply different from what was recorded in the two public newspapers. Although the BBC was the most cited in this newspaper, just like the two previous ones, the percentage lead dropped a little below the two others for the first time. This further strengthens this diversity in the newspaper's foreign news selection. The BBC was the most cited, though followed by the Others category. CNN came third, while Reuters performed poorly with just seven articles at the seventh position.

The *Daily Guide* newspaper recorded 2,863 foreign news articles published within the two-year period, making this newspaper the third highest in terms of its reliance on foreign news articles as sources. Unfortunately, this newspaper recorded the highest percentage of unsourced news stories — with 13.97% constituting the Unsourced category. Table 5.4 presents further details:

Table 5.4 Sources of foreign news in the *Daily Guide*

Sources	Articles	Percentage (%)
BBC World	1,354	47.29
Others	523	18.27
Unsourced	400	13.97
AP	237	8.28
CNN	220	7.68
Own Reporter	54	1.89
Reuters	39	1.36
AFP	36	1.26
Xinhua	0	0
Total	**2,863**	**100**

Source: field data (2015).

The BBC World Service stayed on top with 47.9% of the foreign news carried in the *Daily Guide* — the lowest percentage lead among the four newspapers. Again, the Chinese Xinhua News Agency scored zero in the second private newspaper. The dazzling performance witnessed in the public newspapers so far from the Xinhua News Agency as a source of foreign news in Ghana cannot be extended to the private press. The *Daily Guide* is also the second most diversified newspaper when it comes to sources. The source category of Others recorded 18% of the total news articles for the period under review. AP and CNN recorded modest percentages of 8 and 7 compared to the less than 2% recorded by Reuters, AFP and Own Reporters.

Having outlined the peculiar situations of each newspaper, I proceed now to present the aggregate quantitative view of how the international news agencies competed among themselves as sources for Ghanaian newspapers. The aggregate overview looks a little different from the peculiar trends in the single newspaper analysis. Table 5.5 presents these further details:

Table 5.5 Overview of sources of foreign news in the Ghanaian press

Sources	Articles	Percentage (%)
BBC World	7,720	58.36
Others	1404	10.61
AP	954	7.21
Xinhua	717	5.42
Reuters	591	4.47
Unsourced	587	4.44
CNN	531	4.01
AFP	471	3.56
Own Reporter	253	1.91
Total	**13,228**	**100**

Source: author (2019).

The BBC World Service remains the single most cited source for foreign news in Ghana. AP comes second as the single most cited foreign news source, followed by Xinhua News Agency as the third single most cited for foreign news in Ghana; the Chinese news agency which roughly a decade ago did not have substantial influence emerges here as a strong contender. It is important to note that Xinhua's aggregate performance is slightly above Reuters, AFP and CNN and this influence is in the two most circulating newspapers in Ghana, which are also public newspapers. The use of own reporters and correspondents in covering foreign news in Ghana is less than 2% of the total foreign news articles over the period under study, which signals a sweeping dependence on foreign news organisations. This Own Reporter category also includes Ghana news agency articles. It is crucial to note that unsourced foreign news in the Ghanaian press is not widespread because it largely related to either issues with design or one single newspaper contributing more than 68% of the total error. Table 5.6 shows the composition of unsourced foreign news among the four newspapers.

Table 5.6 Composition of unsourced foreign news

Newspapers	Unsourced news	Percentage (%)
Daily Guide	400	68.14
The Daily Graphic	106	18.07
Ghanaian Times	40	6.81
The Ghanaian Chronicle	41	6.98
Total	**587**	**100**

Source: field data (2015).

If it weren't for the new design of *The Daily Graphic* and the printing errors in the *Ghanaian Times* and *The Ghanaian Chronicle*, unsourced news would have been completely a *Daily Guide* affair and would have not even warranted a mention in this research. But as it is now, unsourced news, which signals poor professionalism, seems to be an issue in the Ghanaian press that warrants a discussion. It is difficult to believe that writing the African story can be such a speculative enterprise with no real sources cited.

To determine the influence each international news agency carried as a source in the Ghanaian newspaper means determining how these foreign news agencies competed among themselves. In this analysis, news cited to the category of Own Reporter and Unsourced foreign news will be taken out of the equation. Figure 5.1 demonstrates the weight of influence carried by each international news agency as a source as against each other.

Fig. 5.1 Weight of influence of international news agencies (100% = 12,388)

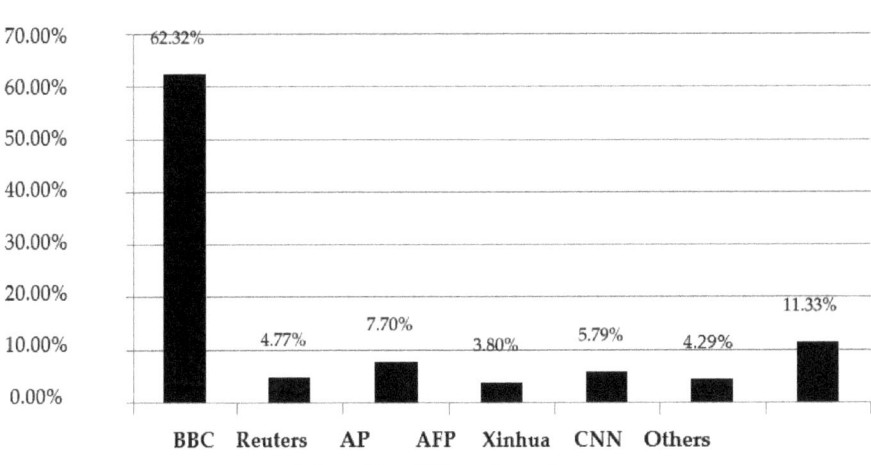

Source: author (2018).

Comparing the performance of international news agencies among themselves meant eliminating the categories of Unsourced and Own Reporter before recalculating the percentages. In such an analysis, the influence of the BBC rises sharply to 62.32%. All the other international news agencies recorded marginal increases in their percentage figure, but the BBC, in particular, recorded a higher increment due to its already high proportional influence among all the four newspapers.

Overview of Africa's Coverage

Having established the international news agencies exerting an influence on how the Ghanaian press reported the continent, this section examines the nature of Africa's portrayal in the Ghanaian press with a focus on the subjects and tone of coverage and the dominant themes of representation. The overarching research question of how Africa was portrayed in the Ghanaian press was answered using subquestions regarding dominant themes, subjects and tone through which the African stories were narrated. The second and third parts of this chapter present the analysis relating strictly to the ethnographic content analysis, which relied on news articles that were selected from the four newspapers.

Subjects of Coverage

The first issue concerning the coverage of Africa in the Ghanaian press is the topics/story types/subjects that received the most coverage. It could be argued that the press's concentration on political reports, as shown in Table 5.7, has rendered a bigger part of the coverage negative since political reports focus on figures of casualties of political conflicts, disagreement of parties, corruption and war. The bias against reporting on history, economy and cultural stories equally indicated the narrow view that was given to many of the things happening on the continent. Mostly, reports were superficial in focus and often written with comparative reference to European democracies. Table 5.7 shows the statistics of the subjects covered:

Table 5.7 Composition of subjects covered on Africa in the Ghanaian Press

Category	Articles	Percentage (%)
Politics	130	72
Social	13	7
Economy	12	7
Personality	9	5
Cultural	8	4
Disaster	6	3
History	2	1
Total	**180**	**100**

Source: author (2019).

The two stories relating to history over the two-year period were about Egypt. Personality related stories did not mention a single African celebrity, except political leaders. The eight stories categorised under culture were also not entirely positive. The *Africa rising* discourse, which has been very much discussed in the current literature, requires contextualisation. First, this discourse became prominent when developed economies were hit by financial crisis. As a result, investors needed new markets for their resources. Second, describing Africa as the next business destination does not necessarily resolve the prevailingly negative media image of Africa imprinted in people's minds for years. Economic and social issues in Africa simply did not receive sufficient reportage in the Ghanaian press; even the few stories that were reported in the Northern media organisations were not repeated in the Ghanaian press.

Tone/Quality of Coverage

The coverage of African countries in the selected Ghanaian press was not different from the negative portrayals that existed in literature about the continent from their Western counterparts. Table 5.8 presents the overview of the tonal coverage of Africa, as per the definitions of Chaudhary (2001, pp. 33–34) and the frameworks set out in this study to identify the tone.

Table 5.8 Tone/quality of coverage of Africa in the Ghanaian press

Tone of Stories	Total	Percentage (%)
Positive	27	15
Neutral	9	5
Negative	144	80
Total	**180**	**100**

Source: author (2018).

80% of stories relating to Africa were negative in nature or belonged to the *Afro-pessimism* discourse. They reported crisis, war, famine and regional political disputes but ignored improvements in these conditions. When considering angles that were excluded from the reports were also never covered in a positive light within this period — for example, the reconciliation of Uhuru Kenyatta and William Ruto. The stories that related to them mostly concentrated on their trial at the International Criminal Court (ICC) and its implications for their victory as President and Vice-president. The positive news articles discussed related to Nelson Mandela in hospital, and Kenya's unity and independence celebrations. Others included appointments of Africans to some eminent United Nations positions.

Dominant Themes

In this sub-section, I deconstruct the dominant themes used by the Ghanaian press in the coverage of Africa through a close engagement with and interpretation of the news articles. Themes are broader than subjects and contain two to three subjects that communicate some ideas beyond individual subjects (see Stevenson, 1984).

The foreign news articles were extensively coded using both inductive and deductive approaches. The 180 foreign news articles selected from the four newspapers were coded all together 359 times. These codes were linked and grouped to reduce the data to manageable size. In all, ten dominant themes were deconstructed with their corresponding frequency and percentages. The total amount of the coded segment of the articles was as well calculated to provide some descriptive view of the intensity of coding as shown in Table 5.9.

Table 5.9 Frequency of dominant themes, from January 2011 to December 2013

Dominant Themes	Frequency	Percentage (%)
War, Crime and Killing	114	31.75
Crises	95	26.46
Terrorism	45	12.53
Colonial Memory	23	6.41
Democracy and Lack of Press Freedom	18	5.01
Irresponsibility	15	4.18
Development and Progress	14	3.90
Diseases and Disaster	13	3.62
Human Rights, Women and Child Abuse	12	3.34
Unrelated Negative Context	10	2.79
Total	**359**	**100**

Source: field data (2015).

These themes were discussed in line with the research objective.

Theme of War, Crime and Killing

This theme included reports of war and fighting, trials and discourses surrounding war crimes, abduction and ransom cases, issues relating to drugs and religious intolerance and its consequent crimes. Where the crimes resulted in killings, the deaths were initially coded as *killing* and later combined with the categories *war* and *crime* due to the blurred nature of these three categories. The theme of *war, crime and killing* represents the most dominant theme through which Africa was portrayed. It is also the most consistent theme, and easy to identify throughout the coding process. That is, much of its attributes were readily manifest. The rampant use of words such as "civil war", "killed", "death", "fierce fighting", "fleeing from war crimes", etc., was visible in all the four newspapers. Examples of some coded segments are as follows:

> THIRTEEN South African soldiers were killed in the Central African Republic as rebels seized the capital over the weekend, President Jacob Zuma has said (*Daily Guide*).

> MORE THAN 100 people are confirmed dead in fierce fighting on Thursday in the capital of the Central African Republic (CAR), Bangui, UN officials say (*The Daily Graphic*).

> Population of a town in eastern democratic Republic of Congo hustling between government rebel forces, residents say. BBC's Ignatius Bahizi, who is on the Ugandan side of the town, says missiles are being fired, killing people. Many people have left their homes since the conflict began in March 2012 (*Ghanaian Times*).

> Two schools were attacked at the weekend, with at least 16 students and two teachers killed. Military spokesman Lt Col Sagir Musa said the militants behind those attacks had used satellite phones to militants following recent attacks (*The Ghanaian Chronicle*).

Apart from these examples which covered war, war crimes and killings generally, there were other stories that related to crimes of piracy along the West African coast and issues of hard drugs.

Using the postcolonial theory demands the questioning and reframing of the portrayal by these news articles regarding not only what was written, but also what was ignored/omitted from the reporting. Significant in this category of omission is the fact that in all these articles which related to the theme of war, crimes and killings, no article assessed the improvements of any of these wars on the continent. The impression was therefore given that no such improvements existed in these situations. The lack of articles discussing improvements on the continent with regards to this theme remains problematic not only because such stories were ignored but also due to the fact that the prominence given to fighting when it erupts is not replicated when progress is made. What was common was that war, fighting and killings became contextual elements for future stories about these countries. This phenomenon will be further discussed under the theme of *negative context*. This contextual background that countries on the continent get tagged with mean that they cannot ever be free from their past. The dominance of the contextual background in many stories gives the impression that the contextual background is pertinent to the present story, framing it as an evolving story, even though the negative context relates to events that happened decades ago.

Theme of Crises

This is the second most widely used theme in telling the African story. Subcategories coded under this theme included: economic crisis, political crisis, regional crisis, refugee crisis, migration crises, controversies, corruption and power-drunk leadership. Significant within this theme is political crisis on the continent, especially in Egypt, Zimbabwe and a few dotted cases in Central Africa. This is because much of the fighting going on in Central Africa was constructed as regional crisis and coded as such in this study. Other important regional crises in this category included Kenya–Somalia conflicts and Sudan–South Sudan conflicts. The flow of refugees within Central and Eastern Africa were covered, especially that of Kenya and Ethiopia hosting Somali refugees. Corruption was described as an unending crisis in some of the articles.

It is factual that the crises in Central Africa have gone on for decades with substantial casualty figures. The news reports highlighted much of the escalation and possible talks to ending the crises. However, the prominence received by the escalations was not equal to attempts at reporting possible negotiations. Also, due to the frequent failure of negotiations and deals, new attempts at peace negotiations were trivialised by the journalists. This act of trivialising attempts at peace making paints a picture of unending crisis. These are examples of coded segments regarding this theme:

> THE signing of an agreement to end the crisis in Mali is likely to delay due to the absence of the rival parties to talks in Ouagadougou, the capital of Burkina Faso, according to officials close to the negotiations (*The Daily Graphic*).

> THE Rwandan President Paul Kagame say the UN peacekeeping force in the Democratic Republic of Congo has "in some cases" made the crises worse (*Daily Guide*).

> SEVENTY generals in the Egyptian armed forces are to be retired, the government has announced. The move comes weeks after President Mohammed Mursi replaced the defence minister and the chief of staff (*Ghanaian Times*).

Journalistic news has such a rudimentary structure that must be followed in a manner that journalists can hardly dissent from. Crisis reporting lends itself more to this rudimentary structure and even though journalists could dig deeper to the root causes of crises, they rarely do it. This leaves most reports on crises hanging on the day or week the event occurred. Apart from the fixed mechanical structure of these news articles, they occupy the journalists only when there is fierce violence or discord. As such, improvements get removed from the agenda not by volition of the journalist but due to their adherence to the profession's ideology.

Theme of Development and Progress

This theme was consciously created to make room for positive reporting because it is natural to assume that there would be a good amount of developmental and progressive stories, especially in the era of *Africa rising discourse*. Subcategories earmarked for coding under this theme included discoveries, positive African heroes, growth and development, and balanced stories with developmental agenda. There was one discovery story and one *balanced* story. The majority of the stories here related to Nelson Mandela of South Africa. There were also three development and growth-oriented stories. Significant among these was the $64.3 million loan facility from Botswana to Zimbabwe that was reported on the website of NewZimbabwe.com. The other positive story was reported by Xinhua News Agency and it was related to the Chinese President's commitment to support Tanzania in her development agenda due to that country's recent progress. Reuters reported the last progress-oriented story which announced the increase in oil production by Libya as a result of stability in the country. However, that story ended with the negative context of the Benghazi attack on the US Embassy that killed four people. The following include examples of coded segments:

> ZIMBABWE'S Finance Minister Tendai Biti, on Monday, said more than $20 billion was needed for infrastructural projects such as road and rail networks and to fully kick-start the re-emerging mining industry. "The thirst for capital in our country is huge and high," Biti said at a ceremony to unveil a 500-million pula (64.3 million US dollars) credit facility from Botswana (*The Ghanaian Chronicle*).

> NIGERIAN AGRICULTURE Minister Akinwumi Adesina has been named Forbes African of the Year for his reforms to the country's farming sector. "He is a man on a mission to help Africa feed itself," said Forbes Africa editor Chris Bishop (*Daily Guide*).

The subcategories captured under this theme did not necessarily paint a very positive picture but carried some optimism that crises and challenges would end. Generally, these stories were non-existent or were too limited to paint a holistically positive picture of the continent:

> Government efforts and preparedness will be further enhanced to ensure the security of lives and property of all Nigerians, irrespective of their locations within the country. On the issue of intelligence gathering, the presidential aide said: "The government has acquired and deployed highly sophisticated security equipment," adding that members of the security agencies have received and continued to receive adequate training "such that our intelligence gathering capacity have witnessed a monumental increase in capacity to gather information" (*The Daily Graphic*).

Throughout the entire period of the study, this was the only message of reassurance and hope carried in the Ghanaian press regarding the efforts of Goodluck Jonathan's government to fight back the Boko Haram insurgency. All the efforts at fighting the insurgency were not reported as such. They were mostly questioned and trivialised, making it look as if Nigeria was incapable of handling the Islamist insurgency.

Theme of Human Rights, Women and Child Abuse

The subcategories of this theme include human rights abuse, in general, and abuse of women and children in particular. These were some of the deductive subcategories that I started coding with. However, not many of the news articles on Africa were narrated using these themes. The stories coded here involved executions, court judgement that promoted abuse of people's rights in authoritarian states and abuse of women and children particularly. Abuses that resulted in "killings" were coded twice. These are some of the illustrations of coded segments:

> GAMBIA has defended the execution of nine death-row prisoners amid a chorus of condemnation led by the United Nations (*Daily Guide*).

> CAMPAIGNERS in Egypt say the problem of sexual harassment is reaching epidemic proportions, with a rise in such incidents over the past three months. For many Egyptian women, sexual harassment — which sometimes turns into violent mob-style attacks — is a daily fact of life. Last winter, an Egyptian woman was assaulted by a crowd of men in the city of Alexandria (*Ghanaian Times*).

The news articles of the entire period failed to report on any positive developments either effected by women and children, or done to/for them. It does not give the sense of any normal child development on the continent, nor of women doing anything noteworthy. All the news articles framed women and children as victims.

Theme of Democracy

This theme contained both positive and negative coverage of the continent. It dealt with issues such as peaceful and non-peaceful elections on the continent, and assessments of the reasons why most sitting African presidents die. Other issues included lack of general freedom, lack of press freedom, military take-overs, leadership challenges and sanctions against countries like Zimbabwe. One particular story read under this theme discussed four countries (Zambia, Malawi, Ghana and Nigeria); this story presented an example of negative reporting on the theme of democracy in Africa, since in attempting to discuss these four countries together, it perpetuated the error of generalisation and homogenisation. In Ghana, the death of President John Evans Atta Mills and the constitutional succession did not involve any violence or dispute. This was also the case in Nigeria for Umaru Musa Yar'Adua. However, the analysis in question ignored these two successes and put them together with Zambia and Malawi simply because all four countries lost a ruling president:

> In Zambia, in Malawi and Ghana and in Nigeria, the death of the presidents was followed by a constitutional succession with a minimum of violence and dispute, and I think this is a very encouraging sign for Africa's development (*Ghanaian Times*).

While this is intended as a positive assessment, it nonetheless is not entirely positive since there is a significant difference between minimum violence and complete absence of violence, as was the case in both Ghana and Nigeria. Several other issues discussed here pointed to press freedom as a sign of good democracy. The following is illustrative of some of the coded segments:

> KENYA'S MEDIA has expressed outrage after-parliament approved a bill imposing regulation on, Journalists. In a late-night sitting on Thursday, MPs voted to set lip a communications tribunal with the power to impose fines for breaching a code of conduct (*The Daily Graphic*).

In this quote, the capacity of Members of Parliament to discuss a law that limits press freedom in a late-night sitting is doubted. However, there are usually several reasons why parliamentary debates run into the night. These include overloaded agenda, late commencement of sessions and many others. But the two feature stories on Kenya and Uganda made no room for such possibilities or mentioned them even in passing.

None of the articles provided explanation for why press freedom is quite problematic in some African states, most of whom are either in transition, transformation or crises. That background information would have been useful because most of the stabilised countries on the continent have decent press freedom records. The idea which required explication was whether press freedom was an ideal element to measure countries in crises. Answers to such questions were rarely given in the stories.

Theme of Colonial Memory

Stories coded under this theme invoked colonial memories in a largely negative way. The issues covered in such stories included harmful histories of the continent, and stereotypical depictions of the continent as the haven of wild animals and a deposit of natural resources. Some other articles portrayed the continent as donor-dependent, usually waiting on saviours from the Northern Hemisphere. A replay of colonial history, and its accompanying discourses and sentiments, has not invoked the necessary guilt in the colonisers; rather it has accorded them a space of superiority. The peculiar case of Mau Mau fighters in Kenya was reported with the announcement of reparations by the British foreign secretary at the time.

Colonial demarcations of natural resources and boundaries have remained a real worry for most Africa nations. The specific cases reported were in Ethiopia, Egypt, Sudan and the Nile:

> In June, UK Foreign Secretary William Hague said Kenya's Mau Mau fighters would receive payouts totalling $32m (£20m) as compensation for being tortured during colonial rule. Mr. Kenyatta said it was important for foreign powers to realise that Africa had come of age and needed respect and fairness in trade not reparation (*Ghanaian Times*).

> FIRST reinforcements to French force in the Central Africa Republic (CAR) are in a bid to restore peace after a rebel takeover. Mainly 200 troops have deployed, with another 500 imminently following former rebel forces who have reportedly been leaving the capital, Bangui, as the troops arrived (*The Daily Graphic*).

The fact that Western countries threaten to freeze aid to countries that have anti-homosexual laws is indicative of the fact that those countries are practically unable to run without aid and would be forced to repel those laws.

Theme of Terrorism

This theme is an extension of the theme of *war, crime and killings*. It is defined as the total deaths resulting from terrorism and terrorist activities in general. It is the third most dominant theme because of the activities of Boko Haram in Nigeria and Al-Shabaab in Somalia and Kenya. Killings resulting from these extremist Islamist groups were coded forty-five times under this theme. Terrorism activities in Southern Libya and Mali were also reported. The most outrageous notion depicted under this theme was that the involvement of Boko Haram in Cameroon and Chad meant that the continent was seriously threatened by activities of Islamists. There are fifty-four countries on the African continent, spread across a vast space of land, and it is difficult to agree with the notion that an activity in Nigeria which has been successful confronted in two neighbouring countries, Chad and Cameroon, threatens the entire continent. These are some extracts of the coded segments:

> RADICAL Islamists in control of northern Mali are becoming "increasingly repressive," Amputating limbs, whipping people in the streets and stoning to death a couple accused of adultery, a human rights group says (*Daily Guide*).

> Mali has been in disarray for much of the year. Islamist and Tuareg separatists seized control of the north of the country and discontented soldiers staged a coup after the civilian administration was unable to regain control of all of the country (*Ghanaian Times*).

> Boko Haram militia has been blamed for a series of deadly attacks in recent years. THE US has designated Nigeria's Boko Haram and Ansaru militant groups as foreign terrorist organisations. The state department described the move as "an important" step to help Nigeria "root out violent extremism". It means US regulatory agencies are instructed to block business and financial transactions with the groups (*The Ghanaian Chronicle*).

Terrorism has a global character, with examples of its activities all over the world. The global nature of the phenomenon was not discussed. The articles rather related terrorism on the continent to poverty, failed governments and corruption. It took the United States of America, for instance, a lot of time to consider Boko Haram as a terrorist group. Until this happened, some of the articles constructed the insurgency as a fight for better living.

Theme of Poverty, Disease and Disaster

This is one of the deductive themes with which I started coding. Items coded here included natural disasters, poverty and diseases such as HIV/AIDs and the six killer diseases in Africa. The data revealed that these were not popular themes of representation under which the African story was narrated. It is however imperative to state that diseases and disasters are opportunistic issues — they are reported as and when they happen. Assuming that a major disaster or disease outbreak had happened during the period under review, the study would have recorded significant amount of these stories. In the case of poverty, newspaper articles do not report on this theme as much as TV and online reportage does. Poverty in Africa was not significantly reported in these newspapers. The omission of articles dealing with either millennium development goals (which later became sustainable development goals) in Africa was not surprising either because these type of news stories do not feature even in the international news agencies themselves. And when the items are not in the international press, then it is likely they will not be in the Ghanaian press, because the latter depends largely on the Northern media organisations for the coverage of the continent. The following are some of the coded segments:

> SOMALIA'S GOVERNMENT has declared the north-eastern region of Puntland hit by a tropical cyclone at the weekend a disaster area (*Ghanaian Times*).

> Rescue operations became more difficult after night fell, South Africa mall roof collapse traps dozens. TWO PEOPLE have died and about 40 are feared trapped after a roof collapsed at the construction site of a South African shopping mall, paramedics (*Daily Guide*).

> SENEGAL'S President Macky Sail's called for the country's Senate to be abolished, with the money saved going for flood relief. Although the low- lying suburbs of the capital, Dakar, flood during most rainy seasons, this year has seen exceptionally high rainfall across West Africa. It is estimated that thousands of people have been left homeless (*The Daily Graphic*).

Accidents that were a result of unforeseen natural disaster were coded under this theme. Findings from government investigations regarding disaster were not cited throughout the coding. Whenever the findings were referred to, they were mainly cited as not credible. Evolving stories attracted attention only when bloodshed or casualties continued.

Themes of Irresponsibility and Negative Context

These two themes revealed by the data were inductively coded and represent instances when actions and decisions of African authorities were described as examples of irresponsible governance, indiscipline, lavish spending, destruction and misuse of state properties without any context. Some protests were constructed as the failure of African governments to improve the living standards of their people. Other stories also imputed a lack of responsible behaviour in ensuring the security of citizens of African nations. Kenyan authorities were accused of ignoring security information offered them before the Westgate mall attack by Al-Shabaab. Therefore, in the heat of the attack, where news reports needed to show solidarity to the people of Kenya and victims' families, they were heavily engrossed in a blame game. The second part of this theme concentrated on the use of past negative events as context to almost every new news article. In providing a context for a story, past negatives were recounted, thereby detracting from the positive elements of the story. This runs through other positive stories within other themes.

Comparing the Coverage of the Ghanaian Press to their Western Counterparts

Afro-pessimism in the Western media has been researched in various studies. Two such studies that have attracted my attention include the work of Beverly Hawk in 1992 titled *Africa's Media Image* and a near replication of Hawk's work recently published by Mel Bunce et al. (2017) under the title, *Africa's Media Image in the 21st Century*. These two publications had two compelling strengths. First, they provided a longitudinal view of Africa's coverage in the Western media which span from 1992 to 2017. Second, the collaboration between journalism scholars and practitioners gave a good balance of theory and practice within this area of research. In this section, I offer a comparison of the coverage of Africa in the Western press, as per longitudinal comparison outlined in Bunce et al. (2017), to what exists in the Ghanaian press. My study is not a replication of either Hawk (1992) or Bunce et al. (2017) and therefore I proceed with the comparison based on caution and with a clear statement of what is comparable and what is not. By these rationalisations, I established the basis for my comparison.

A clear limitation to statistical comparison exists because of differences in study design, structure and periods. Sample sizes and conceptualisation of international news agencies are equally different. In my study, international news agencies referred to all traditional international news agencies (AP, Reuters and AFP etc.) plus international broadcasting media organisations (BBC, CNN, etc.) and their online platforms, and any non-Ghanaian media organisation that was provided as the source for foreign news in the selected Ghanaian newspaper. This conceptualisation was very much guided by what existed in coverage. Apart from statistical comparison, there are other forms of qualitative comparisons that could be made from the conclusion of those two studies in relation to the research topic under investigation. Bunce et al. (2017) selected Ghana as one of its country samples. The international news agencies used in Bunce at al. are covered in my research as well. Both publications used content analysis to determine the subject and tone of the coverage.

The overreaching objective of their research and mine relates to the evolution of *Afro-pessimism* in the Western press either over time or geographical spread. This comparison is useful for two reasons. First, it shows how the Western press coverage of Africa has evolved, as reported by Bunce et al. (2017). It provides a crucial extension to the debate of *Afro-pessimism* and the recent claims of improvements. Second, it opens up the area for further specific research aimed at replicating these studies using African media as cases.

Comparison of Subjects Covered

Much of the previous research, including Bunce et al. (2017) and Hawk (1992), mentions humanitarian/disaster stories as the most prominent subject of *Afro-pessimism*. While Bunce et al. (2017) report a general reduction in this subject in comparison to Hawk (1992) and other studies that followed, my study reveals that *Disaster* coverage in the Ghanaian press was the least covered subject (see Table 5.7). The fact that the coverage of Africa in the Ghanaian press significantly mirrors what exists in the Western press was not surprising because of the high dependency already established. No subject will be prominently covered in the Ghanaian press if it does not abound in the Northern media organisation, the pool from which the journalists in Ghana select their sources.

The subject of *Economy* in my study included stories dealing with economic issues, business and financial activities involving the continent. This subject recorded only 12 stories within the period of 24 months as compared to 130 stories recorded under *Politics*. This represents a contrast to Bunce et al. (2017), where a significant portion of the claims of improvement in *Afro-pessimism* was attributed to the increase in the subject *Business*, which was considered generally positive. Bunce et al. cautioned that the overall increase in *Business* reporting was not uniform across the newswires but was proportionally led by the output of Reuters.

The subject of *Politics*, in this study, included political violence, casualties of politically motivated fighting, political turmoil and disagreements, corruption involving political leaders and war. Out of a total of 180 news articles coded, 130 of them, representing 72%, belonged to this subject. The African continent's newness to Western democratic practice presented an amorphous challenge for the improvement of the continent's media image. Comparing this to Bunce et al. (2017), which coded this subject as *Crime and Conflict*, it could be realised that there was no difference since *Crime and Conflict* recorded an increase in their research as well.

Social stories in this study were concerned with extensions to news stories that provided analysis of social implications, social impact, participation and general sociological foundations of policies and programmes. Usually, sports is included in this category but it was delimited in my study because the coverage needed to be hard news. Many of the stories analysed did not include hard news on sports. Even though the subject of *Social* issues was coded the second highest (13 times), it was still insignificant compared to *Politics*. One of the reasons for this was the fact that social implications of policies are usually analysed in peculiar journalistic genres other than hard/straight news reports. In Bunce et al. (2017), the subject of *Sport* saw an increase in its coverage for the continent in the Western press.

The subject of *Personality* was coded nine times and involved stories about celebrities and popular people who were not acting in the role of politics. The lack of concentration of this subject on African celebrities clearly showed the low level of visibility the African celebrities receive in the press both from Africa and the Northern Hemisphere. Within 24 months, African celebrities or heroes were mentioned nine times, and most often the stories related to Nelson Mandela of South Africa. It is also interesting to note that not all of these nine mentions were positive. There were stories concentrating on the feud within Mandela's family regarding his estate. This subject could not be easily compared with Bunce et al. (2017) because there was no such unique conceptualisation of the subject in that study.

The subject *Culture* was coded only eight times. This was quite astonishing because there are several stories coded in other subjects that have cultural implications. The cultural context of most subjects already discussed were ignored. The reason why this is predominant is because there is very little coverage of this theme in the Western media, from which the Ghanaian press picks its stories. This plays into the globalisation discourse which preaches cultural universality. In fact, no such subjects were specifically investigated in Bunce et al. (2017) and as such no comparison can be made. Africa, as a continent of unique individual countries, has rich historical contexts that must be included in its coverage. It is rather surprising that the subject of *History* was coded only twice in the entire study of 180 articles. Indeed, those two instances related to analysis of Egyptian archival materials. The lack of historical antecedents of most of the subjects that discussed the continent made the coverage look unfair, as if Africa's harsh colonial encounters and contributions to world history were non-existent.

Comparison of Tone/Quality of Coverage

This section presents a comparison of the tone of the coverage which was categorised into positive, negative and neutral/mixed. Following from the themes and subjects already discussed, it is reasonable to state that *Afro-pessimism* dominated the coverage. About 80% of articles were negative, which is contrary to the significant decrease recorded in Bunce et al. (2017). The idea that coverage of Africa has improved in the Western press, as reported in Bunce et al., has not reached the continent yet. The evidence in the case of Ghana proved this because *Afro-pessimism* still dominates the coverage of the continent.

Positive tone represented 15% of the coverage, and this is just 27 articles out of 180. Articles that had an equal or substantial amount of both positive and negative coverage were coded as neutral. These included only 9 articles, representing 5% of the total coverage. The imbalance in the coverage cannot represent a reflection of daily activities of the continent because more of the positive events happening have been ignored. For example, the *Africa rising* discourse did not only represent growing economies and foreign investments but also meant a scramble for Africa's resources. However, it is usually the Chinese investments in Africa that were constructed as a scramble for Africa's resources. In this study, the coverage of Africa is not positive and representative of the daily tragedies and triumphs of its citizens.

Summary

In this chapter, I established the enormous quantitative weight of influence international news agencies carried as a source for the Ghanaian press, from individual points of view to an aggregate picture. The issue of unsourced news was briefly discussed because of its implications for journalistic editorial decision-making and professionalism. I proceeded to deconstruct themes with which Africa was portrayed. The subject and tone of the coverage were outlined. The coverage centred on political subjects, with 72% of the total selected articles. The neglect of African celebrities and personalities was resounding. History, cultural and disaster were among the least-covered subjects. These were followed by social and economic subjects. The outlook of the subjects covered was linked to the tone/quality of the entire coverage. It was established that the excessive slant towards politics meant the coverage had the likelihood of being negative, because most African countries are new to the Western democracy they have come to be measured alongside. In this final part, the findings of RQ1 (a., b. and c.) were compared with Bunce at el. (2017). While Bunce et al. argued for an improvement in Africa's image mostly in the Northern press in recent times, this study reveals that such positive evolutions have not yet reached the mainstream press in Ghana.

6. Postcolonial Trajectories of the Ghanaian Press

Discussing Actors, Conditions and the Power Dynamics

I present the findings of the ethnographic interview, which includes repeated in-depth interviews and newsroom observations designed with significant input from the ethnographic content analysis (ECA) to provide explanatory level meaning to the findings of the initial ECA. During the interview sessions, the journalists and editors were confronted with the results of the ECA. This reconstructive strategy provided the avenue to lead the journalists to appreciate their previous work, a practice they rarely undertake in their daily routines. This chapter deals with the qualitative weight of influence individual international news agencies carry as sources in the Ghanaian press. The mundane newsroom dynamics in terms of condition, actors and practices are analysed. I also offer insights into how intermedia agenda-setting preferences between the Ghanaian press and their foreign counterparts have evolved.

Qualitative Weight of Influence of International News Agencies

The weight of influence on a journalist's editorial decision-making habit cannot be exclusively determined by just what was written in the newspapers and counted through quantitative content analysis. This is because the written news is an ideological construct that can be better understood when investigated beyond its manifest presentation of ideological influences on the journalists who created the news articles, and how these influences affected the entire news-making process. All four newspapers had reporter/editor roles which meant that the foreign pages were part of the special desks headed by page editors, who took full responsibility for whatever appeared on the pages. By this arrangement, the journalists served as reporters as well as editors, in some cases, for their foreign news pages. They made daily news selection decisions. They would receive recommendations from their colleague editors in the editorial conference; but generally, the buck stops at their desk and some of them had no editorial conferences at all. The following themes were unpacked from the interviews and observations.

Theme of Conceptual Substitution

This represents a cognitive processing feature displayed by the journalists through a persistent reference to the specific international news agency that had the most influence on them. The journalists cited the British Broadcasting Corporation (BBC World Service) whenever they needed to refer to an international news agency in answering questions, even when these questions had even nothing to do with the BBC. For example: "If you take the BBC, for instance, they make sure they are covering almost everywhere" (Editor 2 — *Daily Guide*). Another said: "When the BBC or other international news agencies are reporting this stuff, I can't complain" (Editor 7 — *Daily Guide*). They gave responses to questions that had nothing to do with the BBC World Service and still managed to mention the British broadcaster as the yardstick.

The cognitive fixation of citing the BBC as the usual example also became metonymic, that is, while referring to all the international news agencies, the journalists used the BBC, which is just one of them, to represent the whole. Explaining his daily routines as the page editor, the journalist said, "With technology, most nights I go on my phone to the BBC and the next morning I have my stories because I have read them, I just go ahead and follow how things are breaking on from each of these networks" (Editor 3 — *The Ghanaian Chronicle*). The use of the plural form (networks) later in the sentence displayed this metonymy. This conceptual substitution was not limited to only citing examples, there were occasions where the journalists described their preferences by measuring other international news agencies with their perceived qualities of the BBC. They point frequently to the availability of resources to the BBC:

> There is football in Italy and the BBC's team is there even during the campaign and everything because it's money. And someone needs to mobilize these resources and this is something common to the Western press that we do not have (Page Editor 5 — *The Daily Graphic*).

The act of using the BBC World Service's qualities as a measure of other international news media was common and coded across all the interviews. One journalist said, "I diversify my news sources a lot. I go to the likes of CNN, Al Jazeera based on where the news is happening but all in all, I go to the BBC first and see how others fall in line" (Editor 3 — *The Ghanaian Chronicle*). These unconscious cognitive conceptual substitutions highly confirm the quantitative influence presented in the last chapter. The presence of the BBC's qualities in the subconscious minds of these journalists remains largely influential and confirms the British broadcaster's qualitative influence in addition to the enormous quantitative weight found. A comparable case is the Xinhua News Agency, which is well-cited as a source of foreign news, but which is hardly mentioned in any discussion as a benchmark for any qualitative influence.

Theme of Cultural Defeat and Domination

The theme of *cultural defeat and domination* was widely revealed by the data. This was the most coded theme under different sub-themes during the preliminary coding. Even though there were several admissions of bias by the Ghanaian journalists relating to slant and negativity on the part of the international news media against the continent, they ended up suggesting, in the face of the evidence, that they still had no alternatives. In some cases, they measured their alternatives with their perceived qualities of the BBC and other media from the Northern Hemisphere. For instance, in answering the question of whether there was any evidence of *Afro-pessimism* of any kind in the reportage towards Africa that was printed in their newspapers, two journalists answered:

> Oh I know because, maybe, I am a senior journalist. I know that slanting, they have to continue keeping Africa's negative perception. It was a worrying thing; that is why we had to try and do some editing, edit out those that connote extreme negativity (Editor 5 — *The Daily Graphic*).

> There is an old myth that nothing good comes from Africa and so they have to reinforce that. I know this because when they come to Ghana and visit the porch areas of East Legon, they won't take a picture of that, they will take negative ones like the slum of Agbogbloshie (Editor 4 — *The Daily Graphic*).

Another one even asked me to join him watch a YouTube video, he said:

> I watched an interesting introduction of the BBC's Andrew Neil on his show called "This Week" a day after the Paris attack. He recited the might of France as a world power. Compare that to the news a day after there is bombing by "Boko Haram" in Nigeria and you will notice the slant of how two different terrorist acts are described by the same media organisation (Editor 3 — *The Ghanaian Chronicle*).

After these clear admissions of bias by most of the journalists and editors regarding the international news agencies, they then highlighted their inability to do anything about the situation by stating that they simply do not have the resources to counter these biases, and so they replicate them:

> Because we are picking stories from what the BBCs of this world have published, this is mainly what you will get. Sometimes we are not happy to be using all these negatives but that's what they have and the thing is that you aren't there where they covered the event. We do not have the opportunity or the resources to go and cover. Sometimes I wonder if that is all they can cover (Editor 4 — *The Daily Graphic*).

One of them argued that the Ghanaian journalist's incapacity to have alternatives dates back to history. He said, "Even before the advent of the Internet we did not have any other choice, it was difficult to get foreign news except to listen to the BBC radio or VOA. We couldn't afford sending people around Africa" (Editor 7 — *Daily Guide*). Other journalists described the BBC as the most prominent and credible media they knew growing up and, as a result, they have kept learning from the BBC until now. Considering the BBC as the leader of the press in the Northern Hemisphere, these significant praises also came with an admission of a lack of capacity in such a circumstance to be critical of the British broadcaster's coverage. In describing his preferences for any international news agencies, the interviewee said:

> I think besides knowing that other media houses exist, I have been used to the BBC from my infancy. My father in those days had this shortwave radio at one point in time and I switched between the BBC Hausa and English services all day. One is always learning and improving his English language by listening to them (Editor 2 — *Daily Guide*).

This description, apart from being a genuine preference for the BBC, also represents cultural domination emanating from the fact that the BBC was the only alternative available at the time this editor was growing up. In fact, his next assertion was rather revealing. While discussing how he felt about the negative coverage of Africa that has been replicated in his newspaper, he defended the images and added that he did not even believe in the self-rule of the African:

> I don't think I have any course to dispute any of the reports I hear on BBC because I still have this idea that we are not doing well as Africans and due to this sometimes *Yaw* [a Colleague] and I joke over this Kwame Nkrumah's position that the black man is capable of managing his affairs, I think I don't share in those positions because by and large they have messed up governance, the typical African leader tries to go beyond the constitution so that he will stay beyond what the standard tenure he is entitled to and it is like that in most countries in Africa (Editor 2 — *Daily Guide*).

However, responding to the lack of diversity for the sources of foreign news as per earlier content analysis, the journalists made an outstanding admission that showed they are no longer capable of being critical of their childhood preference, the BBC:

> I don't think it is good this way. The graph is quite lopsided. One has to spread one's net to other places maybe because we have put the BBC in that category, it has even become very difficult to critique their presentations which aren't good enough (Editor 7 — *Daily Guide*).

Even though the journalists observed the practical examples of the negativity towards the continent from the press in the Northern Hemisphere and argued that they possess an African perspective; they also depended highly on the Northern press for the coverage of the continent.

Ambivalence towards Africa's Dependency on Northern Media

The dependence on international news media in covering Africa could easily be described from a simple essentialist point of view as some scholars have done using globalisation. However, equally fascinating is the claim by the journalists that an African perspective exists and which they, rather than others, possess. Well, as in the case of the journalists in Ghana, removing some negative adjectives and context elements from the news articles they borrowed from the Northern press was neither detailed nor a requirement of an in-house style guide. The Ghanaian journalists' level of wholesale adoption of "Britishness" because of colonial history is made evident in their comments. While explaining how much responsibility he could assume for the negative images they reproduced from the international media on Africa, one journalist accepted that his weakness is even magnified by his British surname and the boss who knew this, usually told him jokingly he was *British*. "I am maybe biased because I am '.....', so am 'British'. We do sometimes deal with this when the deputy editor calls me 'British' for using more BBC than others. Maybe I am really *British*" (withheld). Another journalist, while responding to lack of diversity in his sourcing of foreign news, explained that he shared the views the BBC carried on most issues because he and his readers are British-inclined:

> It looks like a country like Ghana is British. Don't you think so; you know we worked with the British for many years as a colony. Because of that, we are British-inclined, we prefer the write-ups and views of the BBC to the rest (Editor 1 — *Ghanaian Times*).

After all these endorsements for the BBC, the journalists decided to associate themselves to the credibility of the British broadcaster not only by saying that they are *British* by worldview, but also pointing to the central role the BBC occupies in their daily selections; as one journalist said: "I use BBC a lot. Occasionally I used AP" (Editor 2 — *Daily Guide*). Another journalist said, "I give priority to all international news agencies closest to the place of an event but all in all, I go for BBC first" (Editor 3 — *The Ghanaian Chronicle*). Another journalist also said, "When I am beaten by time and I am quickly looking for news, I first go to the BBC because it's timely and reliable" (Editor 4 — *The Daily*

Graphic). One of them said, "I like the BBC because they are current and reliable. We look forward to their qualities becoming our values too" (Editor 1 — *Ghanaian Times*). In addition to these observations, another journalist had a stronger opinion:

> You will go there because you don't have a choice, they are timely, you pick a story from BBC, compare it with others, at least, the facts won't change. You look generally, globally at what is happening because we share a worldview with them (Editor 5 — *The Daily Graphic*).

The ambivalence comes from the fact that soon after these admissions came the notion of African perspective, which they equally possessed as an element of resistance. It is crucial to state that the form of cultural domination recounted here looks like an essentialist perspective that does not embrace new forms of acceptance and appreciation of this reality. However, the Ghanaian journalists and editors did not only acknowledge biases against the continent in the news that come from the Global North, but they also established that an *African perspective* exists, which they constructed as different from what is communicated by the media from the Northern Hemisphere. An editor claimed that when the Ghana News Agency (GNA) had bureaus around the world, there were different views reported in Ghanaian press about Africa:

> Because the journalists are based in those countries not only to cover war and catastrophe, they did cover the continent better, relating their observations to the Ghanaian context. Apart from understanding the context in which these things happen, they can relate them better to our local context (Editor 6 — *The Daily Graphic*).

Another editor related the *African perspective* to freedom. That is, the GNA represented freedom from the dominant view and projected an African side of the story. The editor of *The Daily Graphic* grew up as a young journalist in that period, and he remembered the *Ghanaianess* in GNA's reports when it had bureaus across the continent in selected strategic cities in the world. One of the page editors gave an example relating to children not wearing shirts. She established clearly that children walking around without wearing a shirt could not exclusively mean poverty, it could be an issue of temperature as well. Therefore, when she was writing about such a scenario, she would not be distracted like an American from New York visiting Ghana for the first time.

In this section, I have established the qualitative weight of influence on the Ghanaian journalists by describing holistically how the newsroom processes work to promote the dependency syndrome of the Ghanaian press on foreign media especially the BBC. I have equally established the significant resistance, with the claim of an *African perspective*, which remains only as an idea because performative options for the practice of resistance available are still mild. I will later establish whether this reliance on foreign media is a form of globalisation or a new form of domination. I will account for the nuances that might arise between globalisation and domination.

Conditions Shaping Foreign News

The circumstances surrounding the news selection processes, the working order of the group, and the actors involved, all together, shape the whole foreign news selection processes providing the framework of operation. These include profitability, economic rationality coupled with advertising bias, routine technological challenges and proximity of journalistic ideology.

Profitability of the Media House

All four newspapers argued that their commitment to foreign news had a positive relationship with profitability which represents the amount of money they make in excess of expenses, variable material cost and other overhead costs. However, their arguments were individually unique. *The Daily Graphic*, the *Ghanaian Times* and *The Ghanaian Chronicle* newspapers argued that even though they would generally increase the support for the foreign news should their profit margins improve, they also suggested that the cost involved in covering the continent comprehensively cannot be accommodated within their current circumstances — an era marked by cost-cutting as a means to either ensure good returns on investments. They suggested that with technological advancements, they do not see how they would defend the high expenditures involved in foreign news coverage when expenses have become the only option left to positively increase profit and shareholders' worth.

According to them, foreign pages have been made *premium pages* for advertising due to the results of market research, which indicate they are among the top read pages. However, the advertising revenue cannot be spent exclusively on the foreign news desk. The newspaper recommends that journalists rely on international news agencies as a way to cut costs. They argued that dwindling national sales as a result of general national economic slowdown does not in itself allow for discussion on foreign engagements.

By their nature and purpose, these newspapers seem to be arguing that they are first and foremost national daily news platforms, and, as a result, they consider foreign news as a *service* to their readers. An editor responded to the question of how foreign news contributed to profitability in this manner:

> Not precisely but this is a local paper so our focus basically is about what we do as a people in Ghana but we don't also live in an island unto ourselves, particularly in the globalised world where you want to know what is happening to others so that it does not affect you (Editor 6 — *The Daily Graphic*).

When confronted again about his worries regarding the dwindling pages for foreign news, another editor repeats his notion of localisation, in which he then rendered foreign news as a service for the readers:

> I'm saying that basically, this is a local newspaper and therefore your focus is on what we do as a nation to be able to provide the news that people require to contribute their quota to nation-building. As I said in the globalised world you want your readers to also have a feel about what is happening around them (Editor 9 — *Ghanaian Times*).

It is clear that he and other editors who have spoken in a similar sense are constructing globalisation as the reason that has underscored their continued commitments to foreign news. Others have cited the migratory flow of Ghanaian people across the globe as the major reason why they must maintain foreign news.

The kind of globalisation described here by the journalist is a one-way traffic phenomenon of excess importation over export. This imbalance could be seen equally in journalism, as the Ghanaian press only receives its information from abroad. There is a lack of active two-way interaction in the ideal notion of globalisation. But through globalisation, migratory flows and other international interactions, different dimensions of proximity mappings and reconstructions have evolved. These proximity issues have forced the Ghanaian newspapers to remain committed to foreign news. In the height of the economic hardships and cost-cutting strategies that are currently implemented by these newspapers, they are but left with only one option, they argued: *depend on international news agencies*.

The *Ghanaian Times* newspaper provided an argument to support their claim of a positive relationship between commitment to foreign news and profitability. They argued that due to their origin as a Pan-African newspaper, any improvement in profit and economic situation could trigger a reduction in their reliance on international news agencies even though they consider the foreign pages purely as a *service* to their readership. But for finances, better coverage of the African continent from the viewpoint of local reporters with a Pan-African perspective was crucial for their newspaper.

Some page editors disagreed with the top management argument on *institutional commitments*. The journalists felt their organisations had not created appropriate environments for the development of originality. They explained that the organisational level failures had exacerbated the situation of dependency on international news organisations. Managements of the selected newspapers have relied on the argument of cost-cutting as a measure of improving profit in an era where newspaper sales are fast dwindling. In such a scenario, no commitment is made towards journalist's comfort to report from abroad. Talking about their experiences in reporting on elections in neighbouring Togo, Côte d'Ivoire and Nigeria, the journalists recounted this feeling:

> I covered elections in Nigeria and Côte d'Ivoire. The resources that the big international news agencies released and what our own have is very intimidating. Ours was limited. To go and speak to someone and language limitation and lack of resources. I cannot afford dinner or go to the Café with my sources. I even had to return quickly because my money was finished (Editor 5 — *The Daily Graphic*).

It is evident from these foregoing arguments that journalists working for *The Daily Graphic* and *Daily Guide* newspapers believe their newspapers could do better in providing support for their coverage of at least neighbouring countries. This opinion is different from the uniform view held by both management and journalists of the two other newspapers, who attributed their reliance on international news organisations to lack of resources. In the case of the *Ghanaian Times* and *The Ghanaian Chronicle*, both management and journalists agree that they are resource-strapped.

Economic Rationality and Advertising Bias

The decision of making foreign news pages *premium advertising pages* emanates from an economic rationality that favours advertising. Audience research results have varied uses, however, in most cases, the intention is to use the audience as baits for advertising. While the management of the newspapers find information gather through research about readers a useful data to sell to adverstisers, many of the journalists felt that was wrong. *The Daily Graphic* newspaper, for instance, previously dedicated two to three pages to foreign news. Now the newspaper dedicates only two half pages. While the page editor found this unhelpful, the managing editor argued that the newspaper needed the money and he explained that the reduction in pages dedicated to editorial content was due to cuts on the number of pages the newspaper prints as a form of cost-cutting strategy. It became difficult for the journalists to maintain a balance of daily tragedies and triumphs on two half-pages compared to three full-pages they had before. This advertising bias means that most stories on the foreign pages needed to be shortened to the extent that they even lost the original context information they came with.

The situation at the *Ghanaian Times* is even worse because the advertising department are able to keep demanding space, until the two pages dedicated to the foreign news are depleted. The practice taking the space dedicated to editorial content for advert occurs because advertisers want to place the advertising on the foreign news pages. The editorial committee at the *Ghanaian Times* has had to sometimes fight for just a half-page for the foreign news.

The *Daily Guide* newspaper has an interesting layout where most leads are squeezed on to the front-page, and continue onto other pages. The editor explained an experiment he conducted to check the foreign page readership significance:

> We attached very big importance to readership of foreign news because a lot of people [are] like me [in that] I started my journalism or newspaper reading from there [...] from reading foreign stories; so I also believe that a lot of people read it [foreign news]. The reason why we got to know that people read the foreign stories is that there was a time [when] we place[d] some ads there and I think it was very disgusting, several people called that they don't want to see the ads there (Editor 7 — *Daily Guide*).

The advertising bias is a condition that cannot result in an improved balance of the tone of coverage because editorial content has to be rejected for advertising. This is closely linked to limited space in journalistic and persuasive writing where the author is expected to put useful information right within the *lead* to win readers to read further. This concept, when married to cuts in printable pages, results in severe limitations to contextual information provided for each foreign news story published in the Ghanaian press.

Routine Technology Challenges

There are a plethora of technical difficulties confronting the newsrooms, including congested networks, slow Internet speed, malfunctioning computers and lack of multimedia work stations. These challenges are visible to any observer who enters these newsrooms. But the challenges have been normalised in a manner that renders them of no effect. However, a closer look at this phenomenon provides a very interesting framework for the workings of foreign news editorial decision-making (news selection).

First, congestion on the network at *The Daily Graphic* and *Ghanaian Times* begins sometime around 13:00 GMT. The page editors of these newspapers are also responsible for other domestic pages, and this preoccupies them in the morning especially because foreign news stories on international news agencies are not usually developed enough to be followed in the morning. By the time they are ready to search for foreign news, most reporters would have returned to the office from their assignments to prepare reports for an editorial conference at 14:00 GMT. These congestions largely limit the diversity of the searches the foreign page editors make. Under these circumstances, the foreign page editors turn to their trusted international news networks and this provides an environment where some specific agencies become most often cited. One editor said:

> You go through all those hustles sometimes and because of the challenges the end result can be affected. Assuming that the machines or computers work faster and we don't have all these IT problems, you could go to certain sources to get news items that are faultless, sometimes others might not even know where this thing is and so there is some challenge (Editor 4 — *The Daily Graphic*).

The second issue is Internet speed. Depending on the services available, the journalists are forced to leave the premises of the organisation to search for a good Internet connection in the city centre. They then upload their stories on a flash drive and bring them to the newsroom for editing. In this scenario as well, diversity is highly affected. It was noticed that the page editors know that the Internet challenges are a frequent issue and, as such, they save some news items in the morning when they arrive so that they can work on these if they encounter Internet issues later in the day. These issues are even complicated by the lack of multimedia workstations in the newsroom, making it impossible for them to record rolling 24-hour international TV stations or monitor radio with the view of writing their news from the broadcast news reports.

Intermedia Agenda-Setting Preferences

The press in Ghana has demonstrated distinct preferences for different international news agencies, with the exception of the British Broadcasting Corporation (BBC) World Service, which was popular across all four selected newspapers. CNN performed very badly in the public press while Xinhua News Agency was the second single most cited international news agency. Contrary to the public press, the Xinhua News Agency scored zero in both private newspapers. The *Daily Guide* and *The Ghanaian Chronicle* never cited the Chinese news agency for any of their items over a period of two years. Rather, they used CNN significantly, which ranked in third position. These differences require a better explication. In this section, I provide these through four themes: Chinese soft power constructed as South–South cooperation; historical background built on a colonial relationship; and informal individual influence built on previous staff contact.

Chinese Soft Power Constructed as South–South Cooperation

China has emerged in the past five decades as a competing economic force in the world. But the entry of China into international news distribution competition with the Northern media organisations was less anticipated. One page editor alluded to this surprise in these words while interrogating the amount of influence Xinhua News Agency carried as a source:

> When you want to go to Asia they [Xinhua News Agency] have something good, but the BBC is an entity by itself, due to years of experience and the influence [...] the English language has throughout the world. Xinhua for instance, I didn't know this; I'm surprised (Editor 3 — *The Ghanaian Chronicle*).

While explaining Xinhua's influence, another page editor linked the agency's influence to the emerging global power of China:

> So, it depends on where the news is coming from and over here in Ghana most people are not really interested, excuse me to say, in the eastern bloc like China, Japan and others. I pick the Chinese stories especially when they have problem with the Islands with Japan and others. I'm trying to bring people's attention to it and the fact that China is growing. At a point, I will think of it because I want detailed news from China to support my position that China has become a super-power. Maybe I might go to Xinhua in the future (Editor 7 — *Daily Guide*).

However, the journalists working for the newspapers that cited Xinhua News Agency most rationalised the Chinese soft power influence as an act of South–South cooperation. The framework of this cooperation is the desire of the periphery nation to disrupt the feudal system of interaction developed at the centre by communicating among themselves more. The argument is that cooperation among the developing nations within the Global South is long overdue. One editor explained their reason for signing the reuse agreement with the Chinese Embassy on behalf of Xinhua News Agency:

> We have some kind of collaboration with Xinhua, which is a Chinese news agency, except that it not very regular, but it can be better; that's the only way, as I said, we don't have the resources to go to Asia. Even covering some neighbouring countries is difficult, [let alone ...] talking about [places] far away in Asia. So the only way is to have some collaboration.

I know that other countries in Asia have very strong news agencies that we can collaborate with. And I'm sure in the spirit of South–South cooperation it will be useful to do what we have done (Editor 6 — *The Daily Graphic*).

Another editor doubted the concept of South–South cooperation, but nonetheless argued that it is far better than the Northern media domination currently reigning:

We need to even have collaboration among ourselves but rather we're having to collaborate with Xinhua, a Chinese news agency. They have approached us for collaboration so that they would be sending us their items and we also send the[m] items. But so far we have only been receiving. That isn't too good but because of their focus on development news, they look far [more] charitable than the Northern media organisations (Editor 8 — *Ghanaian Times*).

The response from the Ghanaian newspapers who have cited the Chinese news agency significantly within the period of the study has so far been mixed but favourable. The journalists refused to describe Chinese influence as another form of domination and lack of diversity in their sourcing of foreign news. They rather insisted on the concept of South–South cooperation as the major reason for their choice. This cooperation is inherently imperial because the Chinese news agency sells their material around the world, but in this case, they offered it for free in the name of cooperation, where the Ghanaian newspapers are expected to file news items for them as well. After signing the agreement, the Ghanaian newspapers are yet to be commissioned to file news items for their Chinese counterpart.

China also offers advantageous training programmes for staff of these two newspapers to spend time in China improving their journalistic skills. The Ghanaian side of this South–South cooperation has been to receive Xinhua News Agency materials. The unequal power arrangement demonstrated by the cooperation is not different from the existing feudal interaction instituted by Northern media. Considering that the Chinese soft power activity of offering news items for free is only operational with two newspapers, one could argue the activity has been successful. Assuming, the agreement is extended to the top ten newspapers in Ghana, we could witness another case of domination which would be rationalised within the concept of South–South cooperation.

Historical Background Built on Colonial Relationships

Scars of the colonial past have never left the colonised states. Examples include language and education. These two elements have rippling effects on others, like trade cooperation and worldview. Some journalists identify this inextricably complex past as the underlying reason why intermedia agenda-setting relationships and preferences look the way they do today:

> Yes, it does; we have a large population of Ghanaians in Britain and they are there because of the colonial time. Between us [Ghana and Britain], at a certain point you didn't even need a visa to go; so, anything about Britain in your paper will attract readership and the same cannot go for news items about Ireland, Finland or Denmark (Editor 7 — *Daily Guide*).

One of the journalists questioned if they could claim independence when their media institutions were directly built on the colonial past, even well after independence:

> I think it's a British influence. Britain colonised this part of the world and the broadcasting system itself was started by the British. I know of a radio station called radio ZOY that is the pioneer[ing] radio station in the country and I think the British Broadcasting Corporation (BBC) signature tune was what they were using in those days when they were rebroadcasting; so we have grown up [...] used to the BBC. We consider anything which emanates from the BBC as the truth sacrosanct. Even *Graphic* newspaper was a British newspaper that was nationalised with no ideological changes (Editor 2 — *Daily Guide*).

The journalists seem to argue that the historical past did not allow for better reflections afterwards on how journalism should be practiced independent of colonial influence. Therefore, British institutions and ideas continued even after independence because the educational system itself was built on the British model and more Ghanaians had studied and lived in the UK than anywhere else. This well-established relationship and institutional culture have become quite compelling to resist by struggling Ghanaian newspapers.

Some of the journalists also suggested that the trust in the BBC among the population is high and any association with that brand's values is highly ranked. The British broadcaster does not have any agreement with newspapers but their rebroadcast radio agreements throughout the country are quite symptomatic of their effort to maintain a hold on this historical advantage via influential institutions. They have led *posh journalism* training either through the British Council or by themselves. Most of these journalists had their childhood experiences dominated by British institutions and practices even before their journalism education. This engagement and familiarity with the BBC's style of reporting remains influential:

> They were my preference because of their language and style of writing. [...] I was also using part of their articles to do my write-ups when I was writing general news. It has helped a lot. So coming to the foreign desk was not so much of a challenge. I was reading these agencies even before I went into journalism. There have been news organisations like the BBC and VOA [Voice of America] who broadcast in Ghana but I like to compare and contrast because of language and content of news coverage (Editor 1 — *Ghanaian Times*).

One editor traced his experiences from the Ghana Army (GA) to the current inextricable historical bond that exist between Ghana and Britain. He argued that historical relationships are more potent than agreements. To him, these remain relevant and evident because most institutions of the state are yet to free themselves of these practices. Another journalist added that, in addition to these relationships, the international news agencies maintain a compelling continuous presence on the continent. The Western international news agencies seem to be the ones largely covering the continent, even though their coverage itself has been described as insignificant:

> Yes, there has been some postcolonial domination, especially with the BBC and Reuters still dominating the Africa scene for newsgathering [...] Their presence and prominence still on the continent has [...] enhanced the type of stories that will shape or reshape society and history whether positively or negatively (Editor 1 — *Ghanaian Times*).

The evolution of intermedia agenda-setting relationship between the Ghanaian press and their international counterparts seemed to be built largely on the historical past and its subsequent entanglements that are visible today, including migration and institutional training that is also dominated by institutions from the Northern Hemisphere.

Informal Relationships Built on Personal Contact

Contacts that journalists met during conferences, meetings and by working together on assignments remain a major determinant of intermedia agenda-setting relationships. I label this set of relationships as informal relationships because there are no formal agreements involved. This happens to be a major source for news about Nigeria in the Ghanaian press. The editor and news editor of the *Daily Guide* both started their journalism careers in Nigeria and they maintain a good relationship with former colleagues who have become major sources of Nigerian news for the newspaper. The Chief Executive Officer (CEO) of *The Ghanaian Chronicle* worked in Nigeria and still maintains contacts there, which his newspaper relies on for news items. Such informal relationships built on contacts of an employee as the determinant of the intermedia agenda-setting relationship represent a more effective way of telling the African story for two reasons: first, the journalists claim that the stories received were contextually more appropriate and are factually and culturally accurate because they were written with Ghana in mind. The *Daily Guide* editors illustrated this with the following examples:

> When the ECOWAS [Economic Community of West African States] human rights court in Abuja, Nigeria, ruled on the case involving the death of a Nigerian student that occurred in Ghana, we got the story the very second the ruling was made. We beat even the BBCs of this world to it (Editor 7 — *Daily Guide*).

Second, the relationship is built on *giving and taking*, allowing their Nigerian friends to also source news from Ghana through them. This reciprocal relationship is useful for reporting the continent. *The Ghanaian Chronicle* newspaper, for example, is trying to convert the CEO's influence in Nigeria into a standing agreement with *Vanguard* and THISDAY newspapers in Nigeria. They have even launched a Nigerian page as part of their foreign news. This page is exclusively dedicated to news from Nigeria because they feel that the sizeable Nigerian community in Ghana deserves more attention. To the editor, the decision to keep a Nigerian page was exclusively based on a market research. In this case, newsworthiness in neighbouring countries means next to nothing. The decision of where to cover in Africa is entirely based on economic reasoning of free news and converting available readership in Ghana into a market.

Journalists' Perspectives on Africa's Media Image in the Ghanaian Press

In this section, I reconstruct, from the perspective of the journalists, why Africa's media image remains negative in the Ghanaian press. I recount the reasoning behind the entire African media image construction in Ghana through three themes: economic hardships and the cost-cutting rationale, proximity of journalistic ideology and the persisting unequal encounter with the Global North. In the first theme, I will discuss economic hardship and its consequent cost-cutting rationale as a major reason, from the perspective of the journalists, which continues to influence the coverage of Africa in the Ghanaian press.

Economic Hardship and Cost-Cutting Rationales

The editors and journalists interviewed are very much aware of the economic hardship the newspaper industry is faced with around the world in the twenty-first century. This notion can even be traced in some of the quotations in Chapter 7, in the section dealing with *conditions of coverage*. However, there is the need to explain how this is linked to the coverage the continent receives in the media. The Ghanaian journalists claim that economic hardships have triggered low newspaper sales and a dwindling advertising income as a result of general corporate austerity in all industries. An editor explained this while responding to the question of whether resources matter in the coverage of Africa:

> Of course, yes! Resources matter a lot and we know. Yet, unfortunately for us in this part of the world newspaper business has become a very difficult one because of resources. First, patronage has gone down, currently because of the economic hardship people can no longer afford to buy newspapers (Editor 9 — *The Ghanaian Chronicle*).

This view, widely held view by journalists, implies that there is a declining income capacity to deal with the proper running of even domestic pages. The editor explained, like three other editors, that the hardships were so severe that they had to close down several district offices:

> In my newspaper's perspective, resources are our problem because at the moment we have to cut down on our regional correspondents because of lack of resources. We used to have two reporters in the city of Tema; some of them we have to even close down their offices because of resources. So, the major problem why we at the *Chronicle* cannot extend our reports to other parts of the African continent is because of resources (Editor 9 — *The Ghanaian Chronicle*).

They equally placed this economic hardship theme within a complex scheme of affairs that made it more complicated to deal with. To them, technology and competition within the newspaper industry itself are so fierce because the readership purchasing power cannot match the price tags of newspapers. One editor answered the question of whether the Ghanaian newspapers can ever be free from relying on the Northern press organisations in newsgathering about the continent:

> No, I don't think so because we don't have the resources. In the first place, the government doesn't give us a subsidy to subsidize the media. Number two, people don't even buy newspapers anymore because of economic hardships which are denying free-market support for newspapers. Today we are selling newspaper GH¢2.50 per day and when you look at it, people are earning a minimum of GH¢9.00. Assuming somebody decides to buy four newspapers, that will [cost] GH¢10.00, which is more than the minimum wage. So, it's affecting their purchasing power when it comes to the newspaper and then again because people will listen to the radio news reviews, they are not motivated to buy. I think that is the fact, a combination of lack of resources and introduction or the influx of technology (Editor 3 — *The Ghanaian Chronicle*).

One significant cost-cutting strategy introduced by all four newspapers in response to the economic hardship was shortening the number of pages of their newspapers. This resulted in limited space for editorial material. One editor described the issue of limited space as an economic strategy because the cost of printing has become burdensome and new technologies have made alternatives to newspapers more common.

Some of the page editors recounted how economic hardships affected the way they reported Africa. However, they disagreed with the idea that improvements in economic fortunes of their newspapers might lead to a better institutional commitment to foreign news. They argued lack of institutional support for editorial activities including foreign newsgathering, is a management choice to some level. They pointed to management fixation with an increase in profit through cost-cutting measures. The page editors of *The Daily Graphic* and *Daily Guide* expressed the feeling that management's commitment to making resources available for editorial activity is weak. They argued that improvements in economic hardship will not change their situation that much.

The claim of journalists that they mirror society implies they cover both the triumphs and tragedies of each day in equal or near-equal proportions. This ideal notion of mirroring society becomes very difficult in the face of limited editorial space. The page editors lamented the phenomenon of limited space and how it renders their coverage lopsided:

> We have a limited space of one page and we must divide it between Africa and the world. You can't just put Africa news alone when there is also a crisis in Asia. If we have had more space or even if we had one full page for African news and one full page for world news, we can carry a lot of stories and even [with] this one page dedicated to both Africa and world news, we still have to take part of it for advertising; how do we capture triumphs and tragedies in this situation? (Editor 2 — *Daily Guide*).

Limited editorial space, which has been caused by economic hardship, is largely a reason for the negative coverage of the continent because the balance between triumphs and tragedies cannot be achieved within such limitations of space. This situation gets even worse when the journalists attempt to place three to four stories on a page. Based on the space available, this leads to unnatural cuts in the length of the story. Sometimes, this is even left for the page designers, with no journalistic training, to do. These sporadic cuts of stories result in the situation where the context of the story is significantly altered. A few experiments witnessed during the newsroom observation showed clearly that the original journalistic pieces being relied on mostly by the Ghanaian journalists are written with a particular structure in mind. For example, bare facts relating to casualties are usually stated in the lead, where the questions of who, what, where, when and how are answered. This is followed with more details on the event, before the background is given to provide context for the entire narrative. From my observation, the cuts in the story length do not respect original structural thinking behind the story and this renders the stories more negative. One editor recognises this as a major disadvantage. She said to keep the original structural outlook requires a technical reconstruction, which is difficult and, in some circumstances, is unavoidable. She spoke about this while responding to why there was unsourced news in their quality newspaper:

> Sometimes I take a story from the BBC and a similar story from Reuters and while cutting I would have to re-write the whole story myself for it to make sense, and, in that case, the story does not belong to either of them [the BBC or Reuters] (Editor 4 — *The Daily Graphic*).

This same limited editorial space prevents the page editors from using features. The genre of features provides details and ideas about a phenomenon and even how it can be resolved but such genres are sparingly used because the journalists need to rework the whole feature story to fit into the space that might be available at the time they are going to print. It is evident that the practice of cutting stories to fit limited editorial space renders some of the stories negative. Taking four stories that had been abridged during my newsroom observations for analysis, I discovered the elimination of contextual background had affected the outlook of the story largely. A typical rewrite of the story also presented several shortcomings, since this reconstruction does not occur within a framework where the Ghanaian journalists can call the original authors for clarification. Much of what a re-write does is to speculate the meaning of the original text as it is. Apart from the contextual difficulties explained, there is also the challenge of medium mismatch. The page editors usually access the online version of their favourite international news agencies. The parameters and requirements of these stories as per the online medium is different. I realised that, usually, the BBC World Service online uses animations, drawings, pictures, artistic impressions and reading and comprehension aids (such as *fact boxes, things to know,* etc.). The original authors have the liberty of developing the African story in a very creative manner because they have space and reading aids to keep readers' interest online. This is the opposite for a Ghanaian press bedevilled with limited space and a lack of similar reading aids in a printed sheet. This affects medium requirements and advantages. What is eventually published is a deconstructed reuse of foreign news articles. Even though this remained an isolated case because the experiments were not widely conducted, a senior page editor with ten years of experience at the foreign news desk accepted that the challenge of medium re-alignment can be tedious, and eventually that affects the selection of stories that are rendered complicated online with animations and artistic impressions.

Proximity of Journalistic Ideology

The concept of what *journalistic news* should look like is usually known among journalists practising in different newsrooms. Due to this common knowledge, journalists borrowing news from each other seem to be reluctant in making changes to the original frames communicated. When the page editors were confronted with the results of the content analysis regarding Africa's negative coverage, they recounted how their professional routines cannot allow them to make significant changes in the stories they borrowed:

> I always countercheck with the other sources. I pick a BBC news [story] and I always read from Reuters, I want to check with the AP (Associated Press). I want to check, so I go to Yahoo, a source we do not even subscribe to, just to find out whether they are a true reflection. You have been to the editorial conference and you saw the heat there. If you change a story significantly and other editors discover ... you will have to produce evidence or facts for the changes and where you got them (Editor 4 — *The Daily Graphic*).

Journalistic stories are structured according to some rules that have not really changed enough over the years. Basically, these rules have become *constructs* and to be seen as professional, one must respect these rules. What is required of a journalist to change a theme that is already communicated to him/her by another journalist is evident from the journalists commissioned to cover the same event, especially when they come with conflicting reports. Sending reporters across the continent rarely happens. On the issue of repetition of negative slant from the Northern press, one editor said:

> When we choose news that is slanted, we just do a little editing, but mostly they too [journalists in the Northern press] know the slant. They have perfected that act; journalists from developing countries cannot go

against it and rewrite the whole story. We don't do enough rewriting of their story... We just pick them most often. We know that there is a slant but where is the evidence before the editorial board? (Editor 2 — *Daily Guide*).

Because journalistic news is an account of someone who has witnessed an event, it becomes difficult for another journalist, who possesses canonical proximity to this ideological construct, to attempt a change. One page editor provided a clearer picture of this:

> Because we are picking stories from what they have produced this is mainly what you will get. Sometimes we are not happy to be using all the negatives but that is what they have and the thing is that you are not there. We do not have the opportunity or the resources to go and cover and those who cover portray the stories differently. This is what they are giving us. Sometimes you wonder is that all that they can cover but our profession demands evidence if you attempt a change or it amounts to some propaganda (Editor 4 — *The Daily Graphic*).

This *proximity in journalistic ideology* coupled with *limited resources* represents a major blockade to any form of resistance to the negative images communicated by the dominant press from the Northern Hemisphere. The major way to resist negative frames communicated by foreign news agencies is to commission one's own reporters, at least in the major cities in Africa. One editor explained how relieved he felt when a reporter of their newspaper lived a short while in China and reported from there for the newspaper.

Some of the editors appealed to some of the journalistic ideological constructs to defend their coverage of Africa. They argued that news must be negative to attract readership, a concept most journalists share. The British-embeddedness and dominance in the Ghanaian education, language and journalism training as earlier established have led to comparative proximity of views carried in media from the Northern Hemisphere. This near sacrosanct reception of news from the Northern press means that the editors share some proximity in the understanding of the news they borrow.

One major journalistic construct that has hardly received any critical interrogation is the perception of journalists about readership taste. The editors seem to argue that readership taste of news about Africa is an element that drives them in their selection. The appeal to readership taste as the reason for publishing seemingly negative and sensational news is largely a construct. It has never been critically questioned by the journalists because they do not cite any scientific study for it. They are usually appealing to common sense understanding within the professional ideology that the news must reflect the readership taste, which they are sure is negative and sensational. In answering the question of why Africa's image remained negative, one page editor answered:

> I think we choose stories not because we intend to effect changes in our societies, but we choose them based on what we think will attract people to them. And, by and large, we are looking at negative stories. I mean you come up with a story and your publishers will not be in tune with it because it will not attract readers, readers will not buy the paper. There will be a reduction in sales. Why? Because it isn't negative (Editor 1 — *Ghanaian Times*).

Senior editors who participated in editorial meetings, where stories were selected, justified their selection based on their years of experience and the claim that they are most familiar with their readership's taste. They argue that this is a taste for bad news and sensationalism. Another page editor recounted his frustrations about how some readers call his boss to complain about the lack of sensational and bad news. He argued that stories involving human interest and soft news are not very much welcomed by the readership.

Publishers and editors have been cited as people who monitored the taste of readers enough to determine what it is that the readers want. In answering the question of lopsidedness between reported triumphs and tragedy in daily news reports, a page editor revealed the publisher's *power* in the interpretation of readership taste. Apart from the fact that there are some isolated cases when the readers have asked for explanations for a certain disaster, there seems to be an established idea among the editors that the readers want to read something sensational and negative. This notion is an *ideological construct* that permeates the practice of normative journalism as per the responses so far extracted. Throughout the ethnographic interview, the journalists and their editors have supported the argument of appealing to the *common-sense notion* about news being negative. In all occasions where I asked for evidence of readership taste, they have not provided proof. They argued that they do not need to do any research to show this. One editor responding to the lack of balance between negative and positive stories on the continent captured the notion vividly in this way:

> In journalism, we have something we call "bad news sells". Now, as a continent, we're supposed to project the positive side of our continent to Africans and to the rest of the world to know the good things that we do but unfortunately, we keep doing it the same way the foreign news does to us. We have always been criticising them that they don't project the positive side of Africa, yet those of us here too do the same thing because of the basic fact that they believe that bad news sells (Editor 9 — *The Ghanaian Chronicle*).

The readership taste has not been investigated carefully because some aspects of it are generally known. The idea that negative reporting is preferred to positive reporting is not debatable, according to journalists. This is a universal journalistic ideology that they seem to have accepted without questioning. Sometimes they argued that progress isn't visible around the West African sub-region, and the readers know this through experience; they argued that this is why they are usually negative in their writing.

Unequal Encounters with the Global North

The journalists recounted the instances in history where they reported from the perspective of their reporters, the ones from the bureaus of Ghana News Agency across the African continent and in selected European and North American cities. They laid a strong claim on an African perspective produced by the agency. One editor said:

> It is difficult now for us. In the past, the Ghana news agency had bureaus in Kenya, London and New York and we were able to write from an African perspective (Editor 5 — *The Daily Graphic*).

Another suggested this same difference and the need to send out their own reporters. The page editor recounted the experience of reporting an election in Togo alongside the international media from the Northern Hemisphere, and questions why what she wrote was so different from what they wrote. And she asked where the journalists working for the

Northern press saw the things they wrote the next day. It looked to her that those journalists were following a template. She recounted:

> Africa should be covered by Africans to every large extent, not completely though. We should be able to attend if there are resources for major events. We should try and get or be represented. [When] I was in Lomé to cover Togo's elections, we didn't see much foreign press there and in fact, they hardly covered the elections. We covered the elections and then, sometimes, I wanted to compare what I had with them... you don't even see it [the news story] there. They [foreign press] will say that [it is] a small country in West Africa, [but] they don't even know where it is. If they are lucky, they will say, West Africa; they even say that it's in East Africa, sometimes (Editor 3 — *The Daily Graphic*).

Another page editor extends the claim of an African perspective by calling for action to make this a reality, because dependence on the media from the Northern Hemisphere cannot produce stories that reveal the continent's uniqueness. This is how he puts it:

> In communicating the African foreign news, it's about Africans themselves taking the initiative of writing their own stories, instead of relying on other networks, because if we continue to depend on other networks, we will disseminate only third-party information. So how can this happen? Unless we have our unique news agency that befits Africa, we will not have to rely on other networks, but I see it as a challenge on my continent (Editor 1 — *Ghanaian Times*).

The journalists seem to support affirmative action, of a sort, in reporting on Africa. This involves a conscious effort to be positive and respectful when writing the African story:

> I am an African; if I am writing something about Mali or Somalia, or sometimes about children, I will not go there, look at the dirty clothes of the children and pitch my story there. I will not do that. The feeling exists first as an African, whether I like it or not. I want to use something else. Why would I want to show an African child in [...] tattered dress? I understand that kids in tattered clothes aren't the only kids around, and [their tattered clothing] does not necessarily mean they are from poor homes (Editor 4 — *The Daily Graphic*).

The feudal system that prevented South–South interaction is still active and limits African journalists in reporting the continent largely. The New World Information and Communication Order (NWICO) report and Johan Galtung and Mari Ruge (1965) have both mentioned this as an element that aggravates dependence. In fact, the world information order, according to the journalists, is strongly linked to the economic order. As such, the never-improving economic situation of the continent, coupled with conflicts of all kinds, has resulted in the closure of national initiatives developed to deal with this. They mentioned especially the Ghana News Agency and PANA press.

The journalists, on the whole, seem to me to be saying that dependence largely accounts for the negative images they reproduced. But at the root of this dependence is a lack of economic resources needed to cover the whole continent. One page editor said:

> Because we are picking stories from what they have produced this is mainly what you will get. Sometimes we are not happy to be using all the negatives but that is what they have and the thing is that you are not there. We do not have the opportunity or the resources to go and cover and those who cover portray the stories differently. This is what they are giving us. Sometimes you wonder if that is all that they can cover (Editor 4, *The Daily Graphic*).

7. Discussing Africa's Media Image in Ghana:

A Synergy of Actors, Conditions and Representations

This chapter discusses the findings of the study in line with the research questions that guided them. I continue to further outline the implications and significance of these findings for the entire study as a unit. I relate the findings to previous research in order to establish the study's contribution to the literature and future research. The creative use of theoretical frameworks that are new to journalism is discussed in the view of their application to this study. The chapter ends with conclusions revisiting the conceptual and theoretical frameworks. I delineate my efforts to negotiate the limitations of this study. This is followed by key contributions to theoretical advances regarding what makes *news*. The general contributions to the state of the art (literature) are also outlined. I finally discuss five approaches that future research should adopt.

RQ1: What Is the Overview of the Coverage of Africa in the Ghanaian Press?

The overview of the coverage of Africa in the Ghanaian press is divided into four subcategories. The first part deals with the subjects of the coverage. The second part outlines the dominant themes through which the African story was told. Third, the coverage is analysed for its tone/quality, i.e. positive, negative or neutral. The fourth aspect relates to a comparison of the sub-questions a. b. and c. between the Ghanaian press and their Western counterparts, pertaining to specific studies.

a. Subjects/Topics/Story Types of the Coverage

Ghana's portrayal of Africa was largely concentrated on the related subjects of politics, economics and social issues, which represent over 86% of the entire coverage over the period of two years. The picture painted with these subjects presents an apparently stagnant continent, whose successes and failures with politics, economics and social cohesion ought to be measured and validated against advanced democracies. In these particular subjects, African voices received little or no agency in the news articles because the stories were told through either their foreign development agents, monitoring organisations or humanitarian officers. The sheer focus on these subjects did not necessarily invoke negative images, except when they were evaluated against already existing standards and ideologies deriving from wherever the original stories were written. The lack of alternative evaluation for issues such as social progress and human development means that the reasoning and the root causes of all sorts of practices emanating from the continent were either ignored or evaluated against dominant perspectives from the Northern Hemisphere.

Stories relating to subjects such as history, culture and personality/celebrities were limited to 10% of the entire review. These stories concentrated on Nelson Mandela, ancient Egyptian archaeological excavations and presidential visits to cities in Europe and North America. Due to such reporting, it is difficult to work out whether or not celebrities exist on the African continent apart from politicians and a few iconic figures like Mandela. When the amount of negatively pitched stories in the entire coverage is juxtaposed with the omission of activities of African celebrities and their charity works, it reveals a trend where one could differentiate between elite celebrities (European celebrities and African politicians) and other celebrities that are involved in decent charity work on the continent but are altogether ignored by coverage.

Mel Bunce (2017) recorded a rise and a sharp decline in *Africa rising* discourse simultaneously. As confusing as these results may sound, the economic stories in that coverage opened up discussions over the issue of Africa as the next business destination. In the attempt to generally discuss ideas about the stagnant economies in the Northern Hemisphere, the Western press portrayed Africa as an alternative destination where the world's capital will grow. As the Northern economies started recovering, the *Africa rising* discourse appeared to diminish. The *Africa rising* discourse was not a dominant subject or theme in the mainstream Ghanaian press coverage of Africa because the concept did not last long enough to reach the continent.

In another attempt to re-conceptualise the *Africa rising* discourse, Rachel Flamenbaum (2017) argues that the discourse did not emanate in the Western world because of its merit. Instead, she perceives the re-appropriation of *Africa rising* discourse by social media users in Ghana as an avenue for an active, positive interpretation of West Africa's postcolonial experiences, which rather lent the concept a useful African agency. Levi Obijiofor and F. Hanusch (2002, 2011) argue that the emergence of social media provides a good opportunity for deconstructing Africa's image. However, the changes recounted by Flamenbaum about Ghana remain just within the remit of social media and do not extend to mainstream media and journalism. The fact that Ghanaian press coverage is lopsided and unable to engage in this positive interpretation, as discovered in this study, is rather a confirmation of their incapacity to act contrary to their ideological understanding of news discourse, which has been handed down to them over centuries as part of a professional co-optation. This *midpoint-position ambivalence* of belonging to a globalised journalism profession and being a custodian of national/regional discourse, as indicated in the work Terje Skjerdal (2012), strongly accounts for the differences in the findings of Flamenbaum on social media and this study's finding on the mainstream print media.

b. Dominant Themes of the Coverage.

The dominant themes of portrayal included war, crime and killing; crises; and terrorism. Consisting of different subjects, these themes were reported as news events and therefore represented actual happenings on the continent. However, it did not appear that other things were happening on the continent except these. It was equally difficult to get a detailed analysis of any of these issues, except the overarching impression of unending war and crises. Terrorism, for example, has long been described as a global threat, but this was hardly evident in the stories. Rather the terrorist acts of groups like Boko Haram and Al-Shabaab were mostly linked to general humanitarian concerns raised by these attacks, which African countries and their leadership are not able to address.

The claim of journalists that they present an objective picture of socio-political events and catastrophes leads to the expectation that after every reportage of a violent outbreak, an equal, or at least substantial, number of reports would follow when calm is restored. The lack of stories reporting improvements on previously reported violent and catastrophic events frames war and fighting as the prevailing events taking place on the continent. The dominant themes of portrayal relating to war, killing, crises and terrorism are eventually used as context for new stories, even though positive changes would have subsequently occurred. It is interesting to note that, irrespective of the subject or issues under discussion, an entire news story, from the lead to the last paragraph, was typically filled with the most poignant calamities. Occasional positive stories reporting progress were often negated with these same negative themes. Beverly Hawk (1992) indicates that, somehow, the journalists feel that a context is required for these African stories in order that the audience in the Northern Hemisphere understands the stories, and these usual themes have, in turn, been continually reused again for this *context* reasoning also in the Ghanaian press. It is systematically established in the literature that these themes have not changed. The works of Robert Stevenson and Donald Shaw (1984), Annabelle Sreberny (1985), Hawk (1992), and Bunce et al. (2017) have confirmed that crises, war and terrorism have not seen any significant reductions and remain the major themes through which the African story is narrated in the Northern press. Ghana's reportage of the continent falls within these same categories. To make room for a balanced analysis of the stories, the *theme of development and progress* was predetermined and searched for throughout the analysis. The analysis showed that the few positive stories were coming from non-mainstream international news organisations. Were a young Ghanaian to rely on just these newspapers as sources of their news about the continent, it would appear evident that no positive developments occur in Africa.

c. Quality/Tone of the Coverage

Based on the subjects and themes of the coverage, 80% of the stories published in Ghanaian newspapers about Africa were negative in tone. This largely negative overview of the continent by the Ghanaian journalists can be explained from two perspectives. First, Stuart Hall (1997) argues that representation does not consist of a straightforward presentation of the world and its relationships, but rather it is a complex notion that relies significantly on meaning emanating from *shared perceptual maps*. Hall then argues that negative representations of a group of people over time shape the group's self-identity, which progressively becomes dependent on how they have been seen by others. But a second intervention by Frantz Fanon (2008) provided a rather critical perspective of this when he argued that the disruption in self-perception of the colonised rendered them susceptible to perpetual disruption of their psychic realm, and, as such, the colonised regularly seek their coloniser's acceptance, even after the colonial encounter, as a form of endorsement. Unfortunately, this endorsement never comes and, therefore, it becomes a standard and a virtue to think and act like the coloniser. The Ghanaian press coverage of Africa has largely supported Fanon's perspective. Based on the empirical evidence of this study, I argue that the Ghanaian coverage of Africa, notwithstanding technological and economic transformations underway on the continent, is severely negative as a result of imitating their Western counterparts.

The argument of improvement in the continent's media image in the Northern press over time, which has been reported by several scholars (Bunce et al., 2017; Nothias, 2017; Obijiofor and MacKinnon, 2016; Scott, 2015; Ojo, 2014 and Scott, 2009) is yet to be witnessed in the Ghanaian press. It can be argued, based on this, that *Afro-pessimism* (among African countries) still largely exist. Then comes the question of why was the thesis arguing for an improved image of Africa not supported in this study. Andy Ofori-Birikorang (2009, p. 106) argues that although the Ghanaian newspapers are "thorough-bred modern postcolonial institutions, they are yet to divest themselves of their recognition as the product of the colonial state, a trend that continually shapes the functional dynamics of their production processes and outcomes". Kwame Karikari (1992) and Burnham Terrell (1989, pp. 136–37) argue that newspapers and other organs of the Western press were "an integral part of white domination".

d. Comparison of a., b. and c. between Ghanaian and Western Coverage

The improvement in the coverage of Africa in the Western press, as reported in Bunce et al. (2017), cannot be supported. Comparing the coverage Africa gets in the Ghanaian press to Hawk (1992) and Bunce et al. (2017), it is clear that the negativity recorded in the 1992 study by Hawk has not changed substantially, although the conditions that necessitated an improvement, as evidenced in the work of Bunce et al. (2017), were expected to be sustained and improved. Bunce recognised and explained how the *Africa rising* discourse peaked so rapidly and dropped so abruptly.

The Ghanaian coverage of Africa appears rather more negative, but with very interesting nuances, like the emergence of the use of Chinese Xinhua News Agency materials. The subjects of comparison did not follow any specific structure. Many of the subjects that Bunce et al. (2017) noted a reduction in reporting on were also less dominant in this study. However, the area of stark difference is *politics*, where much of the coverage in this study clustered; a comparatively smaller space was allotted to the subject of *economy/business*. I argue that this study's contribution relates significantly to the disaggregation of the subjects of *economy* and *politics*, which were treated the same in previous studies. This study reveals that Ghana's coverage concentrated on *politics* and not *economy/business*, which, in a way, confirms the rise and fall of the *Africa rising* discourse.

RQ2: What is the Weight of Influence Carried by International News Agencies as Sources in the Ghanaian Press?

The fact that only 1.9% of the entire coverage of Africa in the Ghanaian press originated from news organisations within the country is indicative of the influence international news agencies have on the logic of reporting Africa even among countries on the continent. The largely dominant role of the Northern media organisations in Ghana's coverage of Africa (about 86%), led by the BBC World Service, does not only represent their quality but also gives an indication that domination has hardly ended. In the determination of the weight of influence of international news agencies on their Ghanaian counterparts, both qualitatively and quantitatively, I conclude that the actors have not changed that much. The very same Northern media organisations still lead the way.

It is, however, crucial not to ignore the performance of Xinhua News Agency for their slight quantitative edge over some international news agencies from the Northern Hemisphere. It is also equally fascinating to state clearly that Ghana remains the only actor in this game that must increase their volume of coverage themselves, because the Xinhua and Al Jazeera news organisations were consciously created to tell specific stories of those countries where they originate, with a logic that in the future would not be different from what the Northern media organisations have to offer. The literature has already established massive financialisation of the Chinese media through private capital (Thussu et al., 2018; Hachten and Scotton, 2016; Xin, 2017) which will soon require a return on investment. This will then push the Chinese media, both home and abroad, to a model not very different from their Western counterparts.

The acceptance and reuse of Western images by the Ghanaian press demonstrates some level of qualitative influence which the Fanonian concept of *internalised oppression* better explains. The situation where the subject of domination is fully aware of the elements of oppression exerted by the oppressor, but yet accepts it as a *natural order of things*, is referred to by Fanon as *epidermalisation of inferiority*. To Fanon, this is unlikely to end as long as the colonised continues to imitate the coloniser in the postcolonial state. The idea that Africans have themselves to blame for remaining poor and consequently incapable of telling their own stories (i.e. that they lack agency) runs across the interviews except for one journalist who linked this to its root cause — the fact that the inequitable encounters Africa lived and continues to live have not ended. In any case, an editor even doubted whether Africa deserves self-rule. I, therefore, argue that depicting the imitations of these actors as a cultural mix and a result of globalisation is erroneous, and conceals this manifest disruption of the psychic realm that is empirically evident in this study. It also hides the emerging hegemony that continues to characterise global news production and distribution worldwide.

Amid this high dependence on international news agencies for the coverage of Africa, the Ghanaian journalists and editors claim they possess an African perspective. This ambivalence has been explained by Homi K. Bhabha's (1994) revision of Fanonian *submissive imitation*. Although Bhabha thinks that psychic realm disruptions are active even in the postcolonial era and re-enacted through contemporary globalisation, he suggests that the concept of the psychic realm disruption is no longer *submissive imitation* — the imitation which assumes that the colonised is a passive alienated subject living on the edges of two worlds and constantly seeking legitimisation. Bhabha forcefully argues that the imitation practised by the colonised is not homogenous but a metonymic resemblance; repetition and difference at the same time. It is a *subversive imitation*. He then introduces the *third space* as a place of hybrid identity that emerges from the fact that the colonised had to live on the edges of two worlds after being psychologically persuaded to imitate their rulers in language, attitude and worldviews. He argues that at the *third space*, the coloniser's superior role at the centre of the postcolonial relationship is disrupted.

The appropriation of an African perspective, the call for a change and the constructions of China's influence as South–South cooperation by these Ghanaian journalists are indicative of this third space. The unending tale of this argument is whether resistance or subversive imitation is an assumed idea or a manifest practice? Even though the journalists recognise the domination under which they write the

African story, they are yet to initiate their response to destabilising the dominant position of the BBC World Service. Marwan Kraidy (2002) argues in support of Bhabha that the fluidity of the postcolonial subaltern is marked by a set of inescapable continuities and interactions that disrupts the essentialist view, that denies the agency of the colonised, with the argument that while imitating the coloniser, the colonised then practices a form of *mimicry* which is a contradictory utterance, and ambivalently unsettles both sides, questioning the basis of the colonisers' authority.

The expedience of empirically testing these ideas through Ghana as a case study were laid out in the country's historical background, but Skjerdal (2012) hints that the appropriation of an African perspective and the heavy reliance on liberal global media concepts reflect the African journalist's appropriation of local identity while at the same time accepting inclusion into a global professional journalism culture. This provides the basis to argue for some kind of hybrid self of the Ghanaian journalists. It is, however, clear that this hybrid self has not been amply demonstrated in practice. The Ghanaian newspapers envisage their agency but have not put into practice a definite effort indicative of Kraidy's argument.

The rising influence of China's Xinhua News Agency was mostly constructed as South — South cooperation aimed at disrupting the position of Northern media. However, the uneven power dynamics of this relationship are not indicative of cooperation. While the editors argued that they are expected to supply Xinhua News Agency with news about Ghana and other neighbouring countries, this is yet to materialise. The cooperation has taken the character of a superior giver, who always gives and a receiver, who usually receives without questioning the source, intents and interests of the giver. The reuse of Xinhua News Agency material in the Ghanaian press, with stories covering issues beyond China, is a real success for China's *public diplomacy* activity across the African continent. While Herman Wasserman (2016) argues that China's *soft power* activities (focusing on editorial decisions of South African media), although vigorously pursued, were massively constrained because the South African journalists did not use news articles beyond China–South Africa relations and BRICS activities. In the case of Ghana, the increasing use of Xinhua News Agency material is also the result of *public diplomacy* activities. This is because out of the four newspapers studied, only the two public newspapers (*The Daily Graphic* and *Ghanaian Times*) who signed an agreement with Chinese officials used Xinhua News Agency □ materials. The remaining two newspapers, which are privately owned, did not use Xinhua News Agency at all. In describing the new form of media imperialism both Chris Paterson (2017) and Thomas McPhail (2014) envisaged China becoming a dominant actor in the African media landscape.

Ignoring the influence of sources on news selection decision-making is tantamount to asserting that there is no relationship between media frames and their root sources. This is also contrary to Hawk's thesis that poor news coverage of Africa is not a victimless crime (Bunce et al., 2017, p. xvi) and as such those committing the crime recognise in what forms they have perpetuated their offences. Sources play a significant role in news construction because the ideology of news hardly permits the receiving journalists to change significantly what their sources say, especially when the source is another journalist. The argument that African journalists are not doing any better than their Northern media counterparts (Obijiofor and Hanusch, 2003; Pate, 1992; Sobowale, 1987) ignores from whose perspective these African journalists covered the continent.

In this study, I have discovered direct reliance on the media from the Northern Hemisphere, which is both indicative of their lingering influential role on the African media and the growing hegemony that the entire journalistic space has experienced when it comes to foreign news production and distribution. These two elements have largely modified the agency of African journalists into submissiveness, although it was widely predicted in Bunce et al. (2017) that with increased participation from local reporters in Africa as the motivating force for African news, the continent now had the chance to claim agency over its image. In light of the requirements from the Western editors and their presumed taste of what their readership wants, such hope has quickly dissipated.

RQ3 (a): What are the Conditions and Practices that Shape the Selection and Placement of Foreign News in Ghanaian Newspapers?

After a thorough description of the coverage of Africa in the Ghanaian press and the weight of influence exerted by international news agencies, as dominant actors, it is useful that the overarching conditions and practices that have provided either an enabling or constraining framework for the coverage are equally explained. This was the rationale for the application of three theories to the foreign news selection process in Ghana.

Aligned with the arguments and framework of Pamela Shoemaker and Stephen Reese (2014), the foreign news eventually selected, on a daily basis, is a product of several conditions, actors and practices beyond the colonial and international power relations. Depending on each unique context, these conditions and practices could either have an enabling or constraining framework for the *message* (news article) the journalists select. Significant among these outlined for discussion include profitability, economic rationality of knowing audiences' taste (advertising bias) and routine technological challenge.

First, the four selected newspapers seem to be working with a similar economic logic even though two are privately owned and the other two are publicly owned. This is because both the public and private selected newspapers rely completely on advertising and circulation income. The government of Ghana, who is the majority shareholder in the two public newspapers, requires a return on her initial investments as an owner. No public funding of any sort exists for any newspapers in Ghana, especially the four selected for this study. The cost associated with keeping their own reporters or buying news items from stringers is unbearable in the face of dwindling advertising and circulation incomes. The plausible logic that these newspapers are arguing is the reduction in the cost of operations. Apart from the *Ghanaian Times* newspaper, which was open to committing more resources to foreign news as a way to give meaning to its original historic mandate as a Pan-African newspaper, the others have argued that no relationship exists between the increase in profitability and commitment of resources to foreign news. By this argument, they have given the news a purely economic tag. The fact that a free version of news on Africa exists does not warrant any economic spending on the coverage of Africa. They supported this by pointing to the existing economic struggle within which the newspaper industry operates. For them, the definition of African news as a social responsibility to correct the continent's media image will not fly in board meetings, which have become a place where profitability rather than *news* (in its social context) occupies a central position in much of the debate.

The second condition, though closely related to the issue of profitability, is the economic rationality that knowing the audiences' taste carries a double-bind for editorial content (see below). The foreign news pages in the four newspapers are premium pages, meaning that they are among the most read pages. The ambivalence this brings is that becoming a well-read page in these newspapers means losing editorial space for advertising. After a foreign news page is made premium, editorial content reduces and, as such, there is a reduction in the diversity of what can be carried. This is quite institutionalised, in that marketing departments have the upper hand in planning the entire newspaper daily. They allocate all advertising first before presenting to the editorial team what exists for editorial content. This confirms the argument, put forward by Rüdiger Schulz (2008), that one needs to acknowledge that readership survey is different from reception research, normally conducted by academics, because even though they have a similar purpose, they are put to very different uses. The paradox that eventually becomes the guiding rule for the journalists is that their knowledge of the taste of the audience cannot be used for any improvements in editorial content because if the page is well-read, then editorial material will have to give way for advertising. Interestingly, less-read pages also risk being turned into a complete advertising page. This advertising bias, in both cases, affects foreign news selection in a way that usually results in only one or two extremely significant news articles on calamities being selected, due to lack of space. The double-bind for editorial content in the political economy of Ghanaian newspapers refers to a situation where managerial role holders at these newspapers demand that readership for editorial contents increase in order to attract advertising on those pages, forgetting advertorials and editorial content, when competing for space in newspapers, have an inverse relationship. This creates a situation where options for the survival of editorial content is limited and each option results in a punitive treatment of editorial content either by reducing the space allocated to editorial content or by turning non-performing pages into a complete advert page.

Third, routine technological challenges have become either an enabling or constraining environment within which the foreign news desks work. Willingness to diversify the sources of international news agencies monitored in a day is dependent largely on the level of congestion on the local Internet speed and access to work-space on the internal network places. When the service is bad, the journalists are not willing to search wider for their news, especially because there is no alternative infrastructure for scooping their news from either live news agency feeds or rolling international news broadcasters. They rely solely on what exists in online, and this makes the whole process Internet-dependent. According to Shoemaker and Reese (2014), there are several influences on the *media message* that are usually not accounted for in the literature because these systemic conditions have mostly been rendered normal at a first glance. Examples of organisational and routine influences were severe among the selected Ghanaian newspapers. This provides a context within which to look at the journalists' work and whether they can appreciate their work as a representation of the continent to which they belong. The crucial preoccupations of these journalists in such circumstances relate largely to what is practically available and feasible under the time constraints within which they deliver the daily news to us.

While discussing the contextual complications which have made it difficult to mirror both triumphs and tragedies of a normal day in foreign news selection in Ghana, it is obvious the literature has grossly ignored these conditions and made them look like they do not have any journalistic influences that are readily visible. In this section, there is no claim of influence either, rather I argue that the entire news selection decision process occurs within some relevant conditions that are ignored by researchers because the literature does not point to those conditions. Nevertheless, they became evident and formed part of the description in this study because of the ethnographic technique and conscious attempt to investigate the *coverage of Africa* beyond the news articles and the journalists themselves, and into the organisational space within which they work.

RQ3 (b): What Are the Challenges of Foreign News Selection in Ghana from the Perspectives of Ghanaian Newspaper Journalists?

After outlining the overview of the coverage, I describe the dominant actors and the overarching conditions within which the entire field operates. The journalists hold certain perspectives on what accounted for the kind of coverage the African continent received in their newspapers. Based on a reconstructive interview strategy, I thematised the discussion under three broad headings: economic hardship and cost-cutting rationales; the proximity of journalistic ideology about the news; and the persisting unequal encounter between the Global North and South.

Economic Hardship and Cost-Cutting Rationale

The journalists relate the sharply decreasing disposable income of the Ghanaian population and reduction in advertising budget of most firms to cutting cost — which is the only option left to increase shareholder's investments. This threat of declining ability of advertising and circulation income to fully pay for the cost involved in producing an edition of the newspaper is further complicated by the suffocating competition in the newspaper industry.

Relating the disposable income to the intense competition means readership would have to select among the newspapers. With an average cost of GH¢2.50 per edition of a newspaper ($0.43), one requires far above the minimum wage per day in Ghana to read even half of the top ten newspapers. The journalists believe the reality of harsh economic conditions within which even educated people have had to live in Ghana has repercussions for the press.

Apart from the readership, they pointed to management policies to cut the number of pages for editorial material to save the newspapers from collapsing. All four newspapers have had a cut in the number of pages as well as space for editorial material. They have argued that the ambition of the libertarian press system as an objective reflection of the daily triumphs and tragedy become unachievable with limited editorial space, which instigated a myriad of difficulties such as an unnatural cut in original stories and the lack of the use of longer genres of news, like feature articles about the African continent.

Other difficulties that result in rendering the stories negative are the elimination of contextual background and mismatch of the medium. The act of re-writing of original stories without further information means relying only on the original story and the eventual reconstruction is hardly better than the original. Medium mismatch occurs when a story using videos, graphics, artistic and forensic impressions and drawings are reduced to only text, and a limited amount of text at that. These challenges presented by economic hardship and the resultant cost-cutting strategies have contributed to the way journalists write about the continent in the Ghanaian press.

I argue that the Ghanaian press coverage of Africa is susceptible to more negativity than is present in its original source because of the confounding structural challenges that the entire foreign news selection and production processes face. This argument is confirmed in the meta-analysis of Susanne Fengler and Stephan Russ-Mohl (2008) who concluded that these rational economic behaviours of media professionals remain a valid context in which to discuss the failures of journalism and blind spots of media coverage.

Proximity of Journalistic Ideology

Ideological proximity between Ghanaian journalists and their international counterparts remains quite visible in the trend of their reuse of news coming from the Northern press. This is largely due to a replication of Western journalism curriculum, and the dominance of Western media assistance in Ghana. The journalists seem to reiterate the notion put forward some years ago by Daniel Patrick Moynihan that democratic media is a space for bad news and anything short of that could not be representative of the true sense of democracy (see Hachten and Scotton, 2016, p. 208). The concept of *news* and its structure is rooted in the dominant ideal type — a *Western libertarian journalism perspective*. This perspective treats the news as a *construct*.

This treatment prevents most journalists from questioning the logic and canonical claims of journalism. For example, the rule-based nature of journalism makes the practice difficult for journalists to change themes communicated to them. In cases where stories must pass the editorial conference test, any visible changes like the original story will be noticed by members of the conference. As such, to ensure that such changes are accepted, one must provide evidence. Oliver Boyd-Barrett (2004) has warned that journalism's fixation on facts leaves no room for an explanation, and, equally, this entire fixation has become ideological. Due to the fact that journalistic accounts are a reconstruction of events either witnessed or briefed about, a receiving journalist is limited in their assessment of stories in a manner that can bring about significant changes in the original story, except in cases where a conscious oppositional re-write is encouraged.

Unequal Encounters and the African Perspective

Some of the Ghanaian newspaper journalists have argued forcefully that an African perspective existed during the era when the Ghana News Agency had bureaus at strategic places around the globe, including the African continent. They argued that the current order of international news flow marks an unequal encounter where the powerful dominates and the vulnerable is reduced to common receivers, for whom all sorts of monolithic strategies have been applied. They stressed that few attempts at challenging this order failed because of the massive economic undertone involved in reporting the continent. Although there is a rapid spread of economic conditions from the North to the South, the economic resources made available to journalists covering some significant African events for the Northern press are intimidating to local journalists. One of the reasons why the continent's media image remains negative is this unequal encounter, because local journalists' reportage is simply different from their Northern media counterparts or their surrogate stringers. The journalists' argument runs contrary to Bunce et al. (2017), who have argued that the deployment of African/local journalists in covering the continent has, in a way, accounted for the improved image they noticed in the Northern press. Although in the same edited volume, Salim Amin (2017) confirms the flaw in this claim — there is a difference between what they independently produce for the local African audience and what their foreign editors commission. The positive issues coming from the continent are just not the news the editors in the North want, but due to the unequal power encounter, it is difficult for journalists from developing countries to succeed in the battle for the deconstruction of the continent's image.

RQ4: What Accounts for the Evolving Intermedia Agenda-Setting Preferences?

Journalistic co-orientation has been vastly described, but usually to determine whether such a relationship exists (Sikanku, 2014; Lim, 2006) rather than accounting for what factors underpin these relationships. Ramona Vonbun et al. (2015) attempt an explanation from a theoretical perspective. This study delimits three empirical findings that have not been cited as a major reason for journalistic intermedia preferences.

Apart from the wide reliance on the BBC World Service across the four selected newspapers, there was a unique trend of how the four selected Ghanaian newspapers reused individual international news media in their coverage of Africa. The nuances were divided into three themes: the construction of China's soft power as South–South cooperation; the appreciation of the historical and colonial background as a defining factor for the enduring relationship (postcolonial complexities); and the use of informal individual contact across the continent.

China's Soft Power and Public Diplomacy

The signing of an agreement with newspapers by the Chinese Foreign Office contributed to Xinhua News Agency's elevated performance as a source of foreign news in Ghana. Two different explanations emerged in light of the data. The *Daily Guide* and *The Ghanaian Chronicle*, both private newspapers in this study, constructed the Xinhua News Agency performance as an element linked with emerging Chinese *soft power* penetration on the continent. Even though the Xinhua News Agency figures surprised them, they argued that Chinese economic activities remain the major determinant of their influence, because ignoring the Chinese rendition of world discourse would amount to missing and failing to report on their progress. Interestingly, these newspapers never for once cited Xinhua News Agency because, to them, Xinhua is not their point of reference for the African news. Herman Wasserman (2016) observes a similar trend in his work in the case of some South African journalists, who refused to cite Chinese news agencies beyond China–South Africa relations.

The second explanation comes from the two public newspapers (*The Daily Graphic* and the *Ghanaian Times*) who have signed the cooperation agreement with Xinhua News Agency. They seemed to be arguing that their use of material from the Chinese news agency represents a South–South cooperation. They recognised themselves that the modus operandi was to share news between China and Ghana but until now they are yet to receive a single request on any issue in Ghana from their Chinese counterparts. H. D. Wu (2016) and Wasserman (2016) have both argued that the reuse of material from the Xinhua News Agency represents a success for the vigorous Chinese soft power activities on the continent. Extending this agreement to the state-funded Ghana news agency in recent times counters Ghana's historical role in the quest to tell the African story, a role that has been largely recognised in the literature (see Ibelema and Bosch, 2009). But, interestingly, this seemed to be justified using the notion of South–South cooperation.

Johan Galtung (1971) argues that a feudal structural system of interaction seems to exist in the communication order promoted by Western democracies that eventually denies periphery nations from communicating among themselves. In the case of the Ghanaian press, China's soft-power success is exclusively linked to public diplomacy activities with two newspapers. Shrouded in unequal power dynamics, the relationship between the Ghanaian public newspapers and Xinhua News Agency looks a lot like a new form of Centre–Periphery relationship, because no exchange is currently taking place. It is difficult to argue that a relationship that is dominated by one party represents South–South cooperation. Rather, it is fair to say that the dominant nations within the South are yet to appreciate the fact that being a semi-periphery or a centre is not a static or given status that cannot change. As soon as a rising periphery nation ignores the underpinning problem of imbalance, a new form of a relationship emerges that is similar to the original concept in the structural imperialism referred to by Galtung. The dynamic nature of the Centre–Periphery news flow has taken a *deterritorialised* nature (see Beer, 2010), where certain semi-periphery nations have become more impactful than some traditional Centre nations.

The Postcolonial Complexities

The colonial encounter in Ghana, like most countries, left two indelible scars through which the coloniser's presence is maintained until today: language and education.

Pragmatically, trade and worldview operate within these two scars that were ideologically instituted as duplicates of the original. Ali Mazrui (1978) establishes that contemporary African countries' identity is traceable to its colonial origins easily. The newspaper journalists in Ghana provided sufficient evidence within this study's findings that the country's history is inextricably linked to its colonial past. Using the BBC World Service dominance as a basis of their argument, the journalists normalised the dependency phenomenon and appropriated British institutions as the only examples they have known. Even though this dominance did not allow for reflections on how to relate to each other on the continent, it is clear that it has formed the foundation upon which everything else is built. They traced the country's media history to the British liberal model and social institutions from military to media assistance as elements that have become so established that it is an effort in futility to oppose them.

They also called for ways to appropriate, for themselves, these established norms as Ghanaian alternatives to the British originals. These narratives are the original goals of a British education in Africa, which Walter Rodney (1981) referred to as the act of turning the African elite into a *fair-minded English-man*. Quite apart from these historical entanglements that might sometimes sound like an excuse for their inability to cause a change in the course of practising journalism, they equally established visible and undeniable migratory linkages between Ghana and Britain. Anya Schiffrin (2010) confirms a real scramble for the postcolonial African journalism practice through media assistance and other kinds of influences. Continuous investment in Ghanaian journalism by international media in different training programmes remains a measure of the International media's quest to keep the status quo. Ahead in this game is the BBC World Service, which has had a peculiarly privileged role since the colonial era, described by Peter Golding (1979) as an authoritative way of mirroring their professional ideologies wherever they went. It was not surprising for the Ghanaian journalists that the BBC World Service occupied a largely dominant role as the source of foreign news about the entire African continent.

The literature dealing with journalistic co-orientation considers these lingering historical and contemporary relationships as *cultural affinity*, or a form of *proximity*. What this study has offered is the argument that we have to disaggregate bundles/concepts of cultural affinity and proximity to account for the unique situations, such as the enduring power imbalance between the colonised and the coloniser that operates in line with the colonial thinking pattern.

Informal Relationships and Personal Contacts

Intermedia agenda-setting between Ghanaian newspapers and their Nigerian counterparts evolved from informal relationships that have been built on the personal contacts of the journalists. Three of the editors lived and worked in Nigeria as journalists. Through their work experience, they built informal working relationships that have allowed for the sharing of news with their Nigerian newspaper counterparts. Apart from these, it became a dominant argument in almost all the four newspapers that they are largely inclined to building on their contacts in conferences and assignments to maintain them as sources.

The issue of relationships became more nuanced as it extended to the country where the editor studied. CNN was widely used by American-trained editors, while those who were British-trained generally preferred Reuters, with the exception of the BBC World Service, which was widely sourced by all the four newspapers as a representative of the British legacy and influential global media. This particular reason for journalistic co-orientation has evolved quite informally but was revealed as a potent means of driving which news agency is selected as the source of foreign news in the Ghanaian press.

Conclusions

This concluding section begins with a recapitulation of objectives and findings; and a look back at how the conceptual and theoretical frameworks assisted in interrogating the purpose of the study. This is followed by limitations encountered and how they were negotiated. The study's contribution to theoretical debates in international news is presented as a guide for future research.

Recapitulation of Purpose and Findings

The coverage of Africa in the Ghanaian press falls predominantly under the concept of *Afro-pessimism*. The substantial concentration on the subjects of politics and, to some extent, on the economy and social vices resulted in dominant themes emerging, such as war, crime, killings, crises and terrorism. The tone/quality of the coverage was largely (80%) negative. Even though the findings were not compared with what the coverage looked like some decades ago, these results clearly show that Africa's media image in the Ghanaian press is as negative as it is around the world. But it is crucial to note that Africa's portrayal in the Ghanaian media is predominantly constructed from the perspective of the Northern press, led by the sweeping influence of the BBC World Service. The BBC's singular influence, for instance, is enabled by the complex colonial and postcolonial trajectories that have lingered and promoted the British foreign broadcaster as the ultimate reference point for most professional journalists in Ghana. Although the BBC is generally an influential international broadcaster, the massive reliance on it for news about Africa, in this Ghanaian case, is not an example of globalisation but an element of domination that never ended.

The rise of Xinhua News Agency from China as an eminent actor, despite being constructed as South–South cooperation, rather reflects the success China's soft-power has achieved. This so-called

South–South cooperation signals looming domination as a result of the unequal power relations that characterises its workings so far.

The international intermedia agenda-setting preferences identified here have largely evolved through three approaches: the enduring historical and colonial relationship, Chinese soft power activities and other informal relationships built around personal contacts of staff of these newspapers.

Considering the entire foreign news selection decision in Ghana as a social subject shaped by myriad influences, the journalists argued that Africa's negative media image is also, in practice, shaped by organisational level elements such as economic hardships and its cost-cutting rationales; their proximity to the dominant normative journalistic ideology; and the uneven encounters between Ghanaian and their Northern press counterparts that have not changed over the years.

The entire foreign news selection process in Ghana operates in three prevailing conditions that individual, organisational and ideological levels of influence have no control over. Three dominant conditions of this nature were deconstructed to improve the continent's image in the near future: profitability; advertising bias underpinned by economic rationality; and routine technological challenges.

Conceptual and Theoretical Framework Revisited

It has been argued already in this study that conceptual and theoretical frameworks provide a cogent approach in tackling data collection and analysis with emphasis on the subjects of interests, processes and the interrelationships between them. Relating these to the arguments of Matthew Miles et al. (2014) and Vincent Anfara and Norma Mertz (2006), it is fair to say that the frameworks do change quite frequently in qualitative research, due to an asymmetrical social world, and, as such, it is prudent to point out which role the frameworks played regarding the determination of the findings to provide further justifications for them.

7. Discussing Africa's Media Image in Ghana

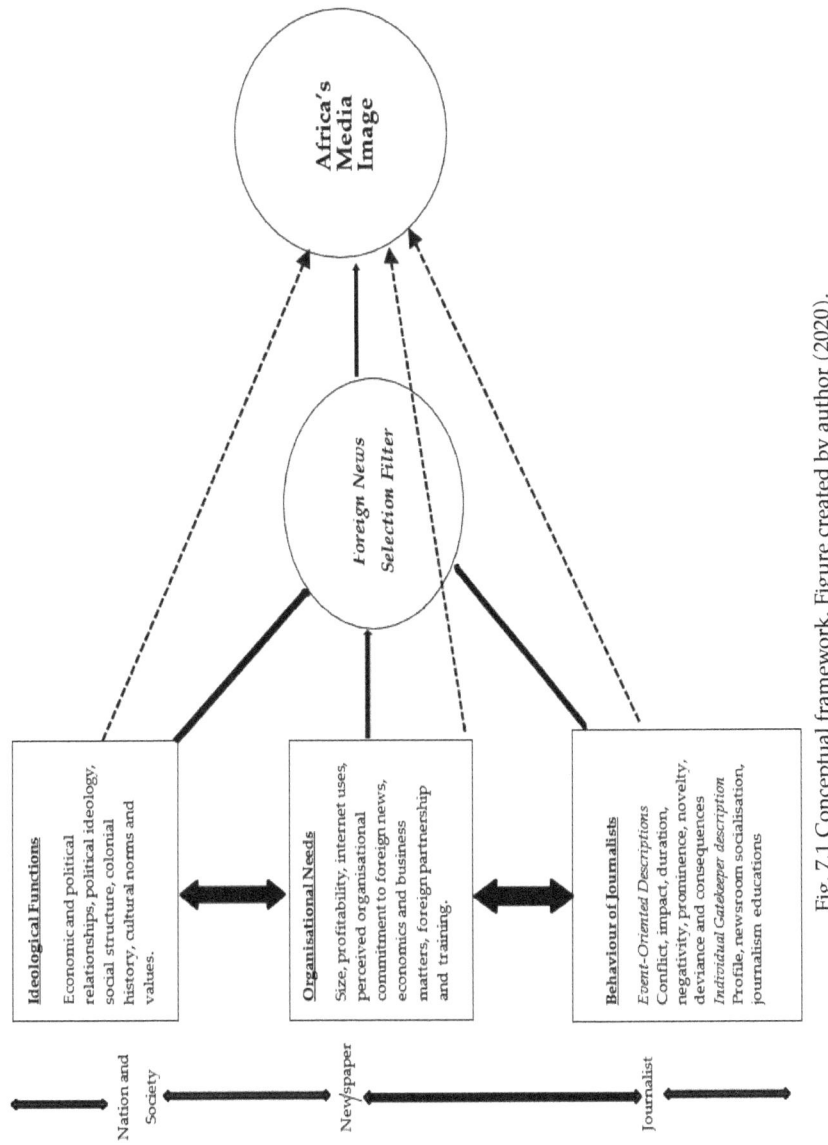

Fig. 7.1 Conceptual framework. Figure created by author (2020).

Figure 7.1, a variation of Figure 3.3., illustrates the development of conceptual assumptions throughout the study and into the study's findings. The three vertical rectangular boxes represent journalists, the newspapers and the Ghanaian society. Movement along this continuum is both reflexive and iterative. The influences of these boxes are unique but cannot be delimited as completely individual because of the interdependent and inter-related symbiotic social framework within which they operate to determine the news content.

The argument that print media journalists as individuals possessed a good appreciation of newsworthiness before joining the newspapers was upheld, since most of the interviewees had prior journalism education that appeared quite effective from their description. However, the assumption that the knowledge they have brought along could be a sole determinant of what news items they select about Africa was not valid, because they described some ideological and organisational conditions that they are required to entirely submit to. In the process, their knowledge is subdued under these conditions. Therefore, the arrow connecting the behaviour of individual journalists directly to the eventual message (Africa's Media Image) is now indicated with dotted lines (showing very little or no influence) instead of full influence indicated in the initial assumption in Figure 3.3. The two other boxes representing organisational needs and ideological functions did not also directly affect the eventual message. Even though there was evidence for journalists leaning towards the style of the colonial master's as a form of measuring quality, it was difficult to establish that foreign news is a ultimately and wholly a product of these ideological influences because there were conditions at the organisational level that this argument had to equally submit to — profitability, specific technological challenges and advertising bias underpinned by economic rationality. Based on these, I argue that foreign news selection decision-making process in Ghana is predominantly a product of the three levels envisaged and there is a mid-point where they converge before exerting their influences (*Foreign News Selection Filter*). Their influences are difficult to delimit entirely. However, the two upper rectangles (organisational level needs and ideological functions) seemed more dominant. Relying on a similar argument by Ofori-Birikorang (2009), I contend that the local newspapers, as modern institutions, have demonstrated in what ways they would like to challenge the ruling order of the postcolonial state. The Ghanaian journalists also mentioned the ideological influence of *single alternative*, which explains the fact that the BBC World Service shaped their childhood before they joined journalism schools not because they wanted it but because it was the only alternative available at the time. The analogies raised here together can be considered as the superior role the ideological functions exert on the two other levels, especially on the individual journalist level.

Negotiating the Limitations of the Study

I should stress that this study would have revealed very broad dynamics if it had studied more countries not necessarily as quantitative research but as a broader yardstick for developing future research on how the African self-identity and speech agency can evolve through the coverage of foreign news. This is because individual countries on the continent have a unique context within which to describe their contemporary agency. As such these findings provide only an in-depth analysis for the Ghanaian case. What could have been useful was to zone the entire continent into colonial experiences and press freedom, and then select areas based on differences and similarities between countries that could provide insightful data. But this requires more time and resources, which this particular study could not support.

The use of ethnographic content analysis (ECA) as a method of qualitative content analysis is an attempt to eliminate major weaknesses of the conventional content analysis by advocating for the collection of numeric and narrative data while conceptualising the text as fieldwork. However, the centrality of the researcher, rather than the code sheet (see Atheide, 1987), presents a real challenge to replications as *a priori coding* is discouraged. Based on the recommendations of Philipp Mayring (2000), this weakness was envisaged and worked on by adopting a *step by step analysis* largely based on theory-driven initial codes in the coding process. It is also useful to indicate that because the study was not entirely conducted using ethnographic content analysis, these weaknesses were further resolved through the interview sessions where some findings were discouraged and eliminated using the insights and arguments of the interviewees.

The use of multiple theories requires that I conceptualise for which level of the entire study a specific theoretical insight applies. To do this, I had to make assumptions based on my explorative knowledge about which variables and people would provide useful insights as was shown in the conceptual framework. For example, to apply the theory of newsworthiness to journalists' behaviour was completely an assumption based on my explorative knowledge and the literature. These assumptions pooled useful insights that would have otherwise been ignored.

Due to the lack of newspaper database in Ghana for the selected newspapers, keyword searches were not used for news article mining. This would have eliminated all the complexities surrounding sampling of newspaper and editions. Rather a multi-stage sampling approach recommended by Daniel Riffe, Stephen Lacy and Frederick Fico (2014) was applied where the newspapers were selected based on their circulation numbers using the Afro-barometer media report as the yardstick. Newspaper circulation figures in Ghana have been contested because some researchers have discovered that the figures, due to advertising, do not reflect reality. But the selections of these newspapers were justified also by the fact that most previous researchers have also relied on these same newspapers due to the consistency they have demonstrated over time.

To identify the sources used for the coverage of Africa in the Ghanaian press, a content analysis was conducted using census method where all editions of the four newspapers over the twenty-four months were sampled. The two constructed week approach was applied to the selection of news articles related to Africa for further qualitative analysis. In place of the keyword search approach, the methodical multi-stage sampling of newspapers, editions and units of analysis have offered the study diversity in the data that was analysed.

The process involved in getting the articles from the selected newspapers into a machine-readable form for the analysis was enormous. The newspapers were found in the University of Cape Coast library periodical archives in Ghana. However, they were bound in a monthly series that was impossible to scan based on the available scanners. I had to turn to Valco Hall library in the same University of Cape Coast, where loose sheets of the newspapers were kept. After borrowing these newspapers, it became evident that there were no optical character recognition (OCR) scans in the entire city. The eventual decision to use an A4 sheet size OCR scanner at the University of Cape Coast Library was timely but also limiting since the dateline was lost, and this meant that quotations from ethnographic content analysis had to be identified using a special alfa-numeric code to identify where they are located in the newspaper article data. Under normal circumstances, these should have been cited as newspaper articles.

The application of two ethnographic techniques to a postcolonial study provided very useful insights, but it also presented real challenges in the analysis because of my immersion in the entire research process. Like other critical interpretive genres (feminist, postmodern and poststructural methodologies), this postcolonial study adopted a creative way of collecting and understanding the data which is explicitly critical and not very much tied to established forms of objectivity. It is crucial to mention that the use of "I" frequently is indicative of this embeddedness, which Zehra Sayed (2016) describes as a common impulse of the critical interpretive inquiry. It is factual that I am Ghanaian and African. My interviewees know this and that closeness to the Ghanaian ways of thinking and doing offered some limiting perspectives especially when applying critical theory and interpretive methodology. Therefore, recognising this limitation becomes a large step towards dealing with it.

Access to the natural environment of the journalists and the application of very rudimentary processes of analysis are forms of research reflexivity aimed at ensuring that opinionated interpretations of the data were eliminated. One useful strategy that neutralised the limitation of my "I" in this study was peer-review, suggested by John Creswell (2014). The quarterly reviews of the School of International and Intercultural Communication (SIIC) offered opportunities to three professors, guest researchers and nine other cohort members of the year group to evaluate the entire study from the beginning to the end.

Key Contributions

Here, I enumerate the contributions of this study to the theoretical debates, advances made in the use of the hybrid methodology in the areas of journalism research, sociology and critical theory. The general contributions to the state of the art in international communication and direction for future research are equally outlined.

New Theoretical Insight into What Makes "News"

News selection research has long been occupied with the age-old question of how events become news. The positivist, object-based proponents in this debate have argued that the nature of news events is a significant determinant of newsworthiness criteria and when an event possesses more of such criteria it tends to have a news value that appeals to journalists (Galtung and Ruge, 1965; Staab, 1990; Harcup and O'Neil, 2001; Eilders, 2006; Schwarz, 2006; Shoemaker, 2006). It is crucial to state that within this object-based approach, several reconsiderations have occurred. Pamela Shoemaker (2006) argues in a commentary that "We should no longer use the prominence with which events are covered as a measure of the event's newsworthiness, and our theories should not use newsworthiness as the sole (or even an important) predictor of what becomes news" (p. 111). J. F. Staab, Christiane Eilders and Andreas Schwarz have all made similar comments that news factors are not the only relevant predictor of news selection decisions because they are just one of several elements. The opposite of this object-based argument is the subject-based argument that news is very much determined by the nature of the selection process, which relies on the political, economic and ideological goals of the news industry (Gans, 2004; Herman and Chomsky, 2008; Van Djik, 2009; Othman et al., 2014). The discord between these two traditions is that they hardly recognise that news selection could be the result of both object- and subject-based factors and that depending on the context, one tradition loses its potency to another. I contribute to this debate by bridging the gap between the two theoretical paradigms by tracing the entire news selection from the individual journalist's appreciation of how the nature of events contributes to the news selection decision. I later weakened the objectivist view of the journalists by showing them the results of their work to seek more critical reasoning that had accounted for the coverage. In this approach, the journalists have revealed the symbiotic nature of these two approaches that have not been properly defined so far. From these findings, I argue forcefully that the decision of what African news is reported in the Ghanaian press on a daily basis is a product of event-oriented factors, organisational needs, conditions and the subconscious ideological elements rooted in the postcolonial mindset. These descriptions go far beyond the news and the journalists to their social milieu, which is very well accounted for in this study.

The claim by the journalists that they had sufficient understanding of what news constituted before even going to journalism school meant that their pre-journalism education was even ideologically influenced by a liberal model — led by the BBC — which was the only option available to them at that time. On this point, I contend that individual appreciation of the event-oriented nature of news criteria, which is usually described as a micro-/individual level element in most research, could itself be borne out of an ideological immersion. To solidify the bridge between the object and subject arguments, I posit in this study that the event-oriented objectivist appreciation of what makes news does exist, but it is quite easily blurred by the practical organisational dynamics and overarching ideology within which the entire news selection process originates and operates.

Journalism and communication studies have had limited interaction with postcolonial studies, even though they have a similar agenda (Thomass, 2016; Shome, 2009; Shome and Hegde, 2002 and Grossberg, 1982). Like the recent attempts of Wasserman (2006) and Toussaint Nothias (2015), this study contributes to the greater dialogue between postcolonial theory and journalism studies. It also offers interesting and new insights into foreign news as produced in the Ghanaian media and the role of international news organisations on this whole process. Overall, it makes for an original and important empirical contribution to the field of journalism and postcolonial studies by arguing, based on its findings, that the kind of dependency syndrome in foreign newsgathering currently occurring in the Ghanaian press was the very element the nationalist press resisted, but ultimately succumbed to, around the time of Ghana's independence. Unfortunately, the re-enactment of these serious colonial complexities has been rather described as globalisation.

Even though some of the Ghanaian newspapers recognise these dominations and have envisaged subversive reuse, I argue that the Ghanaian foreign news *third space* is marked by dormant execution of resistance that dares to dislocate the centrality of the dominant international news organisations. The application of South–South cooperation to the influence of China's Xinhua News Agency is itself underpinned by another unequal power relation, which is largely similar to previous approaches from the Northern Hemisphere. The biggest take-home point here is that the Centre–Periphery model, which described the relationship between developed and developing nations, cannot be pinned to those binary positionalities. As peripheries become semi-peripheries, they tend to re-enact the imbalances that characterised the Centre–Periphery relationship and from there a new model emerges with new positionalities, which are based on power relational capacities, and not on a developed or developing binary.

The theory of agenda-setting has moved to its fourth phase, where researchers are more prone to questioning how the media's agenda is set in the first place, especially in an era where harsh economic conditions have resulted in massive journalistic co-orientations involving dependence of non-elite media on their elite counterparts. What one sees in both national and cross-border investigations of this phenomenon is a strict attachment to the application of statistical analysis to demonstrate whether or not such journalistic co-orientations exist. This study in its open and critical approach to the search for the reasoning behind these journalistic co-orientations discovered that the phenomenon is currently determined by factors that have hardly occupied inter-nation intermedia agenda-setting researchers. Offering an explanatory level analysis, I posit that inter-nation intermedia agenda-setting relationships in Ghana are largely shaped by China's soft power activities, lingering historical and colonial relations and informal relationships built on past work contacts of journalists, editors and owners. These new insights need disaggregation from known factors such as *proximity* and *cultural affinity, because* they are unique in and of themselves.

General State of the Art

I contribute three general insights to the ongoing debate about *Afropessimism* by contesting the literature (Bunce et al., 2017; Bunce 2015; Nothias, 2015; Ojo, 2014; Nothias, 2017; Obijiofor and MacKinnon, 2016; Scott, 2015). I contribute to this debate with a disruption of their argument that Ghana's representation of the continent, to which she belongs, is largely negative and determined mostly by the influence of the press from the Northern Hemisphere. Second, I argue that China's soft power activities are dominant in the Ghanaian newspaper industry through the reuse of Xinhua News Agency materials. This Chinese success has not encountered any impediments, as was recounted by Wasserman (2016) in the South African case. However, the unequal power dynamic within which this success has been achieved in Ghana is no different from the lingering remnants of the colonial encounter. This effectively provides empirical evidence to support Chris Paterson's (2017) inclusion of China as an imperialist actor on the African media landscape. Third, I contribute to the intermedia agenda-setting research by arguing that Ghanaian journalistic co-orientations are determined largely by China's soft power influences, historical but enduring colonial associations with the United Kingdom and personal contacts of the newspaper journalists around the continent. The evolution of this area of research requires empirical evidence (Du, 2013), which was largely provided in this study. This then means *internation intermedia agenda-setting* researchers would have to extend their list of the reasons for the existence of such relationships or recognise that testing only previously established factors does not allow for disaggregation of elements within those factors.

Future Research

This study nonetheless leaves gaps which future researchers can improve on, and here I outline five of these for researchers seeking to work in this area. First, the use of visuals in African representation in the Ghanaian press was not included in this study, but it could offer another interpretation and validation for some of the conclusions of this study. As Nothias (2015) suggests, the visuals infuse a unique corroboration from the semiotic tradition and this has usually been understood as part of the typology of *Afro-pessimism*.

Second, the theoretical battle between the Fanonian *submissive resemblance* (Fanon, 2008) and the *subversive resemblance/hybridity* of Bhabha (Bhabha, 1994; and Kraidy, 2002) requires further investigation supported by wide empirical data and typology of what constitutes resistance. Ideas about African agency has become a way of humanising the discrimination and negative representation the people of the continent have been subjected to. Neither Fanon nor Bhabha provided any clear boundaries for either their *submissive* or *subversive* imitation with which empirical tests could be applied.

The third subject other researchers should aim at resolving is the imbalance in the volume of news between private and public newspapers in Ghana that largely disrupts the sampling equity. Ofori-Birikorang (2009) points to the same issue with health news. I realised equally that the volume of international news produced by the two public newspapers far outweighs their two private counterparts and to achieve balance in the volume of news for the content analysis one will probably require a 2:1 ratio of private–public newspapers. It is crucial to think about this because the sizeable performance of the Xinhua News Agency was only seen in the influential public press. This means I could have found other influential outliers (Al Jazeera and CNN) in the private press, if I had an equal volume of news articles from the private press.

The fourth consideration will be to consider studying the electronic press either separately or together with the newspapers. This might help in describing the resistance issue, since there is a discussion of an emerging African narrative style in local language radio and TV broadcasting that is oppositional to Western journalistic standards and ethics.

Future researchers could look into the geographical composition of foreign news coverage in the Ghanaian press and include more countries with similar and dissimilar press freedom and colonial orientations and language. These could add further colour and depth to the empirical discoveries in this study.

Appendices

Appendix I

Ethnographic Interview Design

Week	Day	Task	Strategy	Notes/Comments/Questions/Remarks
One	One	Introduction to key staff and lunch	Observation	Conversation between participant and myself
One	One	Explaining the research objectives	Conversational/Observation	Conversation between participant and myself: Observing processes
One	Two	Explaining the research objectives in detail and identify activities	Conversational/Observation	Conversation between participant and myself: Observing processes
One	Three	Start serious conversation	Conversational/Observation	Could you describe what you envisaged doing as a journalist when you were training as a journalist? Did you envisage ever working in this capacity? For how long have you been working on foreign news at this newspaper including elsewhere?

One	Three	Identify the interests of the journalist	Conversational/ Observation	Could you describe a typical day behind this desk? Could you describe how you feel reading your paper each morning?
One	Four	Determine the influences on the work of the participants	Conversational/ Observation	Could you tell me what in your view shapes the way you work? Could you please describe what you would have wished shaped much of your work? Tell me about the way you select your news and the processes involved in it up to publication.
One	Five	Identify what the interviewee might want to discuss	Conversational/ Observation	Could you tell me a story about foreign news that stays with me over the weekend? It could be about your wishes, desires, or hopes.
One	Six	Determine the weight of influence of Transnational News Agencies	Observation/ Reconstructive interview	Could you explain why this graph showing the influence of Transnational News Agencies (TNAs) looks like this? Could you explain which TNA is your personal favourite and why that is the case? What do you think your own correspondents covering foreign news will look like? Are there any Kweku Ananse stories that represent our discussion today?

Two	One	Intermedia preference	Conversational interview	Is there any special relationship with a foreign news agency you might want to mention?
				Would you say you follow specific TNAs more than others and do you share their views?
Two	Two	Discover conditions that shape foreign news selection	Conversational interview	Could you tell me what factors in daily experience determine selection of the foreign news?
				Is there a control you exercise over these factors? How do you do it?
Two	Two	Economics	Conversational interview	Does your paper's profitability determine how much you dedicate to foreign news? How do you handle this?
				Are there other factors I cannot see through my observation but you think influences you? Could you describe to me how you know this?
				Tell me anything about this paper's economic rationality and how it influences your content?
Two	Three	The colonial influence	Conversational interview	Could you please tell me about how you overcame colonial influences, if there are any? Language, education, worldviews, access etc.

Two	Four	Africa	Conversational and reconstructive interview	Check this graph for a minute. Ask me for an explanation for anything you don't understand. Could you tell me how you feel about the coverage of Africa in your newspaper? Could you tell me, in your view, what accounted for this? Tell me a story that represents your feelings about Africa at the moment?
Two	Five	Way forward	Conversational interview	What are your experiences in reporting Africa? Who is responsible for these images? How do you think Africa can be better covered? What is the way forward?
Two	Five	Winding down	Observations and reconnection of thoughts	Boiled corn party

Semi-Structured Interviews

1. How much influence do you have on what appears on the foreign page every day?
2. What is your position on the issue that African stories are perceived as a reproduction of foreign news agencies?
3. How do you think your foreign news affects Ghanaians' views of Africa?
4. What level of importance do you think your newspaper attaches to foreign news?
5. How often are foreign news stories discussed at the final editorial meeting?
6. Could you recount concerns and issues you foresee as the major challenges in reporting on Africa?
7. What recommendations would you give as a better way of communicating African foreign news?
8. Would you say the negative images carried in the Ghanaian press are yours or those of foreign journalists from whom you have borrowed material?
9. Do these findings invoke any feelings of postcolonial domination in you?
10. Do you think you will one day be free of relying on foreign news agencies?
11. What shall account for this (if Yes), and if No, what is impeding this process?

Questions for General Manager/Editor

12. Would you say the size of your newspaper influences how much attention you give to foreign news?
13. Do you see any link between foreign news and profitability?
14. What would you say is the biggest challenge of reporting foreign news especially about Africa?
15. What is the way forward?

Appendix II: Code Sheet for Sources

Part I

Date of Article..

Newspaper..

Ownership..

Location...

BBC=1, Reuters=2, AP=3, AFP=4, Xinhua=5, Own Reporter=6, CNN=7, Others=8 and Unsourced=9. For information on how to use the code sheet, refer to Appendix III.

Date	1	#	2	#	3	#	4	#	5	#	6	#	7	#	8	#	9	#	Total
	1		2		3		4		5		6		7		8		9		
	1		2		3		4		5		6		7		8		9		
	1		2		3		4		5		6		7		8		9		
	1		2		3		4		5		6		7		8		9		
	1		2		3		4		5		6		7		8		9		
	1		2		3		4		5		6		7		8		9		
	1		2		3		4		5		6		7		8		9		
	1		2		3		4		5		6		7		8		9		
	1		2		3		4		5		6		7		8		9		
	1		2		3		4		5		6		7		8		9		
	1		2		3		4		5		6		7		8		9		
	1		2		3		4		5		6		7		8		9		
	1		2		3		4		5		6		7		8		9		
	1		2		3		4		5		6		7		8		9		
	1		2		3		4		5		6		7		8		9		
	1		2		3		4		5		6		7		8		9		
	1		2		3		4		5		6		7		8		9		
	1		2		3		4		5		6		7		8		9		
	1		2		3		4		5		6		7		8		9		
	1		2		3		4		5		6		7		8		9		
	1		2		3		4		5		6		7		8		9		
	1		2		3		4		5		6		7		8		9		
	1		2		3		4		5		6		7		8		9		
	1		2		3		4		5		6		7		8		9		
	1		2		3		4		5		6		7		8		9		
Total	1		2		3		4		5		6		7		8		9		

Part II

Direction of the Article..

Thematic Categories..

Frames..

Appendix III

Coding Protocol

Instructions

Part I

This Appendix gives explanations for expressions and symbols used for the different items on the coding sheet (Appendix II). There are five parts to the code sheet — the first four items (followed by dotted lines), and the table. Please, read each item section carefully. Beside each item at the top of the page is a dotted line — this is the space within which you indicate an answer. Your answer should take the form of the relevant digit/number.

Date of Article: Here, indicate the date the newspaper article was published. The date should be designated as Day followed by Month and followed by Year, as in this sample — 01/12/12.

Newspaper: Here, put the relevant number of the newspaper that is being coded. If you are coding *The Daily Graphic*, indicate "1"; the *Ghanaian Times*, indicate "2"; the *Daily Guide*, indicate "3"; and for *The Ghanaian Chronicle*, indicate "4".

Ownership: Here, put the relevant number of the ownership of the newspaper that is being coded. If you are coding *The Daily Graphic* or the *Ghanaian Times*, indicate "1"; and the *Daily Guide* or *The Ghanaian Chronicle*, indicate "2".

Location: Here, put the relevant number relating to the location of the article in the newspaper. You have two options. Indicate the number "1" for articles that appear on the Africa page, and "2" for articles that appear on the World/Global page. Coders for a particular newspaper must use separate code sheets for location "1" and location "2".

Sources Cited: The fifth part of the code sheet is a table which documents sources cited by the newspaper. This part documents which sources are quoted or referred to as the source of a news story/article. The article might attribute some statement to other news agencies, but here we are interested in the final transnational news agency that packaged this article. All the newspapers show this information clearly, apart from *The Daily Graphic*, whose format change neglected to include source information this within the chosen period of the study. For this reason, where *The Daily Graphic* articles are concerned, input the lead into "Google.com" and compare the content and identify the source from here. There are eight options for sources cited. Mark the blank space accompanying the relevant number that corresponds to the source cited. The source numbers are as follows: for the British Broadcasting Corporation (BBC), indicate "1"; for Reuters, indicate "2"; for Associated Press (AP), indicate "3"; for Agence France-Press (AFP), indicate "4"; for Xinhua News Agency, indicate "5"; for Own Reporter at that newspaper, indicate "6". Own reporter means a journalist commissioned by the Ghanaian newspaper for the coverage of an international event. For CNN, indicate "7"; for all other international news agencies, indicate "8"; and for articles for which the source could not be traced, indicate "9".

Part II

Direction of the Article: This refers to the tone/quality of the coverage, and is defined in terms of positive, negative or neutral. For positive news stories — e.g. those that reported harmony within and between nations and nationals, co-operations, development, economic growth, easing of tensions — indicate "1". For negative news are stories — e.g. those suggesting conflict unending, misunderstanding, crisis, border disputes, human and natural disaster, poverty, disease, dumping of toxic waste, scandals — indicate "2". For all other news stories that did not fall into any of the two categories mentioned here, indicate "3", which represents "neutral".

Thematic Categories: The thematic categories the study began with included economic, political, social, disaster and personality news. Other categories are expected to emerge from the data.

Frames: Refer to the MAXQDA code system developed for the qualitative coding of the entire text.

Appendix IV

Due to anonymity agreements accepted during the field research, I identify the journalists by alphanumeric codes. There were ten interviews used in this analysis:

1Tms p1 — Interviewed person 1 works for the *Ghanaian Times* newspaper (1st–16th May 2016).

2Gde p2 — Interviewed person 2 works for the *Daily Guide* newspaper (5th–25th June 2016).

3Crs p3 — Interviewed person 3 works for *The Ghanaian Chronicle* newspaper (26th–10th July, 2016).

4Gph p4 — Interviewed person 4 works for *The Daily Graphic* newspaper (17th May–4th June, 2016).

5Gph p5 — Interviewed person 5 works for *The Daily Graphic* newspaper (17th May–4th June, 2016).

6Gph ed p6 — Interviewed person 6 is the editor of *The Daily Graphic* newspaper (17th May–4th June, 2016).

7Gde ed p7 — Interviewed person 7 is the editor of the *Daily Guide* newspaper (5th–25th June 2016).

8Tms ed p8 — Interviewed person 8 is the deputy editor of the *Ghanaian Times* (1st –16th May 2016).

9 Crs ed p9 — Interviewed person 9 is the news editor of *The Ghanaian Chronicle* newspaper (26th–10th July, 2016).

References

Agbese, A.-O. (2006). *The role of the press and communication technology in democratization: The Nigerian story/Aje-Ori Agbese. African studies.* London: Routledge.

Ainslie, R. (1966). *The press in Africa: Communications past and present.* London: Gollancz.

Akinfeleye, R. A., Amobi, I. T., Okoye, I. E., and Sunday, O. (2009). The continued dominance of international news agencies in Nigerian newspapers: Comparing news coverage of the 2008 elections in America and in Ghana. *African Communication Research*, 2(3), 449–72.

Akinfemisoye, M. O. (2013). Challenging hegemonic media practices: Of "alternative" media and Nigeria's democracy. *Ecquid Novi: African Journalism Studies*, 34(1), 7–20, https://doi.org/10.1080/02560054.2013.767419

Alexa.com. (2009). Top sites in Ghana, http://www.alexa.com/topsites/countries/GH

Alozie, E. C. (2007). What did they say? African media coverage of the first 100 days of the Rwanda crisis. In A. Thompson (ed.), *The media and the Rwanda genocide* (pp. 211–30). London: Pluto.

Altheide, D. L. (1987). Reflections: Ethnographic content analysis. *Qualitative Sociology*, 10(1), 65–77, https://doi.org/10.1007/BF00988269

Altheide, D. L. (1994). An ecology of communication: Toward a mapping of the effective environment. *The Sociological Quarterly*, 35(4), 665–83, https://doi.org/10.1111/j.1533-8525.1994.tb00422.x

Altheide, D. L. (2000). Identity and the definition of the situation in a mass-mediated context. *Symbolic Interaction*, 23(1), 1–27, https://doi.org/10.1525/si.2000.23.1.1

Altheide, D. L., and Johnson, J. M. (1994). Criteria for assessing interpretive validity in qualitative research. In N. K. Denzin and Y. S. Lincoln (ed.), *Handbook of Qualitative Research* (pp. 485–99). Thousand Oaks: SAGE Publications.

Altheide, D. L., and Schneider, C. J. (2013). *Qualitative media analysis* (2nd ed.). Qualitative research methods, Vol. 38. Los Angeles: SAGE Publications.

Altmeppen, K.-D. (2010). The gradual disappearance of foreign news on German television: Is there a future for the global, international, world or foreign news? *Journalism Studies*, 11(4), 567–76, https://doi.org/10.1080/14616701003638459

Amin, S. (2017). Media perspectives: we're missing the story: the media's retreat from foreign reporting. In M. Bunce, S. Franks, and C. Paterson (eds), *Communication and society. Africa's media image in the 21st century. From the "Heart of Darkness" to "Africa Rising"* (pp. 96–98). London: Routledge.

Anfara, V. A., and Mertz, N. T. (eds). (2006). *Theoretical frameworks in qualitative research* (2nd ed.). Thousand Oaks: SAGE Publications, https://dx.doi.org/10.4135/9781412986335

Ankomah, B. (2008). Reporting Africa. *New African Monthly*, June, 12–15.

Ankomah, B. (2011). Reporting Africa. *Global Media Journal African Edition*, 2(2), https://doi.org/10.5789/2-2-28

Anokwa, K., Lin, C. A., and Salwen, M. B. (eds). (2003). *International communication: Concepts and cases*. Belmont: Wadsworth/Thomson Learning.

Ansu-Kyeremeh, K., and Karikari, K. (1998). *Media Ghana: Ghanaian media overview, practitioners and institutions*. Legon: School of Communication Studies, University of Ghana.

Asante, C. E. (1996). *The press in Ghana: Problems and prospects*. Lanham: University Press of America.

Ashcroft, B., Griffiths, G., and Tiffin, H. (1995). *The post-colonial studies reader*. New York: Routledge.

Awoonor, K. N. (1996). Challenges for the media in West Africa. In K. Blay-Amihere and N. Alabi (ed.). *State of the media in West Africa*. Accra: FEF.

Ayres, L., Kavanaugh, K., and Knafl, K. A. (2003). Within-case and across-case approaches to qualitative data analysis. *Qualitative Health Research*, 13(6), 871–83, https://doi.org/10.1177/1049732303013006008

B'béri, B. E. de, and Louw, P. E. (2011). Afro-pessimism: A genealogy of discourse. *Critical Arts*, 25(3), 335–46, https://doi.org/10.1080/02560046.2011.615118

Bach, D. (2013). Africa in international relations: The frontier as concept and metaphor. *South African Journal of International Affairs*, 20(1), 1–22, https://doi.org/10.1080/10220461.2013.783283

Bagdikian, B. H. (2004). *The new media monopoly* (7th ed.). Boston: Beacon.

Barker, M. J. (2008). Democracy or polyarchy? US-funded media developments in Afghanistan and Iraq post 9/11. *Media, Culture and Society*, 30(1), 109–30, https://doi.org/10.1177/0163443708088615

Barthels, M. (2016). 5 key takeaways about the state of the news media in 2016, *Pew Research Center*, 15 June, http://www.pewresearch.org/fact-tank/2016/06/15/state-of-the-news-media-2016-key-takeaways/

Barton, F. (2014). *Press of Africa: Persecution and perseverance*. Lanham: Palgrave Macmillan.

B'beri, B. E. de, and Audette-Longo, M. (2009). Key concepts in the work of Arnold Shepperson: Representing communication and collaboration. *Critical Arts*, 23(2), 153–70, https://doi.org/10.1080/02560040903016909

Becker, L. B., and Tudor, V. (2005). *Non-U.S. funders of media assistance projects*. James M. Cox Center for International Mass Communication Training and Research, University of Georgia, https://www.cima.ned.org/wp-content/uploads/2015/02/CIMA-Non-US_Funding_of_Media_Development.pdf

Beer, A. S. de. (2010). News from and in the "dark continent". *Journalism Studies*, 11(4), 596–609, https://doi.org/10.1080/14616701003638509

Beharrell, P. (1980). *More bad news*. Bad news, Vol. 2. London: Routledge and Kegan Paul.

Berelson, B. (1952). *Content analysis in communication research*. Glencoe: Free Press.

Berger, G. (2014). What it means to work towards excellence in African Journalism Education. In B. Franklin and D. Mensing (ed.), *Routledge research in journalism: Vol. 2. Journalism education, training and employment* (pp. 33–47). New York: Routledge.

Bernard, H. R. (2002). *Research methods in anthropology — qualitative and quantitative approaches*. Walnut Creek, CA: Altamira Press.

Bernard, H. R. (2006). *Research methods in anthropology: Qualitative and quantitative approaches* (4th ed.). Walnut Creek, CA: Altamira Press.

Bertrand, I., and Hughes, P. (2005). *Media research methods: Audiences, institutions, texts*. Basingstoke: Palgrave Macmillan.

Bhabha, H. K. (1985). Signs taken for wonders: Questions of ambivalence and authority under a tree outside Delhi, May 1817. *Critical Inquiry*, 12(1), 44–165, https://doi.org/10.1086/448325

Bhabha, H. K. (1994). *The location of culture*. London: Routledge.

Bhabha, H. K. (1995). Interview with Homi Bhabha. *Artforum*, 33(7), 80–84.

Bookmiller, R. J., and Bookmiller, K.N. (1992). Dateline Algeria: U.S. press coverage of the Algerian war of independence. In B. G. Hawk (ed.), *Africa's media image* (pp. 62–76). New York: Praeger.

Borowski, R. (2012). People's perceptions of Africa. *Race Equality Teaching*, 30(3), 24–27, https://doi.org/10.18546/ret.30.3.07

Bosompra, K. (1989). African news in the world press: A comparative content analysis of a North and South newspaper. *African Media Review*, 3(3), 58–69, http://pdfproc.lib.msu.edu/?file=/DMC/African%20Journals/pdfs/africa%20media%20review/vol3no3/jamr003003005.pdf

Bourdieu, P. (1998). *On television*. Translated by Priscilla Parkhurst Ferguson. New York: New Press.

Boyd-Barrett, O. (2004). Understanding: The second Casualty. In S. Allan and B. Zelizer (eds), *Reporting war. Journalism in wartime* (pp. 25–42). London: Routledge.

Boyle, T. P. (2001). Inter-media agenda setting in the 1996 presidential election. *Journalism and Mass Communication Quarterly*, 78(1), 26–44, https://doi.org/10.1177/107769900107800103

Bunce, M. (2015). International news and the image of Africa: new storytellers, new narratives? In J. Gallagher (ed.), *Images of Africa. Creation, negotiation and subversion* (pp. 42–62). Manchester: Manchester University Press, https://doi.org/10.7228/manchester/9780719091469.003.0003

Bunce, M. (2017). The International news coverage of Africa: beyond the "single story". In M. Bunce, S. Franks and C. Paterson (eds), *Communication and society. Africa's media image in the 21st century. From the "Heart of Darkness" to "Africa Rising"* (pp. 15–29). London: Routledge.

Bunce, M., Franks, S., and Paterson, C. (eds). (2017). *Africa's media image in the 21st century: From the "Heart of Darkness" to "Africa Rising". Communication and society*. London: Routledge.

Campbell, W. J. (1998). *The emergent independent press in Benin and Côte d'Ivoire: From voice of the state to advocate of democracy*. London: Praeger.

Carey, J. W. (1974). Journalism and Criticism: The Case of an Undeveloped Profession. The Review of Politics, 36(2), 227–49

Castells, M. (1996). *The rise of the network society. The information age: Economy, society and culture: Vol. 1*. Malden, MA: Blackwell.

Catenaccio, P., Cotter, C., Smedt, M. de, Garzone, G., Jacobs, G., Macgilchrist, F., Lams, L., Perrin, D., Richardson, J. E., Van Hout, T., Van Praet, E. (2011). Towards a linguistics of news production. *Journal of Pragmatics*, 43(7), 1843–52, https://doi.org/10.1016/j.pragma.2010.09.022

Chang, T.-K., and Lee, J.-W. (1992). Factors affecting gatekeepers' selection of foreign news: A national survey of newspaper editors. *Journalism and Mass Communication Quarterly*, 69(3), 554–61, https://doi.org/10.1177/107769909206900303

Chang, T.-K., Shoemaker, P. J., and Brendlinger, N. (1987). Determinants of international news coverage in the U.S. media. *Communication Research*, 14(4), 396–414, https://doi.org/10.1177/009365087014004002

Chaudhary, A. G. (2001). A comparative content analytical study of negative news in western and third world newspapers. *Asian Journal of Communication*, 11(1), 25–50, https://doi.org/10.1080/01292980109364791

Cohen, A. A. (ed.). (2013). *Foreign news on television: Where in the world is the global village?* New York: Peter Lang.

Cohen, A., and Court, D. Ethnography and case study: A comparative analysis. *Academic Exchange Quarterly*, https://www.thefreelibrary.com/Ethnography+and+case+study%3a+a+comparative+analysis.-a0111848865

Cottle, S. (2009). Global crises in the news: Staging new wars, disasters, and climate change. *International Journal of Communication*, 3, 494–516.

Crane, D. (2002). Culture and globalisation theoretical models and emerging trends. In D. Crane, N. Kawashima and K. Kawasaki (eds), *Global culture. Media, arts, policy, and globalization* (pp. 1–25). New York, London: Routledge.

Creswell, J. W. (2004). *Educational research: Planning, conducting, and evaluating quantitative and qualitative research. Instructor's manual with test bank+Ppt slides*. Upper Saddle River, NJ: Pearson Prentice Hall.

Creswell, J. W. (2012). *Educational research: Planning, conducting, and evaluating quantitative and qualitative research* (4th ed.). Boston: Pearson.

Creswell, J. W. (2014). Research design: Qualitative, quantitative, and mixed methods approaches (4th ed.). Los Angeles: SAGE Publications.

Creswell, J. W., and Miller, D. L. (2000). Determining validity in qualitative inquiry. *Theory into Practice*, 39(3), 124–30, https://doi.org/10.1207/s15430421tip3903_2

da Costa. (1980). News criteria for the selection of news in Africa. In A. L. d. Costa (ed.), *News values and principles of cross-cultural communication* (pp. 6–15). Paris: UNESCO, http://unesdoc.unesco.org/images/0003/000370/037072Eo.pdf

Dakroury, A., and Hoffmann, J. (2010). Communication as a human right: A blind spot in communication research? *International Communication Gazette*, 72(4–5), 315–22, https://doi.org/10.1177/1748048510363627

Danielian, L. H., and Reese, S. D. (1989). A closer look at intermedia influence agenda setting: The cocaine issue of 1986. In P. J. Shoemaker (ed.), *Communication textbook series. Communication campaigns about drugs. Government, media, and the public* (pp. 47–63). Hillsdale, NJ: L. Erlbaum Associates.

Darnton, A. (2005). *Comic relief "public perceptions of poverty", omnibus survey wave 2 findings, summary report*. London: DFID.

Deacon, D., Pickering, M., Golding, P., and Murdock, G. (1999). *Researching communications*. London: Arnold.

Deuze, M. (2008). Understanding journalism as news work: How it changes, and how it remains the same. *Westminster Papers in Communication and Culture*, 5(2), 5–24, https://doi.org/10.16997/wpcc.61

Dierckx de Casterlé, B., Gastmans, C., Bryon, E., and Denier, Y. (2012). QUAGOL: A guide for qualitative data analysis. *International journal of nursing studies*, 49(3), 360–71, https://doi.org/10.1016/j.ijnurstu.2011.09.012

Domatob, J. K. (1988). Sub-Saharan Africa's media and neo-colonialism. *Africa Media Review*, 3(1), http://docplayer.net/31483593-Available-through-a-partnership-with.html

Dover, C., and Barnett, S. (2004). *The world on the box: International issues in news and factual programmes on UK television, 1975–2003*. London: 3WE.

Du, Y. R. (2013). Intermedia agenda-setting in the age of globalization: A multinational agenda-setting test. *Global Media and Communication*, 9(1), 19–36, https://doi.org/10.1177/1742766512463038

Dzisah, W. S. (2008). *The news media and democracy in Ghana (1992–2000)* (Doctoral dissertation, University of Westminster, Westminster, UK).

Eek, H. (1979). Principles governing the use of the mass media as defined by the United Nations and UNESCO. In K. Nordenstreng and H. L. Schiller (eds), *Communication and information science. National sovereignty and international communication* (pp. 173–94). Norwood, NJ: Ablex Publishing Corporation.

Eilders, C. (2006). News factors and news decisions. Theoretical and methodological advances in Germany. *Communications*, 31(1), https://doi.org/10.1515/COMMUN.2006.002

Ekwelie, S. A., and Edoga-Ugwuoju, D. (1985). Ownership patterns of Ghanaian newspapers: An historical perspective. *Gazette (Leiden, Netherlands)*, 35(1), 49–59, https://doi.org/10.1177/001654928503500104

El Zein, H. M., and Cooper, A. (1992). The New York coverage of Africa 1976–1990. In B. G. Hawk (ed.), *Africa's media image* (pp. 121–32). New York, London: Praeger.

Elasmer, M. G. and Bennett, K. (2003). The cultural imperialism paradigm revisited: Origin and evaluation. In M. G. Elasmer (ed.), *The impact of international television. Paradigm shift* (pp. 1–17). Mahwah, NJ: Erlbaum.

Elliott, P. and Golding, P. (1979). *Making the news*. London: Longman.

Evans, M. (2011). Rainbow worriers: South African Afro-pessimism online. *Critical Arts*, 25(3), 397–422, https://doi.org/10.1080/02560046.2011.615142

Fair, J. E. (1993). War, famine, and poverty: Race in the construction of Africa's media image. *Journal of Communication Inquiry*, 17(2), 5–22, https://doi.org/10.1177/019685999301700202

Fanon, F. (2001). *The wretched of the earth* (repr.). Modern Classics. London: Penguin Books.

Fanon, F. (2008). *Black skin, white masks. Get political.* London: Pluto. [originally published 1952]

Feinberg, H. M., and Solodow, J. B. (2002). Out of Africa. *The journal of African history,* 43(2), 255–61, https://doi.org/10.1017/S0021853701008118

Fengler, S., and Russ-Mohl, S. (2008). Journalists and the information-attention markets: Towards an economic theory of journalism. *Journalism,* 9(6), 667–90, https://doi.org/10.1177/1464884908096240

FES. (2014). *African media barometer: The first home-grown analysis of the media landscape in Africa: Ghana 2013.* Windhoek: FES, https://library.fes.de/pdf-files/bueros/africa-media/10807.pdf

Fetterman, D. M. (1984). *Ethnography in educational evaluation.* Sage focus editions, Vol. 68. Beverly Hills: SAGE Publications.

Fielding, N., and Lee, R. M. (1998). *Computer analysis and qualitative research. New technologies for social research.* London: SAGE Publications.

Fiest, S. (2001). Facing down the global village: the media impact. In R. Kugler and E. Frost (eds), *The global century* (pp. 709–25). Washington, DC: National Defense University Press.

Flamenbaum, R. (2017). A "new Ghana" in a rising Africa. In M. Bunce, S. Franks and C. Paterson (eds), *Communication and society. Africa's media image in the 21st century. From the "Heart of Darkness" to "Africa Rising"* (pp. 116–25). London: Routledge.

Foote, J. S., and Steele, M. E. (1986). Degree of conformity in lead stories in early evening network TV newscasts. *Journalism and Mass Communication Quarterly,* 63(1), 19–23, https://doi.org/10.1177/107769908606300103

Franks, S. (2005). Lacking a Clear Narrative: Foreign Reporting after the Cold War. *The Political Quarterly,* 76, 91–101, https://doi.org/10.1111/j.1467-923X.2006.00751.x

Franks, S. (2006). The CARMA report: Western media coverage of humanitarian disasters. *The Political Quarterly,* 77(2), 281–84, https://doi.org/10.1111/j.1467-923X.2006.00771.x

Franks, S. (2005). Reporting Africa: Problems and Perspectives. *Westminster Papers in Communication and Culture,* Special Issue, November 2005, 129–34, https://www.westminsterpapers.org/articles/10.16997/wpcc.46/galley/45/download/

French, H. W. (2017). Media perspectives: how does Africa get reported? A letter of concern to 60 Minutes. In M. Bunce, S. Franks and C. Paterson (eds), *Communication and society. Africa's media image in the 21st century. From the "Heart of Darkness" to "Africa Rising"* (pp. 38–39). London: Routledge

Fuchs, C. (2010). New imperialism. *Global Media and Communication,* 6(1), 33–60, https://doi.org/10.1177/1742766510362018

Fuss, D. (1989). *Essentially speaking: Feminism, nature and difference*. New York: Routledge.

Galtung, J. (1971). A structural theory of imperialism. *Journal of Peace Research*, 8(2), 81–117, https://doi.org/10.1177/002234337100800201

Galtung, J., and Ruge, M. H. (1965). The structure of foreign news. *Journal of Peace Research*, 2(1), 64–90, https://doi.org/10.1177/002234336500200104

Gandhi, I. (1984). *Selected speeches and writings of Indira Gandhi*. New Delhi: Ministry of Information and Broadcasting.

Gans, H. J. (1979). *Deciding what's news: A study of CBS Evening News, NBC Nightly News, Newsweek, and Time*. Evanston, IL: Medill School of Journalism Visions of the American Press Series, Northwestern University Press.

Gans, H. J. (2004). *Deciding what's news: A study of CBS evening news, NBC nightly news, Newsweek, and Time. Visions of the American press*. Evanston, IL: Medill School of Journalism Visions of the American Press Series, Northwestern University Press.

Gavrilos, D. (2002). Arab Americans in a nation's imagined community: How news constructed Arab American reaction to the gulf war. *Journal of Communication Inquiry*, 26(4), 426–45, https://doi.org/10.1177/019685902236900

Giddens, A. (2003). *The consequences of modernity* (repr.). Stanford: Stanford University Press.

Gilboa, E. (2005). The CNN effect: The search for a communication theory of international relations. *Political Communication*, 22(1), 27–44, https://doi.org/10.1080/10584600590908429

Gilroy, P. (2000). *Against race: Imagining political culture beyond the color line*. Cambridge, MA: Belknap Press of Harvard University Press.

Girardet, E. R. (1996). Reporting humanitarianism: Are the electronic media making a difference? In R. I. Rotberg and T. G. Weiss (eds), *From massacres to genocide. The media, public policy, and humanitarian crises* (pp. 45–67). Washington, DC: Brookings Institution.

Gitlin, T. (2003). *The whole world is watching: Mass media in the making and unmaking of the New Left*. Berkeley, CA: University of California Press.

Glaser, B. G., and Strauss, A. L. (1967, 2006). *The discovery of grounded theory: Strategies for qualitative research*. New York: Aldine de Gruyter.

Golan, G., and Wanta, W. (2003). International elections on US network news: An examination of factors affecting newsworthiness. *International Communication Gazette*, 65(1), 25–39, https://doi.org/10.1177/0016549203065001135

Golan, G. J. (2008). Where in the world is Africa? Predicting coverage of Africa by US television networks. *International Communication Gazette*, 70(1), 41–57, https://doi.org/10.1177/1748048507084577

Golan, G. (2006). Inter-media agenda setting and global news coverage. *Journalism Studies*, 7(2), 323–33, https://doi.org/10.1080/14616700500533643

Golan, G. J., and Himelboim, I. (2016). Can World System Theory predict news flow on twitter? The case of government-sponsored broadcasting. *Information, Communication and Society*, 19(8), 1150–70, https://doi.org/10.1080/1369118X.2015.1106572

Goldberg, D. T., and Quayson, A. (2002). *Relocating postcolonialism*. Oxford: Blackwell.

Golding, P. (1977). Media professionalism in the Third World: The transfer of an ideology. In J. Curran, M. Gurevitch and J. Woollacott (eds), *Mass communication and society* (pp. 291–301). Set books (Open University). London: Edward Arnold for the Open University Press.

Gongo, K. (2007). *Distinctly African. The representation of African in the City Press* (Master's dissertation, University of Witwatersrand, Johannesburg), http://wiredspace.wits.ac.za/bitstream/handle/10539/4952/GongoK_Thesis.pdf;jses sionid=4AB2175A8D66BC6F313205DC804299C8?sequence=3

Graphic Communication Group Ltd. (2012). Annual Report, http://corporate.graphic.com.gh/images/pdfs/2012_graphic_annual_report.pdf

Graubart, J. (1989). What's news: A progressive framework for evaluating the international debate over the news. *California Law Review*, 77(3), 629–63, https://doi.org/10.2307/3480564

Groshek, J., and Clough Groshek, M. (2013). Agenda trending: Reciprocity and the predictive capacity of social network sites in intermedia agenda-setting across issues over time. *SSRN Electronic Journal*, https://doi.org/10.2139/ssrn.2199144

Grossberg, L. (1982). The ideology of communication: Post-structuralism and the limits of communication. *Man and World*, 15(1), 83–101, https://doi.org/10.1007/BF01248547

Gruley, J., and Duvall, C. S. (2012). The evolving narrative of the Darfur conflict as represented in *The New York Times* and *The Washington Post*, 2003–2009, *GeoJournal*, 77(1), 29–46, https://doi.org/10.1007/s10708-010-9384-4

Guba, E. G., and Lincoln, Y. S. (2005). Paradigmatic controversies, contradictions, and emerging confluences. In N. K. Denzin and Y. S. Lincoln (eds), *The SAGE handbook of qualitative research* (3rd ed., pp. 191–215). Thousand Oaks, London: SAGE Publications.

Guo, L., and Vargo, C. J. (2017). Global intermedia agenda-setting: A big data analysis of international news flow. *Journal of Communication*, 67(4), 499–520, https://doi.org/10.1111/jcom.12311

Hachten, W. A. (1971). *The muffled drums: The news media in Africa*. Ames: The Iowa State University Press.

Hachten, W. A. (2004). Reporting Africa's problems. In C. Okigbo and F. Eribo (eds), *Development and communication in Africa* (pp. 79–87). Oxford: Rowman and Littlefield.

Hachten, W. A., and Scotton, J. F. (2012). *The world news prism: Challenges of digital communication* (8th ed.). Chichester: Wiley-Blackwell.

Hachten, W. A., and Scotton, J. F. (2016). *The world news prism: Digital, social and interactive* (9th ed.). Chichester: Wiley-Blackwell.

Hahn, O., Lönnendonker, J., and Schröder, R. (eds). (2008). *Deutsche Auslandskorrespondenten: Ein Handbuch*. Konstanz: UVk Verlagsgesellschaft.

Hall, R. (2013). Farming and food in Africa and the mounting battle over land, water and resource rights. *GREAT Insights Magazine*, 3(1), http://ecdpm.org/great-insights/family-farming-and-food-security/farming-food-africa-battle-land-water-rights/

Hall, S. (1986). The problem of ideology; Marxism without guarantees. *Journal of Communication Inquiry*, 10(2), 28–44, https://doi.org/10.1177/019685998601000203

Hall, S. (1997). *Representation: Cultural representations and signifying practices. Culture, media and identities: bk.2*. London: SAGE in association with the Open University.

Hallin, D. C., and Mancini, P. (2004). *Comparing media systems: Three models of media and politics. Communication, society and politics*. Cambridge: Cambridge University Press.

Hamelink, C. (ed.). (1981). *Communication in the Eighties: A reader on the MacBride Report*. Rome: IDOC International.

Hammersley, M., and Atkinson, P. (2007). *Ethnography: Principles in practice* (3rd ed.). London: Routledge.

Hancock, A. and Hamelink, C. (1999). Many more voice, another world: Looking back at the MacBride recommendations. In R. C. Vincent, K. Nordenstreng and M. Traber (eds), *The Hampton Press communication series. International communication. Towards equity in global communication. MacBride update* (pp. 269–304). Cresskill, NJ.: Hampton Press.

Hansen, A., Cottle, S., Negrine, R., and Newbold, C. (eds). (1998). *Mass communication research methods*. Basingstoke: Macmillan.

Harcup, T., and O'Neill, D. (2001). What is news? Galtung and Ruge revisited. *Journalism Studies*, 2(2), 261–80, https://doi.org/10.1080/14616700118449

Harding, F. (2003). Africa and the moving image: Television, film and video. *Journal of African Cultural Studies*, 16(1), 69–84, https://doi.org/10.1080/1369681032000169276

Harrison, J. (2006). *News. Routledge introductions to media and communications*. London: Routledge.

Harth, A. (2012). *Representations of Africa in the Western News Media: Reinforcing Myths and Stereotypes.* Retrieved 2-August 2020 from https://pol.illinoisstate.edu/downloads/conferences/2012/1BHarth.pdf

Hasty, J. (2005). *The press and political culture in Ghana.* Bloomington: Indiana University Press.

Haule, J. J. (1984). International press coverage of African events: The dilemma and the future. *International Communication Gazette,* 33(2), 107–14, https://doi.org/10.1177/001654928403300203

Hawk, B. G. (ed.). (1992). *Africa's media image.* New York, London: Praeger.

Hawkins, R. (1997). Prospects for a global communication infrastructure in the 21st century: Institutional restructuring and network development. In A. Sreberny- Mohammadi (ed.), *Foundations in media. Media in global context. A reader* (pp. 177–93). London: Arnold.

Herman, E. S., and Chomsky, N. (2008). *Manufacturing consent: The political economy of the mass media* (Anniversary edition, with a new afterword by Edward S. Herman). London: Bodley Head.

Hester, A. (1973). Theoretical considerations in predicting volume and direction of international information flow. *International Communication Gazette,* 19(4), 239–47, https://doi.org/10.1177/001654927301900404

Higgins, D. (2014). The Western way: Democracy and the media assistance model, *Global Media Journal,* 4(2), 2–16.

Hoffmann, J. (2010). *Communication rights, democracy and legitimacy: The European Union.* Saarbrücken: LAP LAMBERT Academic Publishing AG and Co. KG.

Holm, N. G. (2016). Best practices of television journalism in Europe: How Anglo- American on-camera styles violate cultural values, Denmark as a case study. *Journalism and Mass Communication Educator,* 60(4), 376–89, https://doi.org/10.1177/107769580506000406

Høyer, S. (2005). The idea of the book. In S. Høyer and H. Pöttker (ed.), *Diffusion of news paradigm. 1850–2000* (pp. 9–16). Gothenburg: Nordicom.

Hume, E. (2004). *The media missionaries: American support of journalism excellence and press freedom around the globe.* Miami: The John S. and James L. Knight Foundation.

Hunter-Gault, C. (2008). *New news out of Africa: Uncovering Africa's renaissance.* New York: Oxford University Press.

Ibelema, M., and Bosch, T. (2009). Sub-Saharan Africa. In A. S. de Beer (ed.), *Global journalism. Topical issues and media systems* (5th ed., pp. 293–336). Boston: Pearson/Allyn and Bacon.

Jacobs, G., Pander Maat, H., and van Hout, T. (2008). The discourse of news management. *Pragmatics,* 18(1), 1–8, https://doi.org/10.1075/prag.18.1.01jac

Jennings, B. M. (2007). Qualitative analysis: A case of software or "peopleware"? *Research in Nursing and Health*, 30(5), 483–84, https://doi.org/10.1002/nur.20238

Johnson, M. A. (1997). Predicting News Flow from Mexico. *Journalism and Mass Communication Quarterly*, 74(2), 315–30, https://doi.org/10.1177/107769909707400206

Jones-Quartey, K. A. B. (1974). *A summary history of the Ghana press, 1822–1960*. Accra: Ghana Information Services Dept.

Karikari, K. (1992). The "Anti-white press" campaign: The opposition of the African press to the establishment of *The Daily Graphic* by the British Mirror Newspaper Company in Ghana, 1950. *International Communication Gazette*, 49(3), 215–32, https://doi.org/10.1177/001654929204900304

Karikari, K. (1998). The press and the transition to multiparty democracy in Ghana. In K. A. Ninsin (ed.), *Ghana: Transition to democracy* (pp. 189–210). Accra: CODESRIA.

Kasoma, F. P. (1996). The foundations of African ethics (Afriethics) and the professional practice of journalism: The case for society-centred media morality. *Africa Media Review*, 10(3), 93–116.

Keane, F. (2004). Trapped in a time-warped narrative. *Nieman Reports*, http://niemanreports.org/articles/trapped-in-a-time-warped-narrative/

Kondracki, N. L., Wellman, N. S., and Amundson, D. R. (2002). Content analysis: Review of methods and their applications in nutrition education. *Journal of Nutrition Education and Behavior*, 34(4), 224–30, https://doi.org/10.1016/S1499-4046(06)60097-3

Kothari, A. (2008). *A study of The New York Times Coverage of the Dafur, Sudan Conflict, July 2003–July 2006* (Master's dissertation, University of Oregon).

Kracauer, S. (1952). The challenge of qualitative content analysis. *Public Opinion Quarterly*, 16(4), 631–42, https://doi.org/10.1086/266427

Kraidy, M. M. (2002). Hybridity in cultural globalization. *Communication Theory*, 12(3), 316–39, https://doi.org/10.1111/j.1468-2885.2002.tb00272.x

Krippendorff, K. (1980). Validity in content analysis. In E. Mochmann (ed.), *Computerstrategien fur die kommunikationsanalyse* (pp. 69–112). Frankfurt: Campus, https://repository.upenn.edu/asc_papers/291/

Krippendorff, K. (2004). *Content analysis: An introduction to its methodology* (2nd ed.). Thousand Oaks, London: SAGE Publications.

Kumar, S. (2014). Media, communication and postcolonial theory. In R. S. Fortner and M. Fackler (eds), *Handbooks in communication and media. The handbook of media and mass communication theory* (pp. 380–99). Chichester: Wiley.

Kuo, E. C. Y., and Xiaoge, X. (2005). MacBride Report 25 Years After. *Media Asia*, 32(2), 63–66, https://doi.org/10.1080/01296612.2005.11726775

Lader, D. (2007). Public attitudes towards development: Knowledge and attitudes concerning poverty in developing countries. *IDS Working Paper*, 353, https://onlinelibrary.wiley.com/doi/pdf/10.1111/j.2040-0209.2010.00353_2.x

Lal Das, D. K. (2008). *Doing social research: A source book for preparing dissertation*. Delhi: Kalpaz Publications.

LeCompte, M. D. (2000). Analysing qualitative data. *Theory into Practice*, 39(3), 146–54, https://doi.org/10.1207/s15430421tip3903_5

LeCompte, M. D., Preissle, J., Tesch, R., and Goetz, J. P. (2008). *Ethnography and qualitative design in educational research* (2nd ed.). Bingley: Emerald Group Pub.

Lent, J. A. (1976). Foreign news content of United States and Asian print media: A literature review and problem analysis. *International Communication Gazette*, 22(3), 169–82, https://doi.org/10.1177/001654927602200304

Lewis, J. (2006). News and the empowerment of citizens. *European Journal of Cultural Studies*, 9(3), 303–19, https://doi.org/10.1177/1367549406066075

Lincoln, Y. S., and Guba, E. G. (1985). *Naturalistic inquiry*. Beverly Hills: SAGE Publications.

Lindlof, T. R., and Taylor, B. C. (2002). *Qualitative communication research methods* (2nd ed.). Thousand Oaks: SAGE Publications.

Lippmann, Walter. (1922). *Public opinion*. New York: Harcourt, Brace and Company.

Loomba, A. (1998). *Colonialism, postcolonialism: The new critical idiom*. London: Routledge.

Lopez-Escobar, E., Llamas, J. P., McCombs, M., and Lennon, F. R. (1998). Two levels of agenda setting among advertising and news in the 1995 Spanish elections. *Political Communication*, 15(2), 225–38, https://doi.org/10.1080/10584609809342367

Mahendran, D. (2007). The facticity of blackness: A non-conceptual approach to race and racism in Fanon's and Merleau-Ponty's phenomenology. *Human Architecture: Journal of the Sociology of Self-Knowledge*, 5, 191–204.

Maier, M. and Ruhrmann, G. (2007). Celebrities in action and other news factors of German TV news 1992–2004 results from a content analysis. *Human Communication*, 11(1), 197–214.

Mano, W. (2005). Exploring the African view of the global. *Global Media and Communication*, 1(1), 50–55, https://doi.org/10.1177/174276650500100112

Mansell, R. and Nordenstreng, K. (2007). Great media and communication debates: WSIS and the MacBride report. *Information Technologies and International Development*, 3(4), 15–36, https://doi.org/10.1162/itid.2007.3.4.15

Mauthner, N. S., and Doucet, A. (2003). Reflexive accounts and accounts of reflexivity in qualitative data analysis. *Sociology*, 37(3), 413–31, https://doi.org/10.1177/00380385030373002

Maxwell, J. A. (2012). *Qualitative research design: An interactive approach* (3rd ed.). Applied social research methods series, Vol. 41. Thousand Oaks, Calif., London: SAGE Publications.

Mayring, P. (2014). *Qualitative content analysis: Theoretical foundation, basic procedures and software solution*. Klagenfurt: AUT.

Mazrui, A. (1978). *Political values and the educated class in Africa*. Los Angeles: University of California Press.

Mbeki, T. (2003). Address at the SANEF Conference on the Media, the AU, NEPAD and Democracy, 12th April 2003, Department of International Relations and Cooperation, Republic of South Africa, http://www.dirco.gov.za/docs/speeches/2003/mbek0412.htm

MacBride, S. (1980). *Many voices, one world: Towards a new, more just and more efficient world information and communication order*. London: Kogan Page.

McCombs, M. (2005). A look at agenda-setting: Past, present and future. *Journalism Studies*, 6(4), 543–57, https://doi.org/10.1080/14616700500250438

McCombs, M. E. (2004). *Setting the Agenda: The mass media and public opinion*. Malden, MA: Polity.

McCombs, M. E. (2014). *Setting the agenda: The mass media and public opinion* (2nd ed.). Cambridge: Polity.

McCombs, M. E., and Shaw, D. L. (1972). The agenda-setting function of mass media. *Public Opinion Quarterly*, 36(2), 176–78, https://doi.org/10.1086/267990

McKercher, C. (2002). *Newsworkers unite: Labor, convergence, and North American newspapers. Critical media studies*. Lanham: Rowman and Littlefield.

Mcnamara, C., and Mong, S. (2005). Performance measurement and management: Some insights from practice. *Australian Accounting Review*, 15(35), 14–28, https://doi.org/10.1111/j.1835-2561.2005.tb00248.x

McPhail, T. L. (2006). *Global communication: Theories, stakeholders and trends* (2nd ed.). Malden, MA: Blackwell.

Mehra, A. (1988). *Newspaper management in the new multimedia age*. Singapore: Asian Mass Communication Research and Information Centre.

Mengara, D. M. (2001). *Images of Africa: Stereotypes and realities*. Trenton, NJ: Africa World Press.

Miles, M. B., Huberman, A. M., and Saldaña, J. (2014). *Qualitative data analysis: A methods sourcebook* (3rd ed.). Thousand Oaks: SAGE Publications.

Miller, J. (2009). NGOs and "modernization" and "democratization" of media. *Global Media and Communication*, 5(1), 9–33, https://doi.org/10.1177/1742766508101312

Minow, N. N. (1961). Television and the public interest. Delivered 9 May 1961, National Association of Broadcasters, Washington, D.C. Transcription by Michael E. Eidenmuller. *American Rhetoric*, https://www.americanrhetoric.com/speeches/newtonminow.htm

Mody, B. (2010). *The geopolitics of representation in foreign news: Explaining Darfur*. Lanham: Lexington Books.

Moeller, S. D. (1999). *Compassion fatigue: How the media sells disease, famine, war and death*. New York: Routledge.

Mowlana, H. (1985). *International flow of information: A global report and analysis*. Paris: UNESCO, https://unesdoc.unesco.org/ark:/48223/pf0000065258

Myers, G., Klak, T., and Koehl, T. (1996). The inscription of difference: News coverage of the conflicts in Rwanda and Bosnia. *Political Geography*, 15(1), 21–46, https://doi.org/10.1016/0962-6298(95)00041-0

Nandy, A. (1988, 1983). *The intimate enemy: Loss and recovery of self under colonialism*. Oxford: Oxford University Press.

National Communications Authority (NCA). (2020). *Authorised VHF-FM Radio Stations as at Second Quarter of 2020*, National Communications Authority: Accra, https://www.nca.org.gh/industry-data-2/authorisations-2/tv-authorisation-2/

National Communications Authority (NCA). (2020). *Authorised VHF-FM Radio Stations as at Second Quarter of 2020*, National Communications Authority: Accra, https://www.nca.org.gh/industry-data-2/authorisations-2/fm-authorisation-2/

Ndlela, N. (2005). The African paradigm: The coverage of the Zimbabwean crisis in the Norwegian media. *Westminster Papers in Communication and Culture*, 2, 71–90, https://doi.org/10.16997/wpcc.43

Neuendorf, K. A. (2002). *The content analysis guidebook*. Thousand Oaks: SAGE Publications.

Nohrstedt, S. A., and Ottosen, R. (2000). Studying the media Gulf war. In S. A. Nohrstedt and R. Ottosen (eds), *Journalism and the new world order* (pp. 11–34). Göteborg: Nordicom.

Nordenstreng, K. (1993). Legal status and significance. In G. Gerbner, H. Mowlana, and K. Nordenstreng (eds), *Communication and information science series. The global media debate. Its rise, fall, and renewal* (pp. 57–68). Norwood, NJ: Ablex.

Nordenstreng, K. (2010). MacBride report as a culmination of NWICO. Keynote at International Colloquium Communication, Université Stendhal, G. 3, Grenoble, 27 –29 January, https://www.researchgate.net/

publication/265036640_MacBride_report_as_a_culmination_of_NWICO/link/5d35b360a6fdcc370a54db21/download

Nordenstreng, K. (2011). Free flow doctrine in global media policy. In R. Mansell and M. Raboy (eds), *Global handbooks in media and communication research. The handbook of global media and communication policy* (pp. 79–94). Malden, MA: Wiley-Blackwell, https://doi.org/10.1002/9781444395433.ch5

Nordenstreng, K. (2012). The New World Information and Communication Order. In A. N. Valdivia et al. (eds), *The international encyclopedia of media studies* (pp. 477–99). Oxford: Blackwell, https://doi.org/10.1002/9781444361506.wbiems023

Nordenstreng, K., and Hannikainen, L. (1984). *The mass media declaration of UNESCO. Communication and information science.* Norwood: Ablex.

Nothias, T. (2012). Definition and scope of Afro-pessimism: Mapping the concept and its usefulness for analysing news media coverage of Africa. *African studies bulletin*, 74, 54–62, https://lucas.leedsac.uk/article/definition-and-scope-of-afro-pessimism-mapping-the-concept-and-its-usefulness-for-analysing-news-media-coverage-of-africa-toussaint-nothias/

Nothias, T. (2015). *Beyond Afro-pessimism? British and French print media discourse on Africa* (Doctoral dissertation, University of Leeds, Leeds).

Nothias, T. (2017). How Western journalists actually write about Africa. *Journalism Studies*, 22(1), 1–22, https://doi.org/10.1080/1461670X.2016.1262748

Nwuneli, O. E., and Udoh, E. (1982). International news coverage in Nigerian newspapers. *International Communication Gazette*, 29(1–2), 31–40, https://doi.org/10.1177/001654928202900103

Nwuneli, O. E., and Dare, O. (1977). The coverage of Angola crisis in the Nigerian press. *Unilag Communication Review*, 1(1), 20–23.

Nyamnjoh, F. B. (2005). *Africa's media, democracy, and the politics of belonging.* London: Zed.

Nyamnjoh, F. B. (2017). Reporting and writing Africa in a world of unequal encounters. In M. Bunce, S. Franks and C. Paterson (eds), *Communication and society. Africa's media image in the 21st century. From the "Heart of Darkness" to "Africa Rising"* (pp. 33–37). London: Routledge.

Nye, J. S. (2004). Soft power and American foreign policy. *Political Science Quarterly*, 119(2), 255–70, https://doi.org/10.2307/20202345

Nye, J. S. (2010). *Cyber power.* Cambridge, MA: Belfer Center for Science and International Affairs.

Obijiofor, L. (2001). Singaporean and Nigerian journalists' perceptions of new technologies. *Australian Journalism Review*, 23(1), 131–51, https://search.informit.com.au/documentSummary;dn=200205150;res=IELAPA

Obijiofor, L. (2009). Is bad news from Africa good news for Western media? *Journal of Global Mass Communication*, 2(3/4), 38–54.

Obijiofor, L., and Green, K. (2001). New technologies and the future of newspapers. *Asia Pacific Media Educator*, 11, 1–13.

Obijiofor, L. (2003). New technologies and journalism practice in Ghana and Nigeria. *Asia Pacific Media Educator*, 14, 36–52.

Obijiofor, L., and Hanusch, F. (2011). *Journalism across cultures: An introduction*. Basingstoke: Palgrave Macmillan.

Obijiofor, L., and Hanusch, F. (2003). Foreign news coverage in five African newspapers. *Australian Journalism Review*, 25(1), 145–64.

Obijiofor, L., and MacKinnon, M. (2016). Africa in the Australian press: Does distance matter? *African Journalism Studies*, 37(3), 41–60, https://doi.org/10.1080/23743670.2016.1210017

Ofori-Birikorang, A. (2009). *Promoting a new health policy in the Ghanaian media: Newspaper framing of the national health insurance scheme from 2005–2007* (Doctoral dissertation, Ohio University, Ohio), https://etd.ohiolink.edu/!etd.send_file?accession=ohiou1249077245&disposition=inline

Ojo, T. (2014). Africa in the Canadian media: *The Globe* and *Mail*'s coverage of Africa from 2003 to 2012. *Ecquid Novi: African Journalism Studies*, 35(1), 43–57, https://doi.org/10.1080/02560054.2014.886660

O'Neill, D., and Harcup, T. (2009). News values and electivity. In K. Wahl-Jorgensen and T. Hanitzsch (eds), *International Communication Association handbook series. The handbook of journalism studies* (pp. 160–74). New York: Routledge.

Opler, M. E. (1945). Themes as dynamic forces in culture. *American Journal of Sociology*, 51(3), 198–206, https://doi.org/10.1086/219787

Östgaard, E. (1965). Factors influencing the flow of news. *Journal of Peace Research*, 2(1), 39–63, https://doi.org/10.1177/002234336500200103

Othman, S. S., Nayan, L. M., and Tiung, L. K. (2014). The elements of news construction model in Malaysia. *Malaysian Journal of Media Studies*, 16(1), 53–62, https://studylib.net/doc/8421388/the-elements-of-news-%20construction-model-in-malaysia

Palmer, J. (2000). *Spinning into control: News values and source strategies. Studies in communication and society*. London, New York: Leicester University Press.

Parenti, M. (1993). *Inventing reality: The politics of news media* (2nd ed.). New York: St. Martin's Press.

Pate, U. A. (1992). Reporting African countries in the Nigerian Press: Perspectives in international news. *Africa Media Review*, 6(1), 59–70, http://pdfproc.lib.msu.edu/?file=/DMC/African%20Journals/pdfs/africa%20media%20review/vol6no1/jamr006001007.pdf

Paterson, C. (2011). *The international television news agencies: The world from London*. New York: Peter Lang.

Paterson, C. (2017). New imperialisms, old stereotypes. In M. Bunce, S. Franks and C. Paterson (eds), *Communication and society. Africa's media image in the 21st century. From the "Heart of Darkness" to "Africa Rising"* (pp. 214–22). London: Routledge.

Prasad, A. (ed.). (2003). *Postcolonial theory and organizational analysis*. New York: Palgrave Macmillan US.

Price, V., and Czilli, E. J. (1996). Modeling patterns of news recognition and recall. *Journal of Communication*, 46(2), 55–78, https://doi.org/10.1111/j.1460-2466.1996.tb01474.x

Reese, Stephen D. and Lee, J. K. (2012). Understanding the content of news media. In H. A. Semetko, H. A. and M. Scammell (ed.), *The SAGE handbook of political communication* (pp. 749–67). London: SAGE Publications.

Riffe, D. (1984). International news borrowing: A trend analysis. *Journalism and Mass Communication Quarterly*, 61(1), 142–48, https://doi.org/10.1177/107769908406100120

Riffe, D., Lacy, S., and Fico, F. (2014). *Analysing media messages: Using quantitative content analysis in research* (3rd ed.). Routledge communication series. London: Routledge.

Roberts, M. S., and Bantimaroudis, P. (1997). Gatekeepers in international news: The Greek media. *The Harvard International Journal of Press/Politics*, 2(2), 62–76, https://doi.org/10.1177/1081180X97002002006

Robins, M. B. (2003). "Lost Boys" and the promised Land: US newspaper coverage of Sudanese refugees. *Journalism*, 4(1), 29–49, https://doi.org/10.1177/1464884903004001110

Robinson, P. (2002). *The CNN effect: The myth of news, foreign policy and intervention*. London: Routledge.

Robson, C. (2011). *Real world research: A resource for users of social research methods in applied settings* (3rd ed.). Oxford: Wiley-Blackwell.

Rodney, W. (1981). *How Europe underdeveloped Africa* (rev. ed.). Washington, DC: Howard University Press.

Rogers, E. M., Dearing, J. W., and Bregman, D. (1993). The anatomy of agenda-setting research. *Journal of Communication*, 43(2), 68–84, https://doi.org/10.1111/j.1460-2466.1993.tb01263.x

Rønning, H. (1997). Institutions and representations. In R. Zhuwararara, K. Gecau and M. Drag (ed.), *Media, democratisation and identity*. Harare: Department of English, University of Zimbabwe.

Rosenblum, M. (1979). *Coups and earthquakes: Reporting the world for America*. New York: Harper and Row.

Ryfe, D. M. (2006). Guest editor's introduction: New institution and the news. *Political Communication*, 23(2), 135–44, https://doi.org/10.1080/10584600600728109

Said, E. W. (1978). *Orientalism*. New York: Vintage Books.

Said, E. W. (2003). Orientalism once more. Lecture given at the Institute of Social Studies, the Hague, the Netherlands, 21 May, https://www.iss.nl/en/media/saidlecture

Sanders, J. (2000). *South Africa and the international media, 1972–1979: A struggle for representation*. London: F. Cass.

Sawant, S. B. (2012). Postcolonial theory: Meaning and Significance. In *Proceedings of national seminar on postmodern literary theory and literature* (pp. 120–26), Nanded, 27–28 January.

Sayed, Z. (2016). *Postcolonial perspective on international knowledge transfer and spillover to Indian news media: From institutional duality to third space*. JIBS dissertation series, Vol. 107. Jönköping: Jönköping University, Jönköping International Business School.

Schiffrin, A. (2010). Not really enough. *Journalism Practice*, 4(3), 405–16, https://doi.org/10.1080/17512781003643244

Schiller, H. I. (1984, 1976). *Communication and cultural domination*. Armonk, NY: M. E. Sharpe.

Schmidt, S. J., and Garrett, H. J. (2011). Reconstituting pessimistic discourses. *Critical Arts*, 25(3), 423–40, https://doi.org/10.1080/02560046.2011.615143

Schoeder, R., and Stovall, J. (2011). The impact of Internet on foreign correspondents' work routines. In P. Gross and G. G. Kopper eds), *Understanding foreign correspondence. A Euro-American perspective of concepts, methodologies, and theories* (pp. 187–93). New York: Peter Lang.

Schorr, V. (2011). Economics of Afro-pessimism: The economics of perception in African foreign direct investment. *Nokoko*, 2, 23–62, https://carleton.ca/africanstudies/wp-content/uploads/Nokoko-Fall-2011-2-Schorr.pdf

Schramm, W. (ed.). (1949). *Mass communications*. Urbana: University of Illinois Press.

Schulz, R. (2008). Readership research. In W. Donsbach (ed.), *The international encyclopedia of communication* (pp. 4115–21). Oxford: Blackwell.

Schulz, W. (1976). *Die Konstruktion von Realität in den Nachrichtenmedien: E. Analyse d. aktuellen Berichterstattung*. Alber-Borschur Kommunikation, Vol. 4. Munich: Alber.

Schwarz, A. (2006). The theory of newsworthiness applied to Mexico's press. How the news factors influence foreign news coverage in a transitional country. *Communications*, 31(1), https://doi.org/10.1515/COMMUN.2006.004

Scott, M. (2009). Marginalized, negative or trivial? Coverage of Africa in the UK press. *Media, Culture and Society*, 31(4), 533–57, https://doi.org/10.1177/0163443709335179

Scott, M. (2015). The myth of representations of Africa. *Journalism Studies*, 18(2), 191–210, https://doi.org/10.1080/1461670X.2015.1044557

Scott, M. (2017). How not to write about writing about Africa. In M. Bunce, S. Franks, and C. Paterson (eds), *Communication and society. Africa's media image in the 21st century. From the "Heart of Darkness" to "Africa Rising"* (pp. 40–51). London: Routledge.

Scotton, J. F., and Murphy, S. M. (1987). Dependency and journalism education in Africa: Are there alternative models. *Africa Media Review*, 1(3), 11–35, http://pdfproc.lib.msu.edu/?file=/DMC/African%20Journals/pdfs/africa%20media%20review/vol1no3/jamr001003003.pdf

Segev, E. (2016). *International news flow online: Global views with local perspectives*. Mass communication and journalism, Vol. 19. New York: Peter Lang.

Sesanti, S. (2009). A case for African culture in journalism curricula. *Communitas*, 14(1), 125–35.

Sharp, J. P. (1993). Publishing American identity: Popular geopolitics, myth and the Reader's Digest. *Political Geography*, 12(6), 491–503, https://doi.org/10.1016/0962-6298

Shiva, V. (2009). Food meets media. *Nordicom Review*, 30, 11–31.

Shoemaker, P. J. (2006). News and newsworthiness: A commentary. *Communications*, 31(1), https://doi.org/10.1515/COMMUN.2006.007

Shoemaker, P. J., and Cohen, A. A. (2006). *News around the world: Content, practitioners, and the public*. London: Routledge.

Shoemaker, P. J., and Reese, S. D. (2014). *Mediating the message in the 21st century: A media Sociology perspective* (3rd edition). New York: Routledge/Taylor and Francis Group.

Shome, R. (2009). Postcolonial studies and communication studies: Mapping new terrains of investigation. *Journal of Global Mass Communication*, 2(3/4), 8–17.

Shome, R., and Hegde, R. S. (2002). Postcolonial approaches to communication: Charting the terrain, engaging the intersections. *Communication Theory*, 12(3), 249–70, https://doi.org/10.1111/j.1468-2885.2002.tb00269.x

Sikanku, E. G. (2011). Intermedia influences among Ghanaian online and print news media: Explicating salience transfer of media agendas. *Journal of Black Studies*, 42(8), 1320–35, https://doi.org/10.1177/0021934711417435

Skewes, E. (2007). *Message control: How news is made on the presidential campaign trail*. Lanham: Rowman and Littlefield.

Skjerdal, T. S. (2012). The three alternative journalisms of Africa. *International Communication Gazette*, 74(7), 636–54, https://doi.org/10.1177/1748048512458559

Slater, D. (2004). *Geopolitics and the post-colonial: Rethinking North–South relations.* Oxford: Blackwell.

Smith, B. O. (1967). Logic, thinking, and teaching. *Educational Theory*, 7(4), 225–33, https://doi.org/10.1111/j.1741-5446.1957.tb01200.x

Snow, D. A., and Benford, R. D. (2000). Clarifying the relationship between framing and ideology in the study of social movements: A comment on Oliver and Johnston. *Mobilization*, 5(1), 55–60.

Sobowale, I. (1987). Image of the world through the eyes of five Nigerian newspapers. *African Media Review*, 2(1), 52–65, http://pdfproc.lib.msu.edu/?file=/DMC/African%20Journals/pdfs/africa%20media%20review/vol2no1/jamr002001006.pdf

Sparkes, V. M. (1978). The flow of news between Canada and the United States. *Journalism Quarterly*, 55, 260–68, https://doi.org/10.1177/107769907805500206

Spradley, J. P. (1979). *The ethnographic interview.* New York: Holt.

Sreberny, A. (1985). *Foreign news in the media: International reporting in 29 countries.* Reports and papers on mass communication, Vol. 93. Paris: UNESCO.

Staab, J. F. (1990). The role of news factors in news selection: A theoretical reconsideration. *European Journal of Communication*, 5(4), 423–43, https://doi.org/10.1177/0267323190005004003

Stake, R. (1995). *The art of case study research.* Thousand Oaks: SAGE Publications

Stevenson, R. L. (1984). Research methodology. In R. L. Stevenson and D. L. Shaw (eds), *Foreign news and the new world information order* (1st ed., pp. 21–36). Ames: Iowa State University Press.

Stevenson, R. L., and Cole, R. (1984). Issues in foreign news. In R. L. Stevenson and D. L. Shaw (eds), *Foreign news and the new world information order* (1st ed., pp. 5–20). Ames: Iowa State University Press.

Taft, R. (1997). Ethnographic research methods. In J. P. Keeves (ed.), *Resources in education. Educational research, methodology and measurement. An international handbook* (2nd ed., pp. 71–75). Oxford: Pergamon.

Terrell, B. (1989). Philosophical investigations on space, time and the continuum. *Philosophical Books*, 30(2), 89–90, https://doi.org/10.1111/j.1468-0149.1989.tb02813.x

Thomass, B. (2016). Inter/national media politics: Approaches to postcolonial studies. In K. Merten and L. Krämer (eds), *Postcolonial studies meets media studies. A critical encounter* (pp. 103–24). Postcolonial studies, Vol. 23. Bielefeld: Transcript.

Thussu, D. K. (2000). *International communication: A critical introduction*. London: Arnold.

Thussu, D. K., Burgh, H. D., and Shi, A. (eds). (2018). *China's media go global* (1st ed.). Internationalizing media studies. London: Routledge.

Ting, T.-y. (2010). Globalization and foreign news coverage. *Journal of Comparative Asian Development*, 9(2), 321–46, https://doi.org/10.1080/15339114.2010.528 295

Tunstall, J. (2008). *The media were American: U.S. mass media in decline*. New York: Oxford University Press.

Ume-Nwagbo, E. N. (1982). Foreign news flow in Africa: A content analytical study on a regional basis. *Gazette (Leiden, Netherlands)*, 29(1–2), 41–56, https://doi.org/10.1177/001654928202900104

Van Djik. (2009). News, discourse, and ideology. In K. Wahl-Jorgensen and T. Hanitzsch (eds), *The handbook of journalism studies* (pp. 191–204). International Communication Association handbook series. New York: Routledge.

Vliegenthart, R., and Walgrave, S. (2008). The contingency of intermedia agenda-setting: A longitudinal study in Belgium. *Journalism and Mass Communication Quarterly*, 85(4), 860–77, https://doi.org/10.1177/107769900808500409

Voltmer, K., and Kraetzschmar, H. (2015). Investigating the media and democratisation conflicts: Research design and methodology of media, conflict and democratisation (MeCoDEM), *Mecodem Series*, http://www.mecodem.eu/wp-content/uploads/2015/06/Voltmer-Kraetzschmar-2015_Investigating-the-Media-and-Democratisation-Conflicts.pdf

Vonbun, R., Königslöw, K. K., and Schoenbach, K. (2015). Intermedia agenda-setting

in a multimedia news environment. *Journalism*, 17(8), 1054–73, https://doi.org/10.1177/1464884915595475

Wasserman, H. (2006). Globalized values and postcolonial responses. *International Communication Gazette*, 68(1), 71–91, https://doi.org/10.1177/1748048506060116

Wasserman, H. (2016). China's "Soft power" and its influence on editorial agendas in South Africa. *Chinese Journal of Communication*, 9(1), 8–20, https://doi.org/10.1080/17544750.2015.1049953

Weber, R. P. (1990). *Basic content analysis* (2nd ed.). Quantitative applications in the social sciences, 0149–192x, Vol. 49. London: SAGE Publications.

Wells, R. A., and King, E. G. (1994). Prestige newspaper coverage of foreign affairs in the 1990 congressional campaigns. *Journalism and Mass Communication Quarterly*, 71(3), 652–64, https://doi.org/10.1177/107769909407100316

Westerstahl, J., and Johansson, F. (1994). Foreign news: News values and ideologies. *European Journal of Communication*, 9(1), 71–89, https://doi.org/10.1177/0267323194009001004

Whitehead, T. L. (2005). Basic classical ethnographic research methods: Secondary data analysis, fieldwork, observation/participant observation, and informal and semi-structured interviewing (Ethnographically Informed Community and Cultural Assessment Research System (EICCARS). University of Maryland, Department of Anthropology.

Wilke, J., Heimprecht, C., and Cohen, A. (2012). The geography of foreign news on television. *International Communication Gazette*, 74(4), 301–22, https://doi.org/10.1177/1748048512439812

Williams, K. (2003). *Understanding media theory*. London: Arnold.

Wolter, I. (2006). Determinants on international news coverage. In N. Carpentier, K. Nordstreng, M. Hartmann, P. Vihalemm, and Cammaerts, B. Pille Pruulmann- Vengerfeldt (eds), *The researching and teaching communications series. Researching media, democracy and participation. The intellectual work of the 2006 European Media and Communication Doctoral Summer School* (pp. 59–72). Tartu: University of Tartu Press.

Wrong, M. (2017). Media perspectives: in defence of Western journalists in Africa. In M. Bunce, S. Franks and C. Paterson (eds), *Communication and society. Africa's media image in the 21st century. From the "Heart of Darkness" to "Africa Rising"* (pp. 30–32). London: Routledge.

Wu, H. D. (2000). Systemic determinants of international news coverage: A comparison of 38 countries. *Journal of Communication*, 50(2), 110–30, https://doi.org/10.1111/j.1460-2466.2000.tb02844.x

Wu, H. D. (2003). Homogeneity around the world? Comparing the systemic determinants of international news flow between developed and developing countries. *International Communication Gazette*, 65(1), 9–24, https://doi.org/10.1177/0016549203065001134

Wu, Y.-S. (2016). China's media and public diplomacy approach in Africa: illustrations from South Africa. *Chinese Journal of Communication*, 9(1), 81–97, https://doi.org/10.1080/17544750.2016.1139606

Xia, B., and Fuchs, C. (2017). The financialisation of digital capitalism in China. *Westminster Institute for Advanced Studies*, 4, 1–32.

Xie, Y., and Cooper-Chen, A. (2009). "According to Chinese media": News flows, the Associated Press and intermedia agenda-setting. *Journal of Global Mass Communication*, 2(3/4), 88–106.

Xin, X. (2017). Financialisation of news in China in the age of the Internet: The case of Xinhuanet. *Media, Culture and Society*, 28(3), 016344371774512, https://doi.org/10.1177/0163443717745121

Yankah, K. (1994). Covering the environment in the Ghanaian media. *Africa Media Review*, 8(1), 47–56.

Yau, J. T. K., and Al-Hawamdeh, S. (2001). The impact of the Internet on teaching and practicing journalism. *The Journal of Electronic Publishing*, 7(1), https://doi.org/10.3998/3336451.0007.102

Yin, R. K. (2011). *Qualitative Research from Start to Finish* (1st ed.). New York: Guilford Publications.

Yin, R. K. (2003). *Case study research: Design and methods* (3rd ed.). Applied social research methods series, Vol. 5. Thousand Oaks: SAGE Publications.

Index

Accra 22–24, 27
Accra Evening News 24–25
Accra Herald 22–23
advertising 51, 53, 56, 109, 144–145, 147–148, 155, 157, 175–176, 178, 186, 188, 190
advertising bias 144, 147–148, 175–176, 186, 188
Africa, media image of 1, 4, 6, 19, 20, 21, 29, 32, 35, 39, 40, 41, 44, 45, 46, 47, 54, 65, 86, 93, 94, 109, 118, 119, 120, 131, 132, 134, 141, 155, 160, 165, 167, 169, 170, 171, 172, 174, 175, 176, 177, 179, 180, 181, 185, 190. *See also* Africa rising discourse; *See also* Afro-pessimism
  dominant themes of portrayal 1, 4, 6, 89–90, 94, 97–98, 103, 105, 109, 117, 120, 125, 129–130, 134, 138–139, 149, 155, 165, 167–169, 180–181, 185
  negative portrayal 1–2, 13–14, 21, 29, 31–32, 35–36, 39–40, 46, 60, 69, 99, 119, 122, 124–125, 134, 141–142, 157, 159–162, 164, 166, 169–170, 179–180, 185, 195
  positive portrayal 39–40, 43, 93, 99, 119, 123–126, 130, 132–134, 162–163, 168–169
  tone of coverage 1, 4, 6, 40, 52, 89, 99, 109, 117, 119, 131, 134–135, 148, 165, 169, 185
    positive 134

African Council on Communication Education (ACCE) 57
African liberation movement 42, 58
African liberation struggle 24
African media 3, 48, 49, 51, 56, 57, 60, 131, 155, 173, 174, 195. *See also* Ghanaian media
African Media Barometer Report 27
African nationalism 28, 49
African perspective 8, 141–144, 146, 162–163, 172–173, 180
African Renaissance 49
African story, the 6, 41, 89, 116, 122, 129, 154, 158, 163, 165, 168, 173, 182
Africa rising discourse 1, 21, 33, 38, 118, 123, 134, 166–167, 170
  context of 33
  decline in 166–167, 170
  rise in 166, 170
Africa's Media Image. See Hawk, Beverly: *Africa's Media Image*
Afro-pessimism 1, 22, 39–40, 46, 61, 92–93, 99, 119, 130–132, 134, 139, 169, 185, 195–196
  evaluation of 40
  evolution of 39
  improvement in 132
Agence France-Presse (AFP) 93, 110–116, 131
agenda-setting 5–8, 63–65, 68–69, 80, 84–85, 90, 137, 152–154, 184, 186, 194–195
  agenda-setting theory 65, 68, 85

intermedia agenda-setting 5–8, 63–65, 68–69, 80, 84–85, 90, 137, 149, 152–154, 181, 184, 186, 194–195
Akinfemisoye, Motilola 4
Algerian War of Independence 35
Al-Hawamdeh, Suliman 53
Al Jazeera 33, 110, 114, 139, 171, 196
Al-Shabaab 128, 130, 168
Altheide, David 94, 106
ambivalence 8, 11, 28, 74–75, 143, 167, 172, 176
Amin, Mohamed "Mo" 43
Amin, Mohammed 33
Amin, Salim 33, 43, 180
Anfara, Vincent 64, 186
Anglophone Africa 23
Ankomah, Baffour 35
Anokwa, Kwadwo 30
Ansu-Kyeremeh, Kwasi 26
Asante, Clement 96
Asante Times 24
Ashanti Pioneer 25
Ashcroft, Bill 70
Associated Press (AP) 93, 110–115, 131, 142, 159
Atta Mills, John Evans 126
audience. *See* readership
Azikiwe, Nnamdi 23, 57–58

Bach, Daniel 31
Bannerman, Charles 22
Bannerman, Edmund 22
Barton, Frank 24
B'Beri, Boulou Ebanda de 32
Beer, A. S. de 46
Benghazi attack (2012) 124
Bennett, Kathryn 81
Berger, Guy 51
Bernard, H. R. 100
Bhabha, Homi K. 72–75, 102, 172, 196
Bloomberg 53
Boko Haram 41, 124, 128, 140, 168
Bookmiller, Kirsten 35
Bookmiller, Robert 35

Bosch, Tanja 22, 46
Bosnia 30, 45
Botswana 124
Bourdieu, Pierre 30
Boyd-Barrett, Oliver 43–44, 180
Brexit 61
British Broadcasting Corporation (BBC) 26, 31, 34, 36, 53, 57, 110–115, 117, 121, 131, 138–144, 149–150, 152–153, 158–159, 171, 173, 181, 183–185, 189, 193
Britishness 142
Bunce, Mel 7, 11, 21, 28, 33, 35, 40, 131–133, 135, 166, 168, 170, 174, 180
Burgh, Hugo de 60
business 16, 31, 33, 53, 60, 85, 119, 128, 132, 155, 167, 170

Cable News Network (CNN) 34, 36, 53, 110–116, 131, 139, 149, 184, 196
Cameroon, Republic of 128
Campbell, W. Joseph 24
Cape Coast Daily Mail 24
Carey, James 44
Castells, Manuel 78
Catenaccio, Paola 92
causal model 66
celebrity 118, 133–134, 166
Central Africa 122, 127
Centre–Periphery model 2, 13, 182–183, 194
Chad 128
Chaudhary, Anju 40, 99, 119
China Central Television 60
China Daily 60
China Radio International 60
China's soft power. *See* soft power: of China
Chinese media 60–61, 171
Citi FM 27
CNBC 53
coding 8, 89, 98, 102–105, 107, 120–121, 123, 125, 129–130, 139, 189
    deductive 102, 120, 125, 129

inductive 91, 102, 120
Cohen, Akiba 66
Cold War 20, 33, 42, 49
Cole, Richard 14
colonialism 11–13, 17, 22–26, 29, 31–32, 35, 41–44, 47–51, 57, 61, 70–75, 127, 133, 142, 149, 152, 169–170, 175, 181, 183–186, 188–189, 194–196
colonial memory 120, 127
colonisation 43, 70, 73
   colonised, the 48, 70, 72–73, 75–76, 152, 169, 171–173, 184
   coloniser, the 72–73, 75, 169, 172–173, 183–184
communication technology 2
communism 12
conceptual design 63, 89, 99
conceptual interview scheme 103–104
constructivism 91
contemporary imperialism.
   See imperialism: contemporary imperialism
content analysis 6–8, 21, 90–99, 106, 108–109, 118, 131, 137, 141, 159, 189–191, 196
   qualitative content analysis 189
   quantitative content analysis 21, 106, 137
Cooper, Anne 46
Cooper-Chen, Anne 69
corruption 13, 36, 43, 118, 122, 128, 132
cost-cutting 55–56, 144, 146–147, 155–157, 178–179, 186
Côte d'Ivoire 146
Coulter, Paddy 41
Crane, Diana 81
credibility 2, 25, 53, 108, 142
Creswell, John 91, 191
crime 98, 120–122, 128, 132, 167, 174, 185
crisis 34, 36, 42, 46–48, 61, 111–112, 119, 122–124, 126–127, 157, 167–168, 185

critical theory 70–71, 91, 191–192
cultural affinity 184, 194
cultural defeat 139
cultural domination 15, 141, 143
cultural globalisation.
   See globalisation: of culture
cultural imperialism. *See* imperialism: cultural imperialism
cultural universality 133
cultural values 51, 71
culture 18, 50–51, 58, 64, 68–69, 72, 74, 82, 92, 100, 105, 118, 152, 166, 173
   ideal culture 100
   real culture 100
Czilli, Edward 34

Dahir, A. L. 36
Daily Nation 47
Danquah, J. B. 24
Dare, O. 47
Darnton, Andrew 45
democracy 50, 59, 80, 120, 125–126, 135, 179
democratisation 12, 18
dependency 3, 8, 17, 19, 50, 80, 113, 132, 144, 146, 183, 193
   cultural dependency 50
Deuze, Mark 53
developed countries 1, 3, 12, 18, 31, 35, 49
developing countries 2, 12–15, 17–19, 28, 36, 42, 47, 49–50, 54, 58, 69, 99, 150, 159, 181, 194
Dierckx de Casterlé, Bernadette 103
digitalisation 52, 55
disease 36, 40, 43, 99, 129
diversity 16, 20, 33, 37, 110, 112–114, 141–142, 148–149, 151, 176, 190
Domatob, J. K. 51
double-bind 176
Doucet, Andrea 106
drugs 121
Du, Ying Roselyn 69
Dzisah, Wilberforce 22

economy 46, 118, 132, 170, 176, 185
  economic hardship 146, 155–157, 178–179, 186
  economic resources 164, 180
  economic strategy 156
  global economy 46
editorial content 147–148, 176–177
education 7, 11, 29, 32, 36, 49–51, 56–58, 61, 72, 78, 83, 152–153, 160, 183, 188, 193
  British model of 152
  Western education 7, 72
Eek, H. 14
  "concept of order" 14
Egypt 118, 122, 125, 127
Eilders, Christiane 66, 82, 192
Elasmer, Michael 81
El Zein, H. M. 46
epidermalisation 71–72, 171
essentialisation 46, 93
essentialism 73, 75, 142–143, 173
ethical issues 8, 89, 107
Ethiopia 122, 127
ethnocentrism 46, 93
ethnographic content analysis (ECA) 6–8, 90–92, 94, 97–98, 109, 118, 137, 189, 191
ethnographic interview (EI) 6, 8, 89–92, 94–97, 103, 109, 137, 161
ethnography 91–92, 100
Eurocentrism 64, 70

Fair, Jo 31–32
famine 40–41, 46, 98–99, 119
Fanon, Frantz 48–49, 71–73, 169, 171, 196
  Black Skin, White Mask 72
  Wretched of the Earth 72
Federal Communication Commission (FCC) 37
Feinberg, Harvey 39
Fengler, Susanne 55, 179
feudal interaction 13, 19, 48, 150–151, 163, 182
Fico, Frederick 93, 190

Fiest, Samuel 55
Flamenbaum, Rachel 38, 167
Foote, Joe 69
foreign development agent 166
foreign policy 34–35, 45, 47, 113
framework
  conceptual 64, 85–86, 105, 190
  theoretical 7, 64, 76, 84
Francophone Africa 39
Franks, Suzanne 36, 55
freedom of expression 18, 25
free flow doctrine 13, 15, 18, 20
French, H. W. 36
Friedrich-Ebert-Stiftung (FES) 95
Fuchs, Christian 35
Fuss, Diana 75

Galtung, Johan 2, 13, 48, 68, 164, 183
  "A Structural Theory of Imperialism" 13
Gandhi, Indira 5
Gans, Herbert 76, 80
García Márquez, Gabriel 15
Ghana Army (GA) 153
Ghana Broadcasting Corporation (GBC) 26
Ghanaianess 143
Ghanaian media 1, 4–8, 11, 23, 27–28, 83, 86, 89–90, 93, 97, 109, 115–120, 124, 129, 131–134, 137, 143–145, 148, 153–155, 158, 165–171, 173, 175, 179, 182, 185, 190, 193, 195–196
  Ghanaian newspapers 4–5, 92, 94, 109, 115, 146, 151–152, 156, 169–170, 173, 176–177, 181, 184, 194
    Daily Graphic, The 25, 27–28, 94–95, 105–106, 109–112, 116, 121, 123–124, 126–127, 129, 139–140, 142–149, 151, 157–160, 162–164, 174, 182
    Daily Guide 27, 94–95, 105, 114–116, 121, 123–125, 128–129, 138, 140–142, 146–150, 152, 154, 157, 160, 181

Ghanaian Chronicle, The 94–95, 105, 113, 116, 121, 124, 128, 138–140, 142, 144, 147, 149–150, 154–156, 162, 181
Ghanaian Times 94–95, 105, 111–114, 116, 121, 123, 125–129, 142–148, 151, 153, 161, 163, 174–175, 182
nationalist press 11, 22–24, 193
post-independence 7, 11, 24–25, 28
pre-independence 7, 11, 28
radio 26–28, 40, 54, 140–141, 149, 152–153, 156, 196
Ghana Institute of Journalism 58
Ghana News Agency 27, 143, 162, 164, 180
Giddens, Anthony 81
"local transformation" 81
Gilboa, Eytan 34
Gilroy, Paul 71
Gitlin, Todd 76
Glaser, Barney 104
Global Financial Crisis 38
globalisation 12, 32, 46, 51, 64, 69, 72–73, 81–82, 133, 142, 144–145, 172, 185, 194
of culture 81
of media 12
global media 12, 14, 33–34, 74, 93, 173, 184
global media debate 14
global media policy 12
Global North 12, 31, 143, 155, 162, 178
Global South 36, 150
Godwin, Ebo 111
Golan, Guy 69
Gold Coast Broadcasting Systems 26
Gold Coast Chronicle 23
Gold Coast Express 23
Gold Coast Independent, The 23
Gold Coast People 23
Gold Coast Times 23
Golding, Peter 57–58, 184
Gongo, Kuselwa 49

Graubart, Jonathan 2
Green, K. 54
Griffiths, Gareth 70
Guardian, The (Nigerian) 47
Guba, E. G. 91
Guo, Lei 63, 65

Hachten, William 23, 25, 52, 55
Hallin, Daniel 82
Hall, Stuart 34–35, 48, 67
Hamelink, Cees 15
Hanusch, F. 21, 38, 54–55, 167
Harcup, Tony 68
Harding, Frances 54
Harth, Amy 42, 44
Hasty, Jennifer 27
Haule, J. J. 61
Hawk, Beverly 7, 11, 20–21, 28, 41, 130–132, 168, 170, 174
Africa's Media Image 7, 20, 130, 155, 165, 188
Hegde, Radha 70–71
hegemony 1, 3, 29, 34, 44, 46, 49, 77, 172, 174
Heimprecht, Christine 66
Hierarchical Influences Model 76, 78, 83
individual level 78–79, 83, 85, 193
organisational level 79, 85, 146, 186, 188
routine level 79–80, 83
social institution level 80
social system level 81, 85
HIV/AIDs 129
homogenisation 20, 80, 93, 126
Huberman, Michael 64, 94
human rights 12, 18, 98, 125, 128, 154
Hume, Ellen 49
Hunter-Gault, Charlayne 56
"Africa's new news" 56
hybridity 70–71, 74–75, 196

Ibelema, Minabere 22, 46
identity 5, 29, 42, 48, 51, 72–74, 78, 169, 172–173, 183, 189

creation of 29
local identity 51, 173
self-identity 48, 169, 189
ideological construct 137, 160–161
ideology 3, 11, 35, 41, 44, 51, 54, 69, 80, 82, 84, 110, 123, 144, 155, 160–162, 174, 178, 186, 193
transfer of 58
imitation 11, 59, 72–73, 75, 172, 196
submissive imitation 73, 172
subversive imitation 73, 172, 196
imperialism 12, 14–15, 32, 35, 81, 174, 183
contemporary imperialism 32
cultural imperialism 12, 81
media imperialism 32, 174
neo-imperialism 35
individualism 78
inequality 2, 13, 17, 19
internalised oppression 71–72, 171
International Association for Mass Communication Research (IAMCR) 18–19, 28
international news agencies 4–8, 48, 90, 93, 106, 109–110, 115–117, 129, 131, 134, 137–142, 145–146, 148–149, 153, 158, 171–172, 175, 177
weight of influence of 4–6, 8, 90, 96–97, 109, 116, 134, 137, 144, 171, 175
international press 3, 129
Western-centric 13
International Programme for the Development of Communication 18
Internet 4, 7, 38, 52, 54, 64, 140, 148–149, 177

Jacobs, Geert 92
Johnson, John 106
Johnson, Melissa 30, 82
Johnson, Wallace 23
Jonathan, Goodluck 124
Jones-Quartey, K. A. B. 24
Jose, Babatunde 24

journalism
African journalism 2–4, 39, 48–49, 51, 54, 57, 59, 62, 163, 173–174, 182, 184
American model of 44, 50–51, 58
journalism education 11, 29, 49–51, 57–58, 78, 153, 188, 193
journalism studies 193
journalistic co-orientation 65, 69, 181, 184, 194–195
journalistic ideology 144, 155, 160, 162, 178, 186
"pack journalism" 46, 55
"parachute journalism" 46, 55
"posh journalism" 153
Western journalism 11, 21, 37–38, 43, 179
Joy FM 27

Kagame, Paul 46
Karikari, Kwame 24–26, 32, 170
Kasoma, Francis 59
Keane, Fergal 31, 42
Kenya 48, 120, 122, 126–128, 130, 162
Kenya–Somalia conflicts 122
Kenyatta, Uhuru 119
killing 40, 42, 98, 121–122, 125, 128, 167–168, 185
King, Martin Luther, Jr. 22
Klak, Thomas 44
Koehl, Timothy 44
Kraetzschmar, Hendrik 97
Kraidy, Marwan 74, 173
Krippendorff, Klaus 92, 107

Lacy, Stephen 93, 190
Lader, Deborah 45
Lal Das, D. K. 98
LeCompte, Michael 106
legitimisation 73, 172
Lent, John 47
Libya 124, 128
Lin, Carolyn 30
Lincoln, Y. S. 91
Lippmann, Walter 31, 43–44, 65

Louw, P. Eric 32

MacBride report. *See* United Nations Educational, Scientific and Cultural Organisation (UNESCO): MacBride report
Macbride, Seán 16
MacKinnon, Mairead 39
Mahendran, Dilan 72
Malawi 125–126
Mancini, Paolo 82
Mandela, Nelson 120, 123, 133, 166
Mano, Winston 50
Mansell, Robin 18
mass media 14, 26, 30, 44, 57, 69
Mau Mau Uprising 127
Mauthner, Natasha 106
Mayring, Philipp 189
Mazrui, Ali 50, 57, 183
Mbeki, Thabo 49
McCarthy, Charles 22
McCombs, Maxwell 68
McKercher, Catherine 53
McPhail, Thomas 50, 174
media agenda 68. *See also* agenda-setting
media content 3, 46, 76–80, 93
media control 1, 12, 25–26, 61, 186
media coverage 36, 40, 41, 44, 179. *See also* Africa, media image of; *See also* global media; *See also* transnational media; *See also* Western media
   contextual background of 40, 99, 122, 158, 179. *See also* negative context
   omissions in 20, 40, 42–43, 55, 93, 99, 121, 129, 166
   sensational 16, 35, 161
media culture 50
media donor 56–57, 59, 127
media frames 3, 174
   negative 45, 46, 160. *See also* Africa, media image of: negative portrayal

media globalisation. *See* globalisation: of media
media imperialism. *See* imperialism: media imperialism
media logic 50
media ownership 4, 37, 53, 55
media representation 5, 20, 27, 31
media texts 32, 74, 98
medium mismatch 158, 179
Mehra, Achal 56
Mengara, D. M. 32
Mertz, Norma 64, 186
Miles, Matthew 64, 82, 94, 104, 186
Millennium Development Goals 36
mimicry. *See* imitation
Minow, Newton 37
Mirror Group 24
Mody, Bella 31, 41, 43–44
Moeller, Susan 40
Morning Telegraph 24
Mowlana, Hamid 13–14
Moynihan, Daniel Patrick 59, 179
Murphy, Sharon 50, 57, 59
Myers, Garth 44–45

Nairobi 43
natural disaster 12, 41, 43, 93, 99, 129–130, 132, 134, 161
natural order 72, 171
negative context 99, 122, 124, 130
negative representation. *See* Africa, media image of: negative portrayal
neo-colonialism 12, 35, 51
neo-imperialism. *See* imperialism: neo-imperialism
neo-liberalism 15
New African 35
news access 92
news flow 1, 2, 3, 5, 7, 8, 18, 48, 63, 64, 65, 180, 183. *See also* free flow doctrine
   Centre–Periphery 183
   international 1–2, 5, 7–8, 63–65, 180
   one-way flow 12

newsgathering
    foreign 53, 96, 157, 193
    global 46
news management 92
news production 29, 33, 92, 172, 174
newsroom 1, 4–5, 32, 53, 57, 94,
    100, 107–109, 137, 144, 148–149,
    157–159
newsroom socialisation 57
news selection 3–6, 8, 11, 29, 63,
    65–69, 80, 82–86, 90, 92, 103, 108,
    114, 138, 144, 148, 174–177, 179,
    186, 188, 192–193
    foreign news selection 5, 8, 11,
    29, 83–86, 90, 103, 108, 114, 144,
    175–177, 179, 186, 188
    object-based approach 67, 192
    subject-based approach 67, 192
newsworthiness 7, 63–68, 82–83, 85,
    154, 188, 190, 192
New World Information and
    Communication Order (NWICO)
    11–12, 14–15, 18–19, 37–38, 163
New York Times, The 36, 46, 53
Nigeria 21, 33, 40–41, 54, 57–58,
    125–126, 128, 140, 146, 154, 184
Nigerian press 47
Nkrumah, Kwame 22, 24–26, 57
Non-Aligned Movement (NAM) 12
Nordenstreng, Kaarle 14, 18, 37
North Africa 39
Northern Hemisphere 2–4, 13, 31, 33,
    38–40, 46, 127, 133, 139–141, 143,
    153, 160, 162–163, 166–168, 171,
    174, 194–195
Northern press 2, 4, 32–33, 40, 44,
    119, 129, 135, 141–142, 150–151,
    156, 159–160, 163, 168–169, 171,
    179–180, 185–186
    dominance of 151
Nothias, Toussaint 47, 92, 193, 195
Nwuneli, O. E. 47
Nyamnjoh, F. B. 24, 48
Nyamnjoh, Francis 4, 42
Nye, Joseph 30

Obijiofor, Levi 21, 38–39, 52, 54–55,
    167
objectivity 34, 59, 66, 191
Ofori-Birikorang, Andy 96, 169, 196
O'Neill, Deirdre 68
optimism 124
Others/Othering 5, 28–29, 32, 37, 39,
    44–45, 75, 98

Palmer, Jerry 66
Pan-Africanism 7, 22, 48, 61, 112, 146,
    175
Pan-African News Agency (PANA)
    48, 61, 164
Pander Maat, Henk 92
participatory paradigms 91
Paterson, Chris 32, 34, 44, 174, 195
Peace FM 27
perceptual map 169
piracy 121
plurality 4, 42
political polarisation 25, 27
politics 5, 30, 82, 84, 118, 132–133,
    135, 166, 170, 185
politics of power 5
postcolonial complexities 181, 183
postcolonial critique 7, 33, 102
postcolonial era 172
postcolonial institution 170
postcolonial press freedom 24
postcolonial studies 70–71, 76, 191,
    193
postcolonial theory 5, 63–64, 69–71,
    85, 121, 193
poverty 30, 36, 40, 43, 45–46, 92,
    98–99, 128–129, 143
power over opinion 30
power relations 8, 51, 79, 175, 186,
    194
Prasad, A. 69
press freedom 11, 15–16, 24–26,
    125–126, 189, 196
Price, Vincent 34
professionalisation 58–59

profitability 144–146, 175–176, 186, 188
Provisional National Defence Council (PNDC) 26
psychic realm 72–73, 169, 172
public diplomacy 60–61, 173–174, 182

Qualitative Analysis Guide of Leuven (QUAGOL) 103
qualitative research 91, 94, 106, 108, 186
  constant comparison 104–105
  keywords-in-context 104
  theme analysis 104–105

race 32, 56, 70–72
racialisation 46, 93
racism 72
Radio ZOY 26
Rawlings, Jerry John 22
readership 21, 30–31, 34, 36–37, 43, 45, 56, 58, 65, 146–148, 152, 155–156, 160–162, 168, 174–176, 178, 181
  African readership 43, 181
  Western readership 20–21, 31, 37, 41
readership taste 36–37, 56, 160–162, 174–176
Reese, Stephen 7, 76–80, 82–83, 85, 175, 177
reflexivity 21, 41–42, 85, 91, 98, 102, 105–106, 188, 191
refugee 122
reliability check 8, 89, 106–107
resistance 3, 8–9, 25, 35, 51, 70, 74–75, 102, 143–144, 160, 172, 194, 196
Reuters 24, 36, 41, 93, 110–116, 124, 131–132, 153, 158–159, 184
Riffe, Daniel 69, 93, 190
Robins, M. 45
Robinson, Piers 34
Robson, Colin 91
Rodney, Walter 50, 183
Rosenblum, Mort 36
Ruge, Mari 48, 68, 164

Russ-Mohl, Stephan 55, 179
Ruto, William 119
Rwanda 45–46, 48

Saldaña, Johnny 64, 94
Salwen, Michael 30
sampling 8, 89, 93–95, 98, 190, 196
Sawant, Shrikant 69
Sayed, Zehra 74, 191
Schiffrin, Anya 59, 183
Schneider, Christopher 27, 94
Schorr, Victoria 31
Schulz, Rüdiger 56, 66, 176
Schwarz, Andreas 68, 82, 192
Scott, Martin 39, 46
Scotton, James 50, 52, 55, 57, 59
Segev, Elad 64
self-rule 22, 24, 57, 141, 172
shareholder 34, 61, 144
Sharp, Joanne 44
Shaw, Donald 168
Shi, Andin 60
Shoemaker, Pamela 7, 66, 76–80, 82–83, 85, 175, 177, 192
Shome, Raka 70–71
Singapore 54
Skjerdal, Terje 51, 59, 167, 173
Slater, David 42
social reality 32, 76, 79
social representation 32
soft power 30, 60–61, 149–151, 173, 181–182, 186, 194–195
  of China 173, 181, 194–195
sole-sourcing 34
Solodow, Joseph 39
Somalia 122, 128, 163
Somavía, Juan 15
South Africa 49, 60, 123, 129, 133, 173, 182
Southern Hemisphere 12–13
South–South cooperation 8, 149–151, 163, 172–173, 181–182, 185–186, 194
Spradley, James 100, 103, 105
Sreberny, Annabelle 19, 168

Sreberny-Mohammadi report 1, 7, 11, 18–19, 28, 34, 38
Staab, J. F. 65–67, 82, 192
Starr FM 27
Steele, Michael 69
Stevenson, Robert 14, 168
Strauss, Anselm 104
subject-object relationship 67
Sudanese Lost Boys 45
Sudan–South Sudan conflicts 122
Sunday City Press 49

Talloires Declaration 37
Tanzania 57, 124
technological challenge 144, 175, 177, 186, 188
technology 2, 12, 16, 29–30, 38, 48, 51–52, 54–55, 57, 61, 138, 156
Terrell, Burnham 170
terrorism 120, 127–128, 167–168, 185
third space 73, 172, 194
Third World and Environment Broadcasting Project 36
Thussu, Daya 60
Tiffin, Helen 70
Ting, T.-y. 30
Togo 111, 146, 162–163
transnational media 35, 50, 93
  corporate 35
triangulation (of data/sources) 8, 89

Ume-Nwagbo, Nwa'ndo 14, 18
United Nations Educational, Scientific and Cultural Organisation (UNESCO) 2, 7, 11–12, 18, 37, 57, 61
  MacBride report 2, 7, 11, 14–18, 28, 34, 38
Universal Declaration of Human Rights (1948) 14

validity check 1, 8, 66, 89, 91, 100, 106–108
van Hout, Tom 92
Vargo, Chris 63, 65
Vliegenthart, Rens 69

Voltmer, Katrin 97
Voluntary Service Overseas 46
Voluntary Service Overseas (VSO) 46
Vonbun, Ramona 181

Walgrave, Stefaan 69
war 14, 25, 35, 43–45, 54, 98–99, 118–119, 121–122, 128, 132, 143, 167–168, 185
Wasserman, Herman 60, 173, 182, 193
West Africa 22, 24, 39, 129, 163, 167
West African Pilot 57
West African press 22, 24
Western ideals 48, 50
Western intervention 36
Western media 2, 7, 14, 21, 29, 31–32, 35, 39, 41–42, 44–45, 51, 54, 61, 130–134, 139, 167, 170, 179
Whitehead, T. L. 100
Wilke, Jürgen 66
Wolter, Ines 31, 55
world press system 13
Wu, H. D. 60, 182

Xie, Yie 69
Xinhuanet 60–61
Xinhua News Agency 8, 60, 110, 112, 114–115, 124, 139, 149–151, 170–171, 173–174, 181–182, 185, 194–196
Xin, Xin 60

Yankah, Kojo 96
Yar'Adua, Umaru Musa 126
Yau, Joanne 53

Zambia 125–126
Zimbabwe 122, 124–125

About the Team

Alessandra Tosi was the managing editor for this book.

Adele Kreager performed the copy-editing and proofreading.

Anna Gatti designed the cover using InDesign. The cover was produced in InDesign using the Fontin font.

Melissa Purkiss typeset the book in InDesign and produced the paperback and hardback editions. The text font is Tex Gyre Pagella; the heading font is Californian FB.

Luca Baffa produced the EPUB, MOBI, PDF, HTML, and XML editions — the conversion is performed with open source software freely available on our GitHub page (https://github.com/OpenBookPublishers).

This book need not end here...

Share

All our books — including the one you have just read — are free to access online so that students, researchers and members of the public who can't afford a printed edition will have access to the same ideas. This title will be accessed online by hundreds of readers each month across the globe: why not share the link so that someone you know is one of them?

This book and additional content is available at:

https://doi.org/10.11647/OBP.0227

Customise

Personalise your copy of this book or design new books using OBP and third-party material. Take chapters or whole books from our published list and make a special edition, a new anthology or an illuminating coursepack. Each customised edition will be produced as a paperback and a downloadable PDF.

Find out more at:

https://www.openbookpublishers.com/section/59/1

Like Open Book Publishers

Follow @OpenBookPublish

Read more at the Open Book Publishers **BLOG**

Global Communications

About the series

Global Communications is a book series that looks beyond national borders to examine current transformations in public communication, journalism and media. Books in this series will focus on the role of communication in the context of global ecological, social, political, economic, and technological challenges in order to help us understand the rapidly changing media environment. We encourage comparative studies but we also welcome single case studies, especially if they focus on regions other than Western Europe and North America, which have received the bulk of scholarly attention until now.

Empirical studies as well as textbooks are welcome. Books should remain concise and not exceed 300 pages but may offer online access to a wealth of additional material documenting the research process and providing access to the data. The series aspires to publish theoretically well-grounded, methodologically sound, relevant, novel research, presented in a readable and engaging way. Through peer review and careful support from the editors of the series and from the editorial team of Open Book Publishers, we strive to support our authors in achieving these goals.

Global Communications is the first Open Access book series in the field to combine the high editorial standards of professional publishing with the fair Open Access model offered by OBP. Copyrights stay where they belong, with the authors. Authors are encouraged to secure funding to offset the publication costs and thereby sustain the publishing model, but if no institutional funding is available, authors are not charged fees. Any publishing subvention secured will cover the actual costs of publishing and will not be taken as profit. In short: we support publishing that respects the authors and serves the public interest.

You can find more information about this serie at:
https://www.openbookpublishers.com/section/100/1

www.ingramcontent.com/pod-product-compliance
Lightning Source LLC
Chambersburg PA
CBHW040903250426
43673CB00064B/1950